Progressivism and the Open Door: America and China, 1905–1921

Progressivism and the Open Door

America and China, 1905-1921

❀ JERRY ISRAEL

UNIVERSITY OF PITTSBURGH PRESS

Library of Congress Catalog Card Number 73-123095
ISBN 0-8229-3210-5

For my mother and father
Sylvia and Arthur Israel
and for my wife Carol

Contents

Acknowledgments

AN EFFORT to integrate separate fields, such as domestic and diplomatic progressivism and American–East Asian relations, relies upon the support of many individuals. The coordination of such support, especially any failure thereof, remains the job of the author.

Lloyd Gardner comes closest to being the exception to this statement of my individual responsibility. His imagination, guidance, confidence, and friendship have been with me and this book from its inception. Warren Susman also shares a central role in shaping everything that follows, as all who know him as teacher and friend will well understand. In addition, I have drawn upon my training with John Higham, Sidney Fine, and Charles Forcey.

Intellectual stimulation has been derived from the written words of many authors mentioned in the historiographical introduction. Others have provided questions, suggestions, encouragement, and dialogue at various stages of my work. I want to thank such historians as Loren Baritz, Warren Cohen, Ronald Formisano, Walter Glazer, Leonard Gordon, Phillip Hosay, Carl Jackson, Helen Kahn, N. Stephen Kane, Peter Karsten, Paul Kleppner, James Lorence, Thomas McCormick, David Montgomery, Noel Pugach, Kenneth Shover, Richard Smethurst, and William Stanton.

Securing relatively unexplored research material has been a key to this work. In addition to the staffs of those libraries and organizations mentioned in the bibliography, I want to acknowledge two extraordinary archivists—Anthony Nicolosi of the Rutgers University Library and William Mobley of the Library of Congress. Also Mr. John O. Crane and Mrs. Martin Egan allowed me access to family papers held privately, for which I am grateful.

Financial support from a Rutgers University fellowship and two University of Texas at El Paso faculty research grants provided necessary typing services at several points in the manuscript's development. The editors of the *American Historical Review* and the *Journal of the Rutgers University Library* have kindly granted permission to reprint portions of material which appeared in an earlier form in their journals. My special appreciation goes to the University of Pittsburgh Press, especially Mr. Frederick Hetzel and Mrs. Eleanor Walker, for preparing and improving this work for publication.

There are a few "invaluables" to be mentioned in conclusion. Professors Gardner and Susman were members of the history department at Rutgers University in the mid-1960s, which in its entirety provided an exciting and challenging environment for graduate work. In particular my thanks to Rutgers friends: David Bernstein, Charles Connell, Lawrence Gerlach, Norman Kaner, Michael Lutzker, and Jeffrey Safford.

I also want to remember here my grandfather, Theodore Herzberg, whose experiences and enthusiasms first inspired me to the possibilities of history.

Finally, those most important people to whom this book is dedicated know, I hope, that for so many reasons, it is a product of their labor and love.

Introduction

A Summary of the Literature as Prelude

The great beasts and the little halted sharp,
Eyed the grand circler, doubting his intent.
Straightaway the wind flawed and he came about,
Stooping to take the vanward of the pack.

> William Vaughn Moody, "The Quarry"

WILLIAM Vaughn Moody's imagery reflects the fascination and dilemma of America in the Far East at the beginning of the twentieth century. The "grand circler" was the United States. All other powers interested in China were the "great beasts" with the Chinese being the "little." America had a role in the Far East: indeed many felt it to be a unique one. Yet even at the "vanward," the United States was but a part of the "pack."

China was America's great market, an extension of the domestic frontier closed by decree of the census and Frederick Jackson Turner in the 1890s. Always more a potential than an actual market, the myth of China's four hundred million customers was an American reality. The United States would transport surplus manufactured goods to sell in China. Through plans to build railways and public utilities in China, surplus capital would also be offered, adding a financial as well as a commercial goal to the Open Door.

China was also to be a market for all types of early twentieth-century progressive American reform. It was this idea of China as a *tabula rasa* for American reform interests that provided a most revealing link between domestic and diplomatic attitudes. Canton, like Chicago, was to be cleansed of crime and corruption. China was to be remade in the American image.

The joint desires for trade, investment, and reform provided a broad-based, almost unquestioned, foundation for American policy. At another level, in the specific formulation of tactics, not goals, American policy witnessed drastic fluctuations. Diplomatic negotiations, especially with Japan and the European powers, from the Root-Takahira agreement to the Washington Conference, must be viewed in relation to developments at home. The great debate in the United States at the turn of the century revolved around the trust, that is, the concentration of industry versus an older competitive tradition. Similarly the debate over tactics in China policy may be stated in terms of cooperation or competition especially with or against Japan. The same forces and pressures were at work in shaping domestic and foreign policy. In both areas the answer attempted would include carefully calculated compromise as in the trade association movement at home and the banking consortium abroad.

This study will concentrate on the facets of interaction between progressivism and American China policy in the early twentieth century. It is intended to advance not only the understanding of this policy and interaction but also the separate and important topics of domestic and diplomatic progressivism. Before beginning, an extended examination of the present state of historical understanding of these subjects is in order.

In a book deserving a place among the significant interpretations of the period, Robert Wiebe has taken a look over his shoulder at efforts to classify the first two progressive decades of twentieth-century American history.[1] The earliest definition of the central theme of those decades was a kind of content analysis, reasoning that the progressives *were* what the progressives *did*. Thus Charles Beard and Harold Faulkner saw that the results achieved were political and social reform and they defined progressivism as a reform movement.[2]

The partial picture derived from such studies produced a biographical method of defining progressives not by what they did but rather by who they were. This approach grew in sophistication from the study of individuals to that of factions, as in Louis Filler's discovery of the era's liberal, crusading journalists. There followed the extension of this form,

1. Robert Wiebe, *Businessmen and Reform: A Study of the Progressive Movement* (Cambridge: Harvard University Press, 1962), pp. 207–11.
2. See in particular Harold U. Faulkner, *The Quest for Social Justice, 1898–1914* (New York: Macmillan, 1931).

first by John Chamberlain and then Morton White and Eric Goldman, in search of the biography of the very mind of the group. Finally in the 1950s emerged the ultimate refinement, a model progressive profile or personality. As perfected by Richard Hofstadter and George Mowry this device provided a clear definition of a progressive.[3]

Despite general acceptance of this approach, the model progressive —a young, midwestern, eastern-educated, Protestant, middle-class journalist or politician—seemed to include every leader in the period. It also failed to identify many who had not already been discovered by more haphazard methods. Sensing this, the latest exponents of the biographical method have attempted to apply it as well to the period's *Varieties of Reform Thought*. Others have begun, however, to ask different questions. Some, like Samuel Hays, have simply wondered if the term *progressive* has any validity or whether the period just blends with earlier and later American history without any personality of its own.[4]

Those like Wiebe who are still unwilling to dismiss such uniqueness have returned to a content study of progressivism rather than the typical progressive. Going back to the idea that there are "certain broad social, political and economic issues," Wiebe, Gabriel Kolko, Allen Davis, and Roy Lubove among others have been struck by problems at both ends of the economic spectrum, those of the underprivileged and social welfare and those of the overprivileged and economic regulation.[5] Combined by the increased responsiveness of government to

3. Louis Filler, *Crusaders for American Liberalism* (New York: Harcourt, Brace, 1939); John Chamberlain, *Farewell to Reform—The Rise, Life and Decay of the Progressive Mind in America* (New York: John Day, 1932); Morton White, *Social Thought in America: The Revolt Against Formalism* (New York: Viking Press, 1952); Eric F. Goldman, *Rendezvous With Destiny* (New York: Alfred A. Knopf, 1952); Richard Hofstadter, *The Age of Reform: From Bryan to F.D.R.* (New York: Alfred A. Knopf, 1956); and George Mowry, *The Era of Theodore Roosevelt, 1900–1912* (New York: Harper & Brothers, 1958), ch. 5.

4. Daniel Levine, *Varieties of Reform Thought* (Madison: State Historical Society of Wisconsin, 1964). See the similar efforts to separate the traditionalists from the modernists in John Braeman's "Seven Progressives," *Business History Review*, XXXV (1961), 581–92. Samuel P. Hays, *The Response to Industrialism, 1885–1914* (Chicago: University of Chicago Press, 1957).

5. Wiebe, *Businessmen and Reform;* Gabriel Kolko, *The Triumph of Conservatism: A Reinterpretation of American History, 1900–1916* (New York: Free Press, 1963); Allen F. Davis, "The Social Workers and the Progressive Party," *American Historical Review*, LXIX (April 1964), 671–88; and Roy Lubove, *The Progressives*

both, these twin problems and the solutions offered to them form the content and results of progressivism. Rejecting overly simplistic stereotypes of progressives as forward-looking heroes or backward-looking villains, revisionists like Wiebe and Kolko have begun to study the delicate relationship between business and government, the desire of businessmen for some sort of regulation and the administration as well as the enactment of such legislation.

Most students of domestic developments in this period pay homage to America's simultaneous "rise to world power" by including a chapter or less on foreign policy. While progressive diplomacy has remained a separate study, its own development reveals a pattern not unlike Wiebe's growth chart for progressivism at home. Looking particularly at the Far East and the Open Door policy, early interpretations, especially those of Tyler Dennett, can be seen as attempts to study policy in terms of its intentions and certainly its results.[6] To Dennett the spirit of the Open Door was not restricted by geography or chronology. In what he called "essentially an intervention policy," Dennett could see American expansion as far back as the Declaration of Independence and as far removed from China as Africa and the Caribbean.

With the figure of Theodore Roosevelt looming ever larger over the period, especially its "big stick" foreign policy, a biographical kind of approach to the Open Door also emerged. Henry Pringle's 1931 treatment depicted a kind of personal triumph symbolized by the typically Rooseveltian statement, "I do not intend to give way and I am year by year growing more confident that the country would back me in going to an extreme." Twenty-five years later in a far-better-researched volume, Howard Beale concurred in the primary impor-

---

and the Slums: Tenement House Reform in New York City, 1890–1917 (Pittsburgh: University of Pittsburgh Press, 1962). Kenneth McNaught, "American Progressives and the Great Society," Journal of American History, LIII (Dec. 1966), 504–20, views the social welfare side but goes overboard in his claims that such "revisionist" views have been broadly accepted already. Wiebe's own more recent survey, The Search for Order, 1877–1920 (New York: Hill and Wang, 1967), for example, develops as the title suggests some interesting points on the organizational character of the period but displays a surprising reversion to biographical explanations in terms of a "new middle class."

6. Tyler Dennett, Americans in Eastern Asia (New York: Macmillan, 1922) and especially Tyler Dennett, "The Open Door Policy as Intervention," Annals of the American Academy of Political and Social Sciences, CLXVIII (1933), 78–83.

tance of Roosevelt on Asian policy.[7] At the same time, others sought
to define the economics and spirit of "dollar" and "missionary" diplomacy in terms of the personalities of William Howard Taft and
Woodrow Wilson.

Just as progressive biography led to profile, so a personal approach
to diplomacy produced broader generalization, such as the monumen-
tal monograph of A. Whitney Griswold, the man-in-the-street history
of Thomas Bailey, the sweeping survey of Foster Rhea Dulles, and
the early published lectures of George F. Kennan.[8] Like the search
for the progressive profile, the first of Kennan's historical essays
removed the content of the Open Door from consideration and introduced an Open Door personality—not the flashy Roosevelt or the
scholarly John Hay, but the unanimously ignored underlings, the
English Hippisley and the American Rockhill. This was not a realisti-
cally ordered foreign policy, Kennan wrote in his famous *American
Diplomacy*. It was, rather, an inexact, misleading, legalistic effort
unconcerned with the power requirements understood only by Roosevelt and friends such as Admiral Alfred Thayer Mahan. If Dennett
was to the study of progressive diplomacy what Faulkner was to the
domestic side, then Kennan was its Hofstadter, with equally broad
acceptance among the majority of historians publishing in the 1950s.

Once again the perfecting of a fundamentally biographical method
left some dissatisfied. The chief critics were those who sensed in the

7. Henry F. Pringle, *Theodore Roosevelt: A Biography* (New York: Harcourt,
Brace, 1931), p. 262; Howard K. Beale, *Theodore Roosevelt and the Rise of
America to World Power* (Baltimore: Johns Hopkins Press, 1956).

8. A. Whitney Griswold, *The Far Eastern Policy of the United States* (New
York: Harcourt, Brace, 1938); Foster Rhea Dulles, *America in the Pacific: A
Century of Expansion* (Boston: Houghton Mifflin, 1938) and *China and America:
The Story of their Relations Since 1784* (Princeton: Princeton University Press,
1946); George F. Kennan, *American Diplomacy, 1900–1950*, Charles R. Walgreen
Foundation Lectures (New York: New American Library, 1951). The many publications of Thomas A. Bailey are most illustrative. From a 1934 meeting with the
historical figure of Roosevelt which resulted in *Theodore Roosevelt and the Japanese American Crisis* (Stanford: Stanford University Press, 1934), Bailey moved to
his similar studies of Woodrow Wilson and to his famed text: *Woodrow Wilson
and the Lost Peace* (New York: Macmillan, 1944), *Woodrow Wilson and the
Great Betrayal* (New York: Macmillan, 1945), and *A Diplomatic History of the
American People* (New York: F. S. Crofts, 1940). The ultimate in the personal
approach was his later *The Man in the Street: The Impact of American Public
Opinion on Foreign Policy* (New York: Macmillan, 1948).

Open Door a real consistency with earlier American policy and with what Wiebe calls the "broad social, political and economic issues." Kennan had stressed the commercial equality and territorial integrity principles of the Open Door as being older, English tactics. Students of Chinese history, especially John King Fairbank, writing simultaneously with Kennan, reminded their readers that the United States had a "traditional China policy" growing out of westward expansion with which the Open Door notes of 1899 and 1900 were perfectly consistent.[9] Equally challenging to the Kennan essays was the appearance in 1951 of Charles Campbell's research into the desire of special business interests for an economic share in the China market rapidly being closed by European spheres of influence. The argument could once again be made that not just Hippisley and Rockhill, but economic pressures of the 1890s had shaped the Open Door policy. In fact, more recent studies from the English side have dismissed the idea that any outside pressure was applied or needed to move the United States toward the Open Door.[10]

Fairbank and Campbell reopened the study of the period's diplomacy to those who viewed its content and results as part of a "political, ideological and military" system. These, who must also then be called revisionists, are concerned, as Wiebe and Kolko are, with the relationship between business and government. Several students of Fred Harvey Harrington, in particular William Appleman Williams, Walter LaFeber, and Thomas McCormick, have done most of the work on this period. Their attention has centered on the link between businessmen, the evolution of the corporate capitalist order, and the development of policy—in this case, foreign. Williams has stressed the Open Door as a compromise in the imperialist-antiimperialist debate of 1898. The Open Door can be viewed then not in personal or unrealistic terms, but as commerical expansionism upon which all could agree and not the more hotly debated territorial expansionism or imperialism.[11]

9. John King Fairbank, *The United States and China* (Cambridge: Harvard University Press, 1948, revised 1954), ch. 14.

10. Charles S. Campbell, *Special Business Interests and the Open Door Policy* (New Haven: Yale University Press, 1951). For the British study see R. G. Neale, *Great Britain and United States Expansion, 1898–1900* (East Lansing: Michigan State University Press, 1966).

11. Walter LaFeber, *The New Empire: An Interpretation of American Expansion* (Ithaca: Cornell University Press, 1963); Thomas McCormick's earlier article, "Insular Imperialism and the Open Door: The China Market and the Spanish-

The study of the link between the domestic and diplomatic natures of the period has hardly begun. Most attempts to relate the two areas have been efforts to support larger theses about one or the other. So in the early literature a favorable view of the reform results of progressivism was usually complemented by the idea that foreign expansion, economic exploitation, or involvement in war would be anathema. Even in the sophisticated studies of a man like Harrington, interest focused on the antiimperialists or those who at least did not fit the evolving expansionist framework. World war became the "betrayal of progressivism." Harley Notter's emphasis on Woodrow Wilson's dislike of the money trust in the 1913 withdrawal from the China banking consortium indicated such thinking in a detailed foreign policy study.[12]

When locating progressives by use of the profile method, the image of an antiimperialist, pacifist reformer was misleading. In this more critical and conservative view of the period, jingoistic, imperialistic, and even militaristic attitudes were the mainstream. In what is certainly the best-known effort to study the link between what he calls the "revered" separate fields of "Progressivism and Imperialism," William Leuchtenberg developed this position.[13] In his pathfinding article Leuchtenberg saw a generally middle-class movement supporting Roosevelt's mild prescriptions to remedy domestic ills and acquiescing in his much more powerful foreign policy of big navies and Caribbean adventures. After Roosevelt this leaderless group still backed Taft's dollar diplomacy and Wilson's use of force in Mexico and eventually Europe.

There was in addition, Leuchtenberg assured, real consistency and

---

American War," *Pacific Historical Review*, XXXII (May 1963), 155–69, and his later monograph, *China Market* (Chicago: Quadrangle, 1967); William A. Williams, *The Tragedy of American Diplomacy*, rev. ed. (New York: Dell, 1962) and the brief *America and the Middle East* (New York: Rinehart, 1958) in which he studies Open Door imperialism.

12. Fred Harvey Harrington, "The Anti-Imperialist Movement in the United States, 1898–1900," *Mississippi Valley Historical Review*, XXII (Sept. 1935), 211–30, and by the same author, *God, Mammon and the Japanese: Dr. Horace N. Allen and Korean-American Relations, 1884–1905* (Madison: University of Wisconsin Press, 1944), Harley Notter, *The Origins of the Foreign Policy of Woodrow Wilson* (Baltimore: Johns Hopkins Press, 1957), pp. 216–17.

13. William Leuchtenberg, "Progressivism and Imperialism: The Progressive Movement and American Foreign Policy, 1896–1916," *Mississippi Valley Historical Review*, XXXIX (Dec. 1952), 483–504.

not just coincidence between reform and imperialism. Both represented mission, social and economic reform at home, and the extension of democracy abroad. Fundamentally racists, whether towards Negroes or Asiatics, would-be progressives had been imperialists in the 1898 debate and accepted every ramification of a vigorous foreign policy—a big navy, the extension of overseas commerce and investment, or the necessity for preparedness following the outbreak of European hostilities in 1914.[14] Zealously utilitarian, progressives were attentive to the twin calls of John Dewey's religious faith in the democratic mission and Herbert Croly's new religion of national reform. Imperialism and reform were joined by the same rationale. They interlocked so as to be almost indivisible and, most important, fed each other large reinforcing doses of mission in the quest for the "promise of American life." To Leuchtenberg, only conservatives could oppose such policies. A curious coalition of 1880-type Mugwump political reformers and modern dress reactionaries like Senator Nelson Aldrich made up the group against something so progressive as Roosevelt's big navy ambitions.

Though professing to study progressivism and the progressive movement and its ideological content and motivations, Leuchtenberg relied heavily on the biographical method of proof. He brought forth the typical imperialist-progressives: Senator Albert Beveridge, boy-diplomat Willard Straight, Croly, and, of course, Roosevelt. To make the case indisputable he moved with ease through the well-known progressive all-star roster: Jacob Riis, Gifford Pinchot, and George Norris supported Roosevelt's seizing of the territory for the Panama Canal in 1903 and Senators Jonathan Dolliver and Robert La Follette were with him on Latin American interventions, the Roosevelt corollary to the Monroe Doctrine. The profile approach was most obvious in repeated references to the Progressive party of 1912 as the movement in toto. Only those openly labeling themselves progressives were considered, thus those Wilson supporters or regular Republican Taft followers who might fit the model were excluded.

The acceptance of this profile approach had far more serious weaknesses than just the methodological. Seeking the basic character of

14. Christopher Lasch's "The Anti-Imperialists, the Philippines and the Inequality of Man," *Journal of Southern History*, XXIV (Aug. 1958), 319–31, is an example of the way the Leuchtenberg thesis serves to explain another of the period's problems.

the period served frequently to dismiss what Wiebe calls the broader issues or the role of those above or below the middle class. Thus Leuchtenberg's perceptive linkage of domestic and diplomatic philosophies is left undeveloped. Were progressivism and imperialism ends in themselves or were they representative of basic conceptions of the society and economy as a whole?

Other investigations of the link between domestic and diplomatic developments in the progressive era have failed to push the borders of the field far beyond Leuchtenberg's. Robert Seager's unpublished dissertation, "The Progressives and American Foreign Policy, 1898–1917," documented the findings of the Leuchtenberg piece. Careful study of 175 representative progressives led Seager to the same reform-imperialism conclusion.[15]

Charles Vevier had sensed the relationship between the progressives and dollar diplomacy even before Leuchtenberg. In his unpublished Master's thesis Vevier developed the link at home and abroad during the period of alienation of the progressives from the Taft administration.[16] Vevier did not go as far as Leuchtenberg in seeing mutual reinforcement as well as the absence of a contradiction between progressivism and imperialism. His argument rested on the premise that progressives were generally unconcerned with foreign policy, thus they were tacit, not active, dollar diplomats. Vevier refused to allow progressive support for "American imperialism" to affect his favorable view of the domestic movement for reform, uplift, and progress.

Vevier's judgments, apart from his somewhat biographical methodology, were straight out of the older content school. Reformers were "good guys" and their silence on the international interests did not convince him that progressivism was fundamentally conservative. Like Leuchtenberg, however, Vevier never asked whether traditional defini-

15. Robert Seager II, "The Progressives and American Foreign Policy, 1898–1917: An Analysis of the Attitudes of the Leaders of the Progressive Movement toward External Affairs" (Ph.D. diss., Ohio State University, 1957). For an example of the work of others adopting the Leuchtenberg biographical approach see Charles Hirschfield, "Brooks Adams and American Nationalism," *American Historical Review*, LXIX (Jan. 1964), 371–92. For the difference between a biographical and a content approach compare this with William A. Williams, "Brooks Adams and American Expansion," *New England Quarterly*, XXV (June 1952), 217–32.

16. Charles Vevier, "The Progressives and Dollar Diplomacy," (Master's thesis, University of Wisconsin, 1949).

tions of imperialism fit the foreign policy of the period. He did not question either if he described a fundamental of the society or one of the many consequences of a still broader progressive consideration of the new industrial society. When he found cleavage among dollar diplomats, the so-called Crane incident of 1909 involving the recall of Charles Crane as minister to China, he failed to pursue its causes or consequences for they could have no significance other than personal or political. All these men were imperialists, weren't they? Or so Vevier reasoned.[17]

Others have attempted to make the link Vevier resisted. None of the reformers are now safe. There are interestingly titled articles like "LaFollette's Imperialist Flirtation" and the Kennanesque conclusions of Ray Ginger, in "Wherein Americans go to live in the clouds," that progressive "self-delusion" in foreign policy was typical of the whole period.[18] Ginger went where Vevier feared to tread. He accepted the Leuchtenberg argument and allowed the imperialism of the progressives to condemn and dismiss the reform nature of the domestic movement as well.

One of the most recent, searching, and critical examinations deriving from the work of Leuchtenberg is Barton Bernstein and Franklin Leib's "Progressive Republican Senators and American Imperialism, 1898–1916: A Reappraisal."[19] Somewhat sympathetic, like Vevier, to the domestic progressive reformer, Bernstein and Leib, nevertheless, take Leuchtenberg's thesis seriously. Interestingly, they do propose that future researchers, like recent students of domestic progressivism, broaden the attitudes sampled to include varieties of progressives—for example, "easterners, southerners and westerners . . . politicians, lawyers, businessmen, and social reformers . . . city dwellers, townspeople and farmers . . . native-born and even . . . immigrants and first-generation Americans." This suggestion, coupled with others, such as investigating "conservatives" as well as "progressives" and hinting at the period's "consensus on the need for overseas commercial expansion

17. Chapter 3 of this work deals with the significance of this incident.

18. Padraic Colum Kennedy, "LaFollette's Imperialist Flirtation," *Pacific Historical Review*, XXXIX (May 1960), 131–44, and Ray Ginger, *Age of Excess: The United States from 1877 to 1914* (New York: Macmillan, 1965), p. 208.

19. Barton Bernstein and Franklin Leib, "Progressive Republican Senators and American Imperialism, 1898–1916: A Reappraisal," *Mid-America*, L (July 1968), 163–205. This article is particularly useful for its up-to-date review of recent research completed or in progress on related subjects.

as a guarantee of domestic prosperity," indicates that, with Bernstein and Leib, the study of the relationships between domestic and diplomatic events reaches towards a stage perhaps akin to the level of discussion by Hays and Fairbank for the domestic and diplomatic areas, respectively.

Still for all their perspective and awareness, Bernstein and Leib are angered by the most shocking of Leuchtenberg's attacks on progressives as imperialists. Finding the domestic record under attack from its foreign policy corollary, they seek to separate the two faces of the period once again so as to preserve a favorable image of domestic accomplishments and share the guilt of imperialism among all Americans, not just reformers.

As seen best in Bernstein and Leib's article, the Leuchtenberg thesis, not the actual relationships between domestic and diplomatic developments, has become the issue.[20] For all its conceptualization, Leuchtenberg's work must still be considered an invitation to discussion and not a final statement. Leuchtenberg himself has never followed up on the article. It is not his major contribution nor his primary focus and should not be allowed to provide a central pivot for all discussions of progressivism at home and America abroad in the early twentieth century.

There must be, and there are signs that, reexamination, and reinterpretation will lead away from praise or scorn for progressivism and imperialism and towards portions of the relationship which have gotten little or no attention. In Arthur Link's *Wilson* an effort is made to pursue the relationship, for example, between progressivism and pre–World War I peace movements as something more than the usual blinding cliches of midwestern isolationism and war as betrayal.[21] Just how deep the ties between peace and progressivism were may be one important question in closing the gap between domestic and diplomatic attitudes and rethinking the dialogue begun by Leuchtenberg. Articles such as Walter Trattner's "Progressivism and World War I: A Reappraisal" and Peter Filene's "Progressivism and the World Peace

20. Bernstein and Leib cite, for example, recent unpublished manuscripts in their possession, such as "Progressivism versus Imperialism: A Critique of the Leuchtenberg Thesis" (John M. Cooper, Jr., 1968) and "California Progressives and Foreign Policy" (Thomas G. Paterson, 1966).

21. Arthur Link, *Woodrow Wilson and the Progressive Era, 1910–1917* (New York: Harper & Row, 1954), pp. 82 ff. and 224 ff. Compare Link with Goldman, *Rendezvous With Destiny*, p. 219.

Foundation" and a recent doctoral dissertation on the Carnegie Endowment for International Peace are indications of research challenging the belief in the Roosevelt-Mahan militarism as the established religion of the period.[22]

In addition, other monographs call into question the present understanding of the progressive-imperialist link. To Paul Varg belongs credit for the most extensive treatment of simultaneous developments at home and abroad. In his *Missionaries, Chinese and Diplomats*, Varg has related the growth of an educational rather than evangelistic missionary movement to the church reforms of the Social Gospel in America.[23] Restricted by his subject to the social welfare side of the period, Varg does allude to the "religious aspect of the broader socioeconomic and political movement that looked beyond the limits of national boundaries." In his description of the missionary as urban social worker, interested in the range of issues from education and the role of women to temperance both alcoholic and narcotic, Varg has gone furthest in specifying the actual role of the progressive idea in foreign contact. His work suggests the possibility of exploring beyond the catchall term *imperialism*, be it of the power or economic variety. Varg notes the missionary desire to view "the answers to Chinese needs in the Western forms of society with which they were familar, in terms of public education, an improved technology, in scientific experimentation in agriculture and Western democratic political institutions." He implies then that progressives were not just imperialists, but a special breed whose reform program grew out of their own domestic environment or orientation. Imperialism or progressive imperialism, at least as expressed in the workings of the Open Door, may be viewed as part of a broader approach designed to order the world in a uniquely progressive way. In this vein, others are at work in relating specifically progressive organizations to foreign policy. Of special interest is the highly original article of Claude Fike, "The

22. Walter I. Trattner, "Progressivism and World War I: A Reappraisal," *Mid-America*, XLIV (July 1962), 131–45 and Peter Filene, "The World Peace Foundation and Progressivism, 1910–1918," *New England Quarterly*, XXXVI (Dec. 1963), 478–501. Michael Lutzker's doctoral dissertation on the Carnegie Endowment for International Peace, "The 'Practical' Peace Advocates: An Interpretation of the American Peace Movement, 1898–1917" (Rutgers University, 1969).

23. Paul Varg, *Missionaries, Chinese and Diplomats: The American Protestant Missionary Movement in China, 1890–1952* (Princeton: Princeton University Press, 1958), pp. vii, 3–4, 66–67, 75–76, 91–97, and 116–24.

Influence of the Creel Committee and the American Red Cross on Russian-American Relations, 1917–1919."[24]

Such questioning leads in the same direction as the revisionism now under way in the separate fields of domestic and foreign policy of the period. Since Leuchtenberg and the others grasped only a partial consequence and not a cause, perhaps the broader issues to be raised are the relationship of business to reform and the corollary desire of such businessmen-reformers to develop and shape the corporate capitalism of the early twentieth century.

In his survey of the turn of the century's response to industrialism Samuel Hays calls for a study of the dynamics of foreign expansion. He sees it as a revealing outward expression of the new coping with organization and industrial change on the part of business and government alike.[25] Thomas Paterson takes a hesitant and obvious yet necessary first step in his article, "American Businessmen and Consular Service Reform, 1890's to 1906."[26] Even more revealing are some of the conclusions of Charles Forcey in his study of the editors of the *New Republic*. Progressives, at home and abroad, had a love affair with efficiency, something Hays and Samuel Haber have perceived as well.[27] The elaboration of this trend domestically led to the movement away from laissez faire and trustbusting toward industrial consolidation. So too in foreign affairs Croly and Straight, two of Leuchtenberg's chief examples, sought the analogous transition from an internationally competitive Open Door to a closely cooperative one. Forcey tends to accept the Leuchtenberg position that there was no necessary contradiction between progressivism and what he still chooses to call impe-

24. Claude E. Fike, "The Influence of the Creel Committee and the American Red Cross on Russian-American Relations, 1917–1919," *Journal of Modern History*, XXI (June 1959), 93–109.

25. Hays, *Response to Industrialism*, p. 204, says, "The literature of American foreign policy is abundant but deals mainly with formal diplomatic relations rather than with the dynamics of expansion and of co-operation and conflict among peoples. Economic or cultural expansion has not received comprehensive treatment."

26. Thomas G. Paterson, "American Businessmen and Consular Service Reform, 1890's to 1906," *Business History Review*, XL (Spring 1966), 77–97.

27. Charles Forcey, *The Crossroads of Liberalism: Croly, Weyl, Lippmann and the Progressive Era, 1900–1925* (New York: Oxford University Press, 1961); Samuel Hays, *Conservation and the Gospel of Efficiency: The Progressive Conservation Movement, 1890–1920* (Cambridge: Harvard University Press, 1959), and Samuel Haber, *Efficiency and Uplift: Scientific Management in the Progressive Era, 1890–1920* (Chicago: University of Chicago Press, 1964).

rialism. Yet his own work shows that such a view is static, partial, and merely illustrative of a much broader, evolving relationship between business and government at home and abroad. It is here, for example, that a relationship is obvious between the Open Door as a synthesis of territorial and commercial expansionism and progressivism as a compromise between the rationalization of industry and the free enterprise tradition. The imperialist and antiimperialist movements and the trust and antitrust campaigns were part of the same historical period. They were also partners in sharing the same historical frame of mind.

There is then the need for general reexamination of progressivism and Open Door foreign policy drawing on earlier efforts but barring no one or no idea failing to meet an expected image, be it humanitarian reformer or middle-class conservative. Such an approach should not be designed to reinforce any particular definition nor to reopen debate on any particular thesis. It must articulate and analyze the attitudes and actions of the many diverse, but related, elements obviously at work throughout the period.

Progressivism and the Open Door: America and China, 1905–1921

1

Alice in Wonderland

Through the China Looking Glass and What America Found There

ON the 16th of the Moon at the hour of ssu, September 14, 1905, 9:00 A.M. to 11:00 A.M., America's oft-proclaimed princess, Alice Roosevelt, met the empress dowager of China. While this real life version of "the dream child moving through a land of wonders wild and new" may not have been filled with Lewis Carroll's logical nonsense it contained a fascination similar to that of the fictional Alice's famous flight. In a vocabulary foreign to the usual State Department communication, American Minister to China W. W. Rockhill described the preparations to Secretary of State Elihu Root: "the Department of the Imperial Household will send a large chair with yellow loops to the Lang Jun Garden, in which Miss Roosevelt will be conveyed to the Jen Shou Throne Hall of the Summer Palace for Audience."[1]

Although the familiar White Rabbit, Dormouse, and Queen of Hearts were not in attendance, Theodore Roosevelt's daughter Alice surrounded herself with an equally interesting cast of characters. Only the

1. On Alice's trip see W. W. Rockhill to Elihu Root, Sept. 20, 1905, U. S. Dept. of State Dispatches (hereafter cited as Dispatches), vol. 128, National Archives (hereafter cited as NA); Alice Roosevelt Longworth, *Crowded Hours* (New York: Charles Scribner's Sons, 1933), pp. 71, 73, 91 ff. William Phillips, *Ventures in Diplomacy* (Boston: Beacon Press, 1952), pp. 23–24. A fascinating recent study and text of the Lewis Carroll classic is Martin Gardner, *The Annotated Alice* (New York: Clarkson N. Potter, 1960).

ladies of the party joined in the imperial audience but the entourage to the Far East in the early autumn of 1905 included American senators and congressmen and the usual crowd of reporters mostly concerned with the latest details in the touring romance of the president's daughter and her prince, Nicholas Longworth.

A closer inspection of the roster of passengers reveals that this extended Asiatic trip was more than just a social or romantic visit. Certainly the junket was planned to coincide with the deluge of praise heaped on Roosevelt for his part in the recently completed Portsmouth negotiations to end the Russo-Japanese War. The president's desire to represent his government officially as well as personally explained in part the presence of Secretary of War William Howard Taft. Among the others in the party were railroad builder E. H. Harriman and Mabel T. Boardman, successor to Clara Barton as leader of the reorganized American Red Cross. The appearance of these three hints that Alice's adventures in the Chinese wonderland were in fact part of the first general taking stock of America's position in China since the promulgation of the Open Door notes of 1899 and 1900 and the coming to office of Roosevelt in 1901.[2]

Several changes and crises in the summer of 1905 made such a rethinking of policy necessary. John Hay was dead and the loss of the Open Door's chief spokesman, especially when the power balance of the Far East was changing with Japan's military success against Russia, placed greater stress on the diplomacy of Roosevelt and the knowledge of those like Taft who advised him on Far Eastern affairs. More directly, Taft's visit resulted from the need to soothe Chinese sensitivities on the issue of exclusion of Chinese immigrants and visitors from the United States. Excited by insult and injury in the Pacific states especially, Chinese merchants were enforcing a general boycott of American goods which Taft hoped to stop. While American trade suffered, railroad and investment hopes took an equally devastating blow when the plans of the American China Development Company to build a Canton-Hankow railway were dashed with Chinese cancellation of the original concession. The future of other such plans for China and Manchuria explained Harriman's interest in making the long trip.

2. Theodore Roosevelt to William Howard Taft, Sept. 2 and Sept. 4, 1905, Theodore Roosevelt Papers (hereafter cited as TRP), series 2, vol. 57, Library of Congress (hereafter cited as LC); Taft to Mabel Boardman, Sept. 16, 1905, Mabel Boardman Papers, LC; and Mabel Boardman, "An Audience With the Dowager Empress of China," *The Outlook*, XC (Dec. 12, 1908), 824–28.

Finally, in the midst of these setbacks, indeed the cause of them many felt, political, administrative and educational reforms had not yet lived up to the promise held for them in the empire. A representative of a major organization in the social welfare field, Mabel Boardman could look for herself and others who could not make the trip to see what needed to be done.

Plans for the Open Door in Action

Despite the general need for a reconsideration of policy, which justifies 1905 as a turning point in the story of America's relations with China, the concept of a wonderland still seems appropriate for the image of China in the United States at that time. Generalizing about this powerfully pervasive idea and yet unrealized dream of China's potential, Robert Divine has noted perceptively that "Americans had developed a romantic view of China, visualizing it a vast potential market for American goods, American culture and American democracy." It was this view, or a variety of it, that Alice and her friends brought in 1905. Since the Open Door notes and the beginning of the Roosevelt years, there was the increased sense that opportunity would finally be realized in China as indeed it would also be at home. As the cartoonist for *Judge* sketched it, Roosevelt would now say to both his poker partners, China and Uncle Sam, "Come now, gentlemen, it is time to throw aside that worn-out deck and try one which will give both of you a square deal."[3]

It is true that the president was among those whose ideas on the future of America's role in the Far East fit into a larger pattern of domestic and international development. Confident of America's need and ability to expand ever westward, Roosevelt stressed, even before he inherited the White House, the need not to "avoid the responsibilities that confront us," lest the country bow to England and Germany, "the great progressive, colonizing nations."[4] A system-builder himself, Roosevelt's ideas were sharpened and reinforced by the other master planners gathered around him. In one of the rare truly give-and-take situations between the intellectual and the political realms, the H

3. Robert A. Divine, *The Illusion of Neutrality* (Chicago: University of Chicago Press, 1962), p. 25. *Judge,* XLIX (Aug. 5, 1905).

4. Theodore Roosevelt, *The Strenuous Life: Essays and Addresses* (New York: Century, 1902), pp. 6–7, 34. This is a collection of four essays given between April 1899 and Sept. 1901.

Street world of Brooks and Henry Adams, John Hay, W. W. Rockhill, and Alfred Thayer Mahan produced an Open Door policy, a minister, a secretary of state, and a president to support it, and fertile minds to give it structure and definition. Much has been said of these men and the expansionism they preached yet it should be noted that each in his way dealt with the problems of China and Asia at the turn of the century.[5]

While Hay circulated the famous notes, written in large part by Rockhill, calling for commercial equality and territorial integrity in China, Brooks Adams had already defined this constant westward flow in his *Law of Civilization and Decay*. Now seeking to have America apply that basic law, after the second round of Open Door notes, Adams wrote to Hay, "We hold command in the East, with possible consequences which I cannot measure but which are certainly greater than anything which has happened since 1870."[6] To capture economic supremacy which meant in Adams's mind blocking others, especially Russia, from trying to do the same, America had to strengthen its military might and ensure a permanent international market for its products. Picking up Adams's words and ideas, in his first State of the Union address Roosevelt called for American military and economic power to expand the frontier of the United States westward to the interior of China.[7]

The president captured the mind of Admiral Mahan who had in 1900 applied his own law of civilization, the influence of sea power on the problem of Asia. Much of Mahan's strategic thinking explained Adams's fear of Russia, a land power, taking a preponderant role in

5. Walter LaFeber, *The New Empire: An Interpretation of American Expansion* (Ithaca: Cornell University Press, 1963), ch. 2. Among the many discussions of the meetings of this group one of the best appears in Tyler Dennett's *John Hay: From Poetry to Politics* (New York: Dodd, Mead, 1933), pp. 289–90.

6. Brooks Adams to John Hay, Aug. 17, 1900, John Hay Papers, container 18, LC; Brooks Adams, *Law of Civilization and Decay* (New York: Macmillan, 1895).

7. Discussion of the use of Adams's ideas by Roosevelt can be found in Howard K. Beale, *Theodore Roosevelt and the Rise of America to World Power* (Baltimore: Johns Hopkins Press, 1956), pp. 159 ff. and 174–75, and in William A. William's "The Frontier Thesis and American Foreign Policy," *Pacific Historical Review*, XXIV (Nov. 1955), 387. See also Brooks Adams, *America's Economic Supremacy* (New York: Macmillan, 1900), and two articles on Adams: William A. Williams, "Brooks Adams and American Expansion," *New England Quarterly*, XXV (June 1952), 217–32, and Charles Vevier, "Brooks Adams and the Ambivalence of American Foreign Policy," *World Affairs Quarterly*, XXX (April 1959), 3–18.

China. Mahan's influence can also be seen as a motivation for Hay's sending of the second Open Door notes after the relief expeditions of European armies had been mobilized to defeat the antiforeign Boxer Rebellion. Less often noted in connection with Mahan is his certainty that the future of the world would be determined by the character of the civilization China received. He, too, like Brooks Adams, emphasized the need to rush through the newly opened door with large supplies of Western, specifically British and American–Anglo-Saxon commerce and thought.[8]

More an observer of life than a participant in it from the time of the death of his wife in 1885, Brooks's older brother, Henry Adams, was perhaps most symbolic of America's position in China, as he was of so much else in American history as well. In 1900 Adams was interested in the whole drama developing in the Far East, likening it to a novel by Alexandre Dumas.[9] Whether he sensed it or not, Adams had since 1886 been looking to China for a magic formula for his personal future just as his brother and friends searched for the future of the country and civilization. In the darkness immediately following his wife's death and before discovering his own fascination with the Middle Ages, Adams joined artist friend John La Farge on a visit to the Orient which got them as far as Japan. There they encountered Ernest Fenellosa, a student of Eastern culture and more importantly for Adams, a cousin of his dead wife. Fenellosa, like Ezra Pound, sought his own future in China, an artistic or spiritual open door, a renaissance to be sparked not by classical antiquity but by China which Pound called a "new Greece." Adams found Fenellosa an ineffective tyrant, a kind of Buddhist St. Dominic who made him yearn for some old New England "Calvinism with leanings toward the Methodists."[10]

For all his cynicism Henry Adams was deeply captured with the dream of China. In 1886 he reported his conclusion to John Hay:

8. Alfred Thayer Mahan, *The Influence of Sea Power Upon History, 1660–1783* (Boston: Little, Brown, 1890) and the same author's *The Problem of Asia* (Boston: Little, Brown, 1900).

9. Allan Nevins, *Henry White: Thirty Years of American Diplomacy* (New York: Harper & Brothers, 1930), p. 171.

10. See the exceptionally interesting article by Donald Richie, "Henry Adams in Japan," *Japan Quarterly*, VI (Oct.–Dec. 1959), 434–42; also Van Wyck Brooks, *Fenellosa and His Circle* (New York: E. P. Dutton, 1962), p. 67; and Lawrence Chisolm, *Fenellosa: The Far East and American Culture* (New Haven: Yale University Press, 1963).

"China is the only mystery left to penetrate. I have henceforward a future. As soon as I can get rid of history, and the present, I mean to start for China, and stay there." Combining past and future, Adams divided his time upon his return to writing his famous study of the administrations of Jefferson and Madison and learning Chinese. For all the effort, Adams never got to the future, even though, as his biographer points out, he was still planning the "ultimate exploration" after twenty more years of globe-trotting.[11] In retrospect Adams's unrealized dream represents the failure of Americans at the turn of the century to realize their dreams for the Chinese wonderland. Despite this intriguing historical analogy, Adams's fascination with China reveals, more importantly, that even a man intent on painfully wrenching himself from his own life and world could be caught in the pervasive hope that the future could be found in China and perhaps only there.

There were others far removed from H Street in Washington who also saw America's role in the Orient as part of a broader domestic and international pattern. The most persistent theme in all such ideas was the involvement of the United States, at least economically if not politically, in the Pacific as an outgrowth of American westward expansion toward the frontier. Frederick Jackson Turner, often linked with but by no means a part of the Adams's circle, had developed such a frontier thesis to explain all of American history. In reviewing later the situation at the turn of the century Turner thought it highly logical that "having colonized the Far West, having mastered its internal resources, the nation turned to deal with the Far East, to emerge in world-politics of the Pacific Ocean."[12]

Others sounding much like Mahan and Adams stressed America's

11. Ernest Samuels, *Henry Adams: The Middle Years* (Cambridge: Harvard University Press, 1958), pp. 312, 321, 344, 475.

12. Frederick Jackson Turner, *The Frontier in American History* (New York: Henry Holt, 1920). The concept of the frontier and expansion has been explored in Williams's "The Frontier Thesis and American Foreign Policy." On Turner see also Lawrence S. Kaplan, "Frederick Jackson Turner and Imperialism," *Social Science*, XXVII (Jan. 1952), 12–16. Of the many treatments of the West in a general sense see three works in particular: Loren Baritz, "The Idea of the West," *American Historical Review*, LXVI (April 1961), 618–40; Herbert Heaton, "Other Wests Than Ours," *Journal of Economic History*, VI (Supp. VI, 1946), 50–62; and A. Grenfell Price, *The Western Invasions of the Pacific and Its Continents: A Study of Moving Frontiers and Changing Landscapes* (New York: Oxford University Press, 1963).

favorable geopolitical position, the civilizing burden of the Anglo-Saxon, and a strong fear of Russia in China. Representative of such thinking are the words of four men with seemingly different orientations: university president James Angell, Methodist missionary James Bashford, economic geographer O. P. Austin, and New York mayor Seth Low.

Speaking to a University of Michigan baccalaureate audience in June of 1900, James Angell felt the United States had a "widening horizon" from which it could not retreat. The horizon was a new era in commercial life. The United States had surplus products to distribute and five thousand miles of Pacific Ocean in which to do it. The United States could not be excluded from any land in Asia which was "washed by the waves of the Great Sea." Angell's conclusion was apparent: the "Young Giant of the West" must "yield a great influence over China's people in respect to commerce, to education and to religion."[13]

Bishop Bashford's view of the development of civilization was much like Brooks Adams's, from the Fertile Crescent ever west to the Mediterranean, the Atlantic and finally the Pacific. Sea power, especially with the proposed Panama Canal, gave the commercially and industrially rich United States a chance to dominate Chinese civilization. Religious power was still more pivotal. Or as Bashford confidently wrote, "the Chinese themselves in breaking away from an ancient civilization can readily be led to accept a western, Christian, Protestant civilization."[14] Adopting a verse form the bishop summarized his feelings on China and America:

> God took care to hide that country
> Till he prized his people ready
> Then he chose me by his whisper
> And I found it, and it's yours
>
> Yes "America's God's Country"
> Yes a best of all creations

13. James B. Angell, "The Widening Horizon," unpublished baccalaureate address, New York Public Library (hereafter cited as NYPL), June 17, 1900; and also Angell's interest in China of the same period, "The Crisis in China," *Atlantic Monthly*, LXXXVI (Oct. 1900), 433–37.

14. James W. Bashford, *The Awakening of China*, Missionary Research Library (New York: Union Theological Seminary, 1907); the poem may be found in Bashford's Diary, XXXVII, 96, also among the James Bashford Papers of the Missionary Research Library.

What's the use of going further
Till I crossed the range to see

God forgive my pride I'm nothing
It's God's present to our nation
Anybody might have found it
But his whisper came to me.

Somewhat more prosaically, O. P. Austin, chief of the Treasury
Department's Bureau of Statistics, added a scientific explanation for
America's role in China. Once again the dominant idea was that civilization had progressed from Europe to America and now to Asia, following the setting sun. The great railroad building of the nineteenth
century was to be matched by developing cable communications across
the Pacific so as to knock at the commercial doors of East Asia, something Secretary of State William Seward had also perceived three decades earlier. From Austin's perspective America's unique place came
not from sea power, education, or God but from equatorial currents
flowing west from the place where an isthmian canal would enter the
Pacific toward the newly acquired Philippines, then north along the
coast of China and Japan until deflected east across the north Pacific
"to the American coast and then . . . down the United States to the
point of beginning."[15]

Seth Low, mayor of New York in 1902 and later president of both the
commercial American Asiatic Association and the industrial National
Civic Federation, combined these ideas in "The Position of the United
States Among the Nations."[16] America, Low observed, had always been
a world power. The interest in twentieth-century China could then be
explained as just part of the constant theme of growth or, as Low captured the spirit of American expansion, "a nation cannot live to itself
alone, and continue to be either great or strong." The large land and
sea space the United States commanded, its traditions of education and
self-government, and the new opportunity of the Panama Canal all

15. O. P. Austin, Address to the National Geographic Society reprinted in
National Geographic Magazine, XVI (Sept. 1905), 399–423. For the historical
importance of geopolitics see Charles Vevier, "American Continentalism: An Idea
of Expansion, 1845–1910," *American Historical Review*, LXV (Jan. 1960), 323–
35, and Charles Vevier, "The Collins Overland Line and American Continentalism," *Pacific Historical Review*, XXVIII (August 1959), 237–53.

16. Seth Low, "The Position of the United States Among the Nations," *Annals
of the American Academy of Political and Social Science*, XXVI (July 1905),
1–15.

meant that the Open Door would be an imposition of the ideals and productivity of the American people on the race for foreign trade in China.

While most of these plans for the United States in the Orient were general and vague, economist Charles Conant deserves credit for the best-defined such system as set forth in a series of seven articles between September 1898 and August 1900.[17] With an interest in banking, Conant's most original contribution was the linking of outlets for American capital in China to the more widely heralded opportunities for American products and progressive civilization. In particular he stressed America's ability to bring electricity and railroads to China and to equip these heavy industries with power machinery necessary for production and communication. The more usual commercial and civilization-saving themes of the Open Door were present as well. In a sentence best capturing the policy of John Hay with the philosophy of Brooks Adams, Conant stated the basic assumption of those who sought to build a system for the future out of America's role in the Far East:

If all the markets were open, if all the opportunities for labor and for employing the fruits of labor were free to men of all nations upon equal terms, that nation would confess its cowardice and decadence which was not willing to trust its fate on the economic field to the energy, inventive genius, and productive power of its people.[18]

The Open Door was then, at least to some of those important in its adoption, enforcement and reception at home, not an empty set of legalistic phrases about equality of opportunity and territorial integrity but a basic plan or system for the opening of Chinese markets and minds to American products, money, and ideas. The conclusion that such an opening was necessary came mostly from the understanding of the evolution of civilization ever westward. The realization that America was uniquely qualified to take the initiative in filling this opening emerged from various economic, geographic, religious, and patriotic perspectives and was reinforced by the seeming abundance of material wealth found in the United States.

17. Charles Conant, *The United States and the Orient* (Boston: Houghton Mifflin, 1900). Conant's articles were published between 1898 and 1900 in *North American Review, Forum,* and *Atlantic Monthly.*
18. Ibid., p. 188.

Economic Aspirations

Professor Walter LaFeber has demonstrated how the idea of a surplus at home, especially in the 1890s, could produce strong expansionist tendencies abroad.[19] In the depression years after 1893 Americans frantically sought solution of the problem of an obviously maldistributed domestic economy by finding markets for a production surplus that few at home could afford. By 1901, however, Open Door expansionism was a positive rather than a negative concept. From strength rather than weakness, American involvement in foreign affairs in the first years of the twentieth century was guided by the twin beliefs that not America but the world, or at least China, needed saving and that the United States was the only country qualified to do it.

Certainly that China should be saved mostly to be an outlet for an American manufacturing surplus remained uppermost in many minds. Before the Senate and in numerous magazine articles, Indiana Senator Albert Beveridge set forth what reads like a grade school primer on the realities of the corporate capitalist order.

"What America is looking for is trade," Beveridge asserted. Commerce was a nation's food and when prosperous a country's diet would be mostly exotic foreign food. "We cannot live upon ourselves," he warned. "We must dispose of our surplus abroad, and upon the sale of our surplus abroad depends the prosperous condition of all our commerce." Moving from introductory political economy to elementary political geography Beveridge made his plan clear: "The most populous portion of the surface of the earth does not control its own markets. This portion of the earth's surface is Asia, and especially the Empire of China with its 400,000,000 of consumers."[20]

These customers attracted many Americans. On the day he was shot in Buffalo, William McKinley sketched the problem that had dominated and would continue to dominate so much of his and his successor's time. "What we produce beyond our domestic consumption," McKinley declared, "must have a vent abroad."[21] Wisconsin Senator Robert

19. LaFeber, *The New Empire*, ch. 4.

20. See Beveridge's Jan. 9, 1900, speech before the Senate: U.S. Congress, Senate, 56th Cong., 1st Sess., Jan. 9, 1900, *Congressional Record*, XXXIII, 704–12. Also his article, "The White Invasion of China," *Saturday Evening Post*, CLXXIV (Nov. 16, 1901), 3–4.

21. A complete text of the Sept. 5, 1901, McKinley speech may be found in *Review of Reviews*, XXIV (Oct. 1901), 432–34.

La Follette, later a leading congressional insurgent and avowed defender of the people versus big business, echoed similar sentiments in supporting the 1900 acquisition of the Philippines. He advised, "We will be ready to conquer our rightful share of that great market for the world's commerce, we can legally and morally reserve unto ourselves perpetual commercial advantages of priceless value to our foreign trade for all time to come."[22] Commercially, at least in theory, China was just the perfect example of Russell Conwell's fashionably popular concept of "acres of diamonds," as in fact one American journalist did describe it. America's geographical position, stable economy, farm and factory productivity, and abundant resources made failure remote. Equality of opportunity, meaning no territorial spheres of influence as developed by European powers in the 1890s, was all that was needed. *The Nation* defined the commercial as opposed to territorial expansionism of the Open Door: "We do not need to seek an unfair advantage. An open door and no favor infallibly means for the United States . . . the greater share and gain in the commercial exploitation of China."[23]

Secretaries of State Hay and Root in the period from 1899 through 1905 were, as Hay put it, "alive to the importance of safeguarding our great commercial interests in that empire."[24] Despite this awareness and such tangible results as the new commercial treaty of 1903 with China designed to enlarge opportunities, open new ports, and abolish internal restrictions to trade, a huge gap remained between the potential and the realized advantages of American commerce in China.[25]

In some areas of the United States, the south in particular, exports of cotton goods, especially to Manchuria, were of major importance

22. Padraic Colum Kennedy, "LaFollette's Imperialist Flirtation," *Pacific Historical Review*, XXIX (May 1960), 134–35.

23. Frederick McCormick to Howard McCormick, Oct. 1, 1902, Frederick McCormick Papers, Cornell University Library; *Nation*, LXXII (May 9, 1901), 368–69. For a clear statement in practice of this philosophy see Secretary of the Treasury Shaw to the American Bankers' Association, Oct. 11, 1905, TRP, series 1, box 98.

24. John Hay to Paul Dana, March 16, 1899, in William Roscoe Thayer, *The Life and Letters of John Hay* (New York: Houghton Mifflin, 1908), II, 241.

25. Elihu Root, *The Military and Colonial Policy of the United States: Addresses and Reports by Elihu Root* (Cambridge: Harvard University Press, 1916), p. 105, and Charles S. Campbell, *Special Business Interests and the Open Door* (New Haven: Yale University Press, 1951), p. 9.

to a domestic industry. Manchuria was in fact the very spot taken more
and more to be most naturally suited for development by the United
States. It was there that Russian competition was most seriously felt
because of the presence of a Russo-Chinese bank and Russian opposition to the opening of ports for American commerce. However, the
frontier nature of Manchuria's "pioneer belt," so like Montana and the
Dakotas, and the belief that the great Manchurian populations were
"energetic and progressive" convinced many that cotton could be followed by a flood of other overproduced American goods.[26] Yet even
in Manchuria, despite the implorings of the Asiatic Association, the
broader-based Committee on American Interests in China, and the
even-more-general National Association of Manufacturers, the potential
market had not even begun to be realized. Though exports increased
after the turn of the century, Asian markets in general still lagged
behind European and other North American outlets, with business
amounting to some $104.7 million in 1901 as against $1,136.5 million for
Europe and $196.5 million for North America.[27]

A group of Americans, railroaders and bankers, did seek to extend
American interest beyond commerce and to capture the opportunity
immediately. As engineer William Barclay Parsons proclaimed in
McClure's Magazine in 1900, "We of today are concerned not with
what China will do eventually with progress but with what we ourselves can and should do with it now."[28] The *we* in this case was the

26. For a southern view see *Charlotte Daily Observer*, April 19, 1901, found in
William E. Griffis Papers, Rutgers University Library, New Brunswick, N. J. There
is a tremendous amount of official correspondence and historical literature on the
subject of Manchuria. For messages of American ministers E. H. Conger and
W. W. Rockhill, see in particular John Hay Papers, boxes 11 and 13 and container 22, LC; and Dispatches, vol. 117, National Archives. For two scholarly
articles from an interesting perspective see C. Walter Young, "Economic Factors
in Manchurian Diplomacy," *Annals of the American Academy of Political and
Social Science*, CLII (1930), 293–307, and "Manchuria as a Demographic Frontier," *Population Index*, II (Oct. 1945), 260–74.

27. Statistics are taken from the report of consul Henry B. Miller published in
New York Daily Tribune, March 5, 1901, found in the Griffis Papers, box 28, and
from the research of Phyliss Ibach Smith for which I am greatly indebted. See also
Journal of the American Asiatic Association, II (Feb. 8, 1902), 20–22, and Albert
K. Steigerwalt, *The National Association of Manufacturers, 1895–1914* (Ann
Arbor: Bureau of Business Research, 1964), pp, 57–59.

28. William Barclay Parsons, "The American Invasion of China," *McClure's
Magazine*, XIV (April 1900), 499–510.

American China Development Company composed of Parsons, former China minister Charles Denby, A. W. Bash of Seattle, New York lawyer Clarence Cary, and a group of stockholders including E. H. Harriman of the Union Pacific, Jacob Schiff of the investment house of Kuhn, Loeb and Company, and the presidents of the National City and Chase National Banks. Out of this group came the plan to build a railroad from Hankow to Canton on a concession granted by China. Such a scheme was of course in keeping with the ideas of a man like Charles Conant that through the introduction of heavy capital industry in the power and transportation fields there could be obtained what Denby described as a "foothold in the east" and the "boundless riches of her [China's] mines and the hoarded wealth of centuries."[29] While railroad investment plans would become an important part of American-Chinese relations, the hopes of the Development Company were no better realized than those of American exporters. The complete collapse of the group's concession and the question of future attempts would be the reason for E. H. Harriman's joining the Alice Roosevelt entourage. Before that can be considered in the context of 1905, however, the third element making up the Open Door policy, not commerce or investment but reform, must be understood.

Reform Impulses

The failure of the Boxer Rebellion, designed to end foreign control of China's affairs, strengthened rather than weakened the hand of the Western allies now tied together by the second Open Door notes, military cooperation, and the financial settlement or indemnity demanded of China. As *World's Work* reviewed the situation in 1901 it was apparent that the failure of antiforeign insurrection and the dawn of a new century would spell the awakening of China from the somnolence of centuries and "what we regard as progress will be greatly accelerated." The image of the sleeping Chinese was so prevalent that it may liter-

29. William R. Braisted, "The United States and the American China Development Company, 1895–1911," *Far Eastern Quarterly*, XI (Feb. 1952), 147–65. Charles Denby, "Our Relations With the Far East," *Munsey's Magazine*, XX (Jan. 1899), 515–20. Thomas McCormick has done the most research into the period when the company's plans were developing. Consult his dissertation, "A 'Fair Field and No Favor,' American China Policy During the McKinley Administrations, 1897–1901" (University of Wisconsin, 1961).

ally be said that Americans felt China could become overnight what one diplomat called "thoroughly progressive, thoroughly American." W. W. Rockhill, drafter of the Open Door notes, negotiator at the 1901 indemnity proceedings, and student of Chinese affairs, felt there was no alternative for the empire save "develop or decay." Reform, Rockhill wrote for *Collier's,* must "come from without . . . under direct pressure from abroad."[30]

Reform and progress were seen necessary for their own sake but also as the hinges to swing open the door to commerce and investment opportunities in China. Thus the three elements of American policy would work hand in hand as Seth Low understood when, before the Asiatic Association in 1902, he toasted prosperity, good government, peace and commerce.[31] The very indemnity resulting from the Boxer Rebellion was the prime tool in fitting together the various pieces of the Open Door policy. It was to become eventually a most successful instrument when used to educate Chinese students in the United States after 1907. Such a program developed a useful link between American attitudes and the soon-to-be-influential elements of the Chinese political and business communities.

In the first years of the century, the indemnity was seen in an even-more-basic economic sense as a way to reform China's nonexistent currency system by placing it on a gold standard. Personally chosen by Roosevelt, Charles Conant, Cornell political scientist Jeremiah Jenks, and labor expert Hugh Hanna worked as a commission on international exchange to achieve such a standard although they were soon compromising and hoping to achieve at least a bimetallic or even a trimetallic system including copper and silver but based on a gold standard.[32] Less directly involved in economic reform, others were concerned with what Parsons had scorned as "what China will do eventually with progress." Evidence of the hope for a new era in China "pregnant with opportunities" came at the St. Louis Louisiana Purchase Exposition of 1904 and

30. *World's Work,* III (Dec. 1901), 1475–76, and W. W. Rockhill, "The Outlook in China," *Collier's,* XXVIII (Jan. 4, 1902), 9.

31. W. W. Rockhill quoted in the *Journal of the American Asiatic Association,* II (May 1902), 114; Low's toast appears in the same volume of the *Journal* (Nov. 1902), p. 310.

32. The complex currency negotiations can be traced through a series of official sources, the most important of which are: Conger to Hay, Jan. 3 and Jan. 9, 1903, Dispatches, vol. 122; Hugh Hanna to Hay, Sept. 19, 1903, Hay Papers, box 12, LC, and finally Rockhill to Elihu Root, Dec. 11, 1905, Dispatches, vol. 129.

the establishment of an East Asiatic Committee working in conjunction with the American Museum of Natural History, the Metropolitan Museum of Art, and Columbia University. Headed by Morris Jessup of the Natural History Museum and distinguished Columbia anthropologist Franz Boas, this committee sought a great Oriental school in America in order to gain a deeper understanding of the peoples and countries of East Asia. Nowhere was the relationship between the reform and commercial goals of the Open Door more clearly shown than in the membership of the East Asiatic Committee. Working in behalf of what Boas himself labeled "our commerce and political intercourse" was a roster reading much like a Who's Who of the America China Development Company, including Parsons, Schiff, Harriman, and Cary, as well as James J. Hill of the Great Northern Railway and John Foord of the Asiatic Association.[33]

Missionaries had been the major American group striving to awaken the sleeping Chinese before 1900 and remained so after as well. As Paul Varg notes, however, after 1900 education generally replaced evangelism as the missionaries worked to implant their kind of Christian progress in a China they felt moving in new, challenging, perhaps revolutionary directions. Once again as Kenneth S. Latourette, leading student of Christian missions in China, has noted, missionaries came as part of "the desire of merchants, manufacturers, and investors for access to the markets, and the raw materials of China." Yet their dream, for they too like Adams saw China as past, present and especially future, was an economic advance or invasion combining a "political revolution, a moral advance, an intellectual renaissance, a religious reformation and a nineteenth century of scientific and industrial development."[34]

Education was the key to unlock the door to Chinese reform, or so

33. *Journal of the American Asiatic Association*, III (Feb. and May 1903), 7, 108, 110.

34. Paul Varg, *Missionaries, Chinese and Diplomats: The American Protestant Missionary Movement in China, 1890–1952* (Princeton: Princeton University Press, 1958), pp. 71, 77, 81–85, 119. Two excellent treatments of the missionary-merchant-reform link are Kenneth S. Latourette, "Christianity in China," *Annals of the American Academy of Political and Social Science*, CLII (1930), 63–71, and S. Earl Taylor and Halford E. Luccock, *The Christian Crusade for World Democracy* (New York: Methodist Book Concern, 1918), p. 64. For a more limited view there is James M. McCutcheon, "The Missionary and Diplomat in China," *Journal of Presbyterian History*, XLI (Dec. 1963), 224–36.

Americans believed. Every imperial edict establishing schools or abolishing ancient examinations as the sole criterion for civil and military office was hailed as a sign of progress, a modernization, and a transfer of values to Western standards. Still, more argued, the world must surely educate China.[35] While foundations were being built for bringing Chinese to the United States, Americans helped to establish places of higher learning in China. Under the auspices of the United Board for Christian Colleges, American schools were begun after 1900 to join such institutions as Hangchow Christian and the University of Nanking which had been started in 1845 and 1888 respectively.[36] Medical colleges were also founded, and one of them, the Hsiang Ya Medical College—which eventually became Yale-in-China at Changsha—deserves special mention.

Imbued with the spirit of John Hay's words that "the storm center of the world has gradually shifted to China" where world politics would be decided for the next five centuries, a group of Yale undergraduates met in February 1901. They discussed what their role could be now that, as Yale Reverend Harlan Beach had proclaimed, "dawn had broken on the hills of T'ang" and China had "opened her doors."[37] With nothing but what one later recalled as "consummate self-assurance," Yale men led by recent graduates Warren Seabury and J. Lawrence Thurston set out to "tell the world what was the matter with it."[38]

They had little plan but a pragmatic, flexible attitude troubling to more doctrinaire missionaries. By mid-1903 they concluded that only

35. Conger to Hay, Sept. 13, 1901, and June 16, 1902, Dispatches, vols. 114, 116. An excellent study of values and standards is Y. C. Wang, "Western Impact and Social Mobility in China," *American Sociological Review*, XXV (Dec. 1960), 843–55.

36. Taken from John Barrow, "American Institutions of Higher Learning in China, 1845–1925," *Higher Education*, IV (Feb. 1, 1948), 121–24.

37. Publications on Yale-in-China include only officially sanctioned studies such as Reuben Holden, *Yale-In-China: The Mainland, 1901–1951* (New Haven: Yale-In-China Association, 1964); Reginald Wheeler, *Flight to Cathay* (New Haven: Yale University Press, 1949); and Anson Phelps Stokes, *A Visit to Yale-In-China, June 1920* (New Haven: Yale Foreign Missionary Society, 1920). See also the inspirational Harlan P. Beach, *Dawn on the Hills of T'ang* (New York: Student Volunteer Movement for Foreign Missions, 1899). The Sterling Memorial Library of Yale houses the seldom-used archives of Yale-in-China which, under the name of the New Asia College, is still functioning in Hong Kong.

38. The recollections of A. B. Williams in 1944 are reported in Holden, *Yale-In-China*, pp. 9, 77.

a new institution, a great Christian educational center, a veritable Yale-in-China could win over to them the leaders of Chinese society. "Win the leaders," Thurston wrote to Beach, "and we win the Empire." As was so often the case, the real rather than the idealized Open Door forced them to remove themselves to the remote Hunan province. From their school Henry W. Luce, father of the more well-known magazine editor, wrote to New Haven. In Hunan they had "a clear field to work out a consistent and harmonious plan from the lower schools to the higher." As a consequence they could "exert a wide influence on a large body of people. We may work together," Luce sincerely hoped, "for God, for China and for Yale." By 1906, the institution, which would eventually include a school of arts and sciences and a preparatory school in addition to the medical college, was working as a center for the "uplifting of leading Chinese young men toward civilization" and the establishment of a "stable and progressive government" though not so rapidly nor as significantly as Luce may have dreamed.[39]

A part of Yale-in-China's course work was devoted to the non-religious technical and engineering work. This was in keeping with a part of American education for China which concentrated on the more practical future concerning river and forest conservation so as to pre-serve the richness all so hopefully foreseen for China and its friends. American forester Gifford Pinchot visited China in 1902 and reported on an incredibly lovely, rich, and beautiful landscape especially in Manchuria. Yet Pinchot also observed Shanghai's filth and Manchuria's unbelievable death rate.[40] While Pinchot traveled, others worked to restore China's rivers and canals. If commerce was to be unloaded at Shanghai, the Whangpoo River must be made navigable. If it was then to be shipped into the interior, the thousand-mile Grand Canal system leading toward Peking must be made more modern and effective than the prevailing form which dated back to the very year Columbus had discovered the New World.[41]

39. J. Lawrence Thurston to Beach, June 8, 1903, Yale-in-China Archives, Thurston-Seabury correspondence, 1903–1906 file; Henry Luce to Prof. Reed, May 10, 1904, Yale-in-China Archives, Henry Luce file. See also a 1906 progress report in the Thurston-Seabury correspondence.

40. Gifford Pinchot, *Breaking New Ground* (New York: Harcourt, Brace, 1947), pp. 218–22.

41. On the Whangpoo see Rockhill to Hay, July 30, 1901, Dispatches, vol. 113. For canals there is the article of the United States consul George E. Anderson, "The Wonderful Canals of China," *National Geographic Magazine*, XVI (Feb. 1905), 68–69.

Herbert Hoover was also in China before and after the Boxer Rebellion as a mining and railway engineer. He too visited the far reaches of the empire and was struck by the need to bring the mind and tools of Western administrative machinery to agrarian, impoverished China so as to make it a suitable market for American trade and democracy. With the example of the isthmian canal so fresh in its mind, the American Asiatic Association thought engineers like Hoover more important than educators. In August 1902 the journal of the association summarized its feelings on China and the future: "the supreme figure in the modern world is the engineer, and the supreme test of any material position is efficiency." There was only one test: "If it makes for greater economy, it will prevail, if it makes for needless waste, it will fail. The rule runs the same whether the thing tried by it be a tool, a labor-policy, a ship-canal, a government or a human institution."[42]

One other domestic organization joined in the drive for reform in China. Implored by John R. Mott of the Student Volunteer Movement for Foreign Missions not to be "satisfied with exerting influence on one side of the world," Fletcher Brockman and D. Willard Lyon of the Young Men's Christian Association sailed for China in the mid-1890s. The Association, as it soon came to be known in China, set itself up by 1899 in the great cities, Shanghai in particular, as an organization for businessmen residing in the port. It soon became China's first all-embracing social work group.[43] Feeling a religious need to bring Jesus of Nazareth to the "Open Door in Paotingfu," as well as a desire to be a part of the reorganization of China's national systems of finance, army, and education, the YMCA did most of its work correcting urban woes, much like those they sought to eradicate in America—gambling and prostitution. To replace these the Association, under the influence of Robert Lewis in Shanghai and the not-to-be-outdone Princeton-in-Peking movement, sponsored industrial edu-

42. Herbert Hoover, *The Memoirs of Herbert Hoover* (New York: Macmillan, 1952), I, 37–71. *Journal of the American Asiatic Association*, II (Aug. 1902), 172.

43. D. Willard Lyon, *The First Quarter Century of the YMCA in China, 1895–1920* (Shanghai: Association Press, 1920) found in the Missionary Research Library at Union Theological Seminary. Galen Merriam Fisher, *Public Affairs and the YMCA, 1844–1944*. (New York: Association Press, 1948), 161–64. The files of the YMCA World Service may be consulted at the organization's national headquarters in New York. On the origins of their work in China see John R. Mott to Fletcher Brockman, Jan. 3, 1899, YMCA World Service Papers, x951, folder (1898–1900), and Lyon to Mott, May 24, 1900, also in x951, folder (1898–1900).

cation through lectures. China's upper-class literati heard all about the steam engine, the railway, and the electric telegraph in the Association's effort to teach the "languages, commercial customs and business methods of the west."[44]

There were then few areas in which Americans of many different backgrounds did not feel they could succeed just as they could at home with large doses of such education. In political reform, equal attention was paid to the empress dowager's rumored conversion to representative government with Chinese dispatched to study international governmental structures.[45] "Progressive and humanitarian" efforts were also inaugurated to abolish slavery, to develop postal, telegraph, and customs services, to modify the existing penal code by eliminating "slicing, exposure of the head, beheading of the corpse, strangulation and branding," to build an army and navy, and most symbolically to outlaw the ancient female tradition of foot-binding.[46] In fact while a suffragette movement gained support in the United States, the role of women in Chinese society was stressed by American reformers in the Far East. The duty of a Chinese woman was to be married in a polygamous society where concubinage was common. One in ten thousand Chinese women could read and write. Two hundred thousand girls a year did not survive infancy. The field was open for America's feminists and Lillian Wald, Mrs. John R. Mott, the National American Women's Suffrage Association, and the Women's Boards of Foreign Missions repeated that all other reforms and opportunities depended on this one. "All workers in reforms realize," a suffragette advised Minister Edward Conger, "the advance in civilization is relative to the status of women."[47]

44. See the letter of Prof. Jay Rodger in the YMCA World Service Papers, x951.01, China Report Letters 1898–1913; also a letter from Robert Lewis to Mott, May 1, 1905, World Service Folder, 1905. The scientific revolution hoped for is described in Charles Keyser Edmunds, "China's Renaissance," *Popular Science,* LXVII (Sept. 1905), 387–98.

45. Paul Reinsch, "China Against the World," *Forum,* XXX (Sept. 1900), 67–75; W. A. P. Martin, "China Transformed," *World's Work,* XII (Aug. and Oct. 1906), 7844–48 and 8115–25; Wu Ting Fang, "Chinese and Western Civilization," *Harper's Monthly Magazine,* CVI (Jan. 1903), 190–92.

46. Rockhill to Root, July 19, 1905, and April 24, 1906, Dispatches, vols. 127, 130, and John Gardner Coolidge to Hay, April 26, 1905, Dispatches, vol. 127.

47. Kate Gordon to Conger, Oct. 14, 1901, and Conger to Hay, Dec. 4, 1901, both in Dispatches, vol. 115; Mrs. John R. Mott's view can be found in *Evangel,* II (May 1899), 6–9, found as well in John R. Mott Papers, FA546, Yale Divinity School Library; see also Lorsa Maxon Holmes to Lillian Wald, Jan. 4, 1900, Lillian Wald Papers, file case 1, drawer 1, NYPL.

Writing in 1905, missionary spokesman Arthur Smith surveyed the China reform field and concluded proudly, "China had more progress in the preceding five years than any other nation upon the face of the globe." From the effort expended at least, it would seem that Smith's conclusion could not but be correct.[48]

Problems with the Chinese Stereotype

Although almost all shared some part of the dream of America in China's future, some, like Mark Twain, dissented. In his "To the Person Sitting in Darkness" Twain announced his complete support of the Boxer's antiforeign drive of 1900. "It is all China, now, and my sympathies are with the Chinese," declared a man never reconciled to the Gilded Age and what came after. Striking out at his missionary critics, Twain stated what was almost a unique negation of the commerical, investment, and reform ambitions of the Open Door: "We have no more business in China than in any other country that is not ours."[49] In an earlier characterization of the Chinese, Twain had found them a harmless race when let alone—quiet, peaceable, free from drunkenness, and most industrious.[50] Seeing the 400,000,000 Chinese as stereotypes, Twain was here far more in step with his peers than in his views of the Open Door. Ironically, the persistent American image of the Chinese, which Twain shared, usually pictured a people who could not but benefit from the very involvement Twain so openly protested.

John Chinaman, to use the popular term of the day, was helpless yet

48. Smith's progress report is cited in Bashford, *The Awakening of China,* p. 17. John Foster wrote frequently on the subject. Representative is an address to the National Geographic Society entitled "Present Conditions in China" found in the George Kennan Papers, box 85, LC.

49. Mark Twain, "To The Person Sitting in Darkness," and "To My Missionary Critics," *North American Review,* CLXXII (Feb. and April 1901), 161–176, 520–524. Consult the useful William Gibson, "Mark Twain and Howells: Anti Imperialists," *New England Quarterly,* XX (Dec. 1947), 435–70.

50. Mark Twain, *Roughing It* (Hartford: American Publishing Co., 1872), ch. 54. On stereotype views of the day see for example *McClure's Magazine,* XVI (Dec. 1900), 134–40; *National Geographic Magazine,* XII (Dec. 1901), 434–36; and the very useful material gathered in the Griffis Papers, box 28, folder 3. For historical treatment see Harold Isaacs, *Scratches on our Minds: American Images of China and India* (New York: John Day, 1958), passim, and Ssu-yu Teng, "The Predispositions of Westerners in Treating Chinese History and Civilization," *Historian,* XIX (May 1957), 307–27.

industrious, frugal yet honest, indifferent yet successful in business. He could be wise, friendly, reliable, and scholarly, or ignorant, cruel, lazy, and backward. These images were widespread, from Elihu Root who believed the Chinese helpless yet capable of the highest arts of civilization to muckraker Lincoln Steffens who seemed to feel that the Chinese could predict the weather but could only be employed to fish and launder.[51]

The determining factor was that a Chinese in China had all the good virtues, while a Chinaman in the United States took on all the bad habits.[52] The years after 1900 brought about West Coast agitation over Japanese immigration and the subsequent Gentlemen's Agreement of 1907. During the period the issue of Chinese exclusion was by no means settled either. Since 1882 the door to the United States had been closed to Chinese laborers, once so sought-after for work on the transcontinental railroad. Congressional intent had been to cut off cheap labor competition. The exclusion bill rested deeply, however, on the untrustworthy part of John Chinaman's image.

Theodore Roosevelt was representative of the deep cleavage between optimism about the future of America in the Far East and dislike of the Chinese as people. A great admirer of Japan, Roosevelt cannot be taken as one paranoiacally fearing a "yellow devil," yet his "dissatisfaction with the Chinese attitude" fit with that of many who did have such fears. Roosevelt's negative image of the Chinese was the complete contradiction of what he felt America should be. "We cannot play the part of China," he began his essay, "The Strenuous Life," and "be content to rot by inches in ignoble ease within our borders." Roosevelt warned that "China has already found that in this world the nation that has trained itself to a career of unwarlike and isolated ease is

51. See an address by Root delivered at Canton, Ohio, Jan. 27, 1903, in Root, *The Military and Colonial Policy of the United States*, p. 16. Also Lincoln Steffens's letters to Laura Suggett, Aug. 19, 1925, and to his son Pete, Aug. 14 and Sept. 19, 1929, as reprinted in Ella Winter and Granville Hicks, *The Letters of Lincoln Steffens* (New York: Harcourt, Brace, 1938), II, 705, 845–46, 857. Also Lincoln Steffens, *The Autobiography of Lincoln Steffens* (New York: Harcourt, Brace, 1931), I, 439.

52. The relationship between Chinese in America and in China is pursued in two recent dissertations: John B. Gardner, "The Image of the Chinese in the United States, 1885–1915" (University of Pennsylvania, 1961) and the weaker Robert McClellan, Jr., "The American Image of China, 1890–1905" (Michigan State University, 1964).

bound to go down before other nations which have not lost the manly and adventurous qualities."[53]

Even those intimately connected with Chinese commerce, such as former minster to Siam John Barrett, could not dismiss the "great danger to the United States" and its "progressive ideals" posed by the "vast hordes of China."[54] Yet certainly Barrett was horrified when such exclusionist sentiment led to an effort to restrict even the temporary entrance into the United States of those people, merchants, teachers, students, travelers, and government officials whose influence was needed to make possible American commerce, investment, and reform in China. Such an event took place right under Barrett's eyes as special commissioner for Asia at the St. Louis Exposition of 1904. In what was supposed to be "splendid cooperation" and a new era, employees of the Chinese exhibit were subject to Treasury Department regulations for admission including the posting of bonds and the furnishing of photos as well as ordered not to leave the fairgrounds and to exit from the country not more than thirty days after the end of the exposition. When this humiliation, which almost caused the withdrawal of the Chinese, was followed the next year by the detainment of members of the family of the mayor of Shanghai at the port of Boston, Chinese merchants responded with the first full-scale boycott of American goods. As one historian has noted, Barrett would surely have preferred a policy whereby influential Chinese could "come in but close the door behind you." *The Nation* perceptively pointed out, however, that America's negative image of the Chinese was having disastrous effects on the interests of the Open Door in China, in this case with a boycott hurting American trade. "The attitude of our Government," *The Nation* scolded, "is one of distrust and contempt and smacks of the same spirit which makes the average American look upon every Chinaman as an underfed and overworked laundryman, to be kicked or stoned if the policeman's back is turned."[55]

53. See Roosevelt to Rockhill, Aug. 29, 1905, TRP, series 2, vol. 57. See also Roosevelt, *The Strenuous Life,* p. 6; Egbert Oliver, "The Rise of American Understanding of Asia," *United Asia,* IX (June 1957), 149–56.

54. John Barrett, "America in the Pacific," *Forum,* XXX (Dec. 1900), 478–91.

55. See *Journal of the American Asiatic Association,* III (May 1903), 108; Conger to Hay, July 3, 1903, Dispatches, vol. 123; for information on the Shanghai mayor's family see the recollections of William Phillips in the Oral History Research Project, p. 21, Columbia University Library. Also Bruno Lasker, "Come

Problems Threaten Plans

Little evidence exists to show that the boycott had any real influence on trade, outside of a portion of South China.[56] Still such a boycott had important repercussions. It explains the presence of Taft simultaneously with Alice Roosevelt. It can be seen as partly responsible for a reconsideration of American tactics if not goals in the Far East. Roosevelt was under pressure from those who feared the results of the boycott on American business. As in the 1882 congressional debate, those opposing exclusion or in this case pressuring for a relaxation of existing standards agreed that workers must be restricted but that influential Chinese must not be offended. In commercial and not humanitarian terms, the boycott stood as a direct threat to the hopes of the Open Door.[57]

From every quarter the same theme ran across the President's desk. Seth Low besieged Roosevelt to restore good relations with the privileged class of China if America was to have any influence in that country's awakening. On the floor of the Senate, Joseph Foraker accused the closed door of having robbed America of a market. Letters from George Perkins of United States Steel, the Portland Chamber of Commerce, and the British American Tobacco Company and alleged phone calls from Standard Oil argued the same way. *The Nation* felt that for once justice would spell dollars and cents. James J. Hill, spokesman for railway and shipping interests, thought the boycott "the greatest commercial disaster America has ever suffered." Former Secretary of State John Foster feared the consequences should China reciprocate by barring the same kind of Americans as there were Chinese barred in the United States. Foster thought that such a disaster would mean an "effective stop to all American enterprises in

---

in But Close the Door Behind You: Chinese Exclusion in the United States," *Pacific Affairs,* XVI (Sept. 1943), 344–47, and *Nation,* LXXXII (Feb. 22, 1906), 147, 152.

56. Dorothy Orchard, "China's Use of the Boycott as a Political Weapon," *Annals of the American Academy of Political and Social Science,* CLII (1930), 212–61; Alvey Adee to William Loeb, Sept. 21, 1905, Roosevelt Papers, series 1, box 97.

57. John Higham's *Strangers in the Land: Patterns of American Nativism, 1860–1925,* rev. ed. (New York: Atheneum, 1963), p. 25, deals with the general setting for exclusion; for the 1882 debate see U. S., Congress, Senate, 47th Cong., 1st sess., March 6, 1882, *Congressional Record,* XIII, 1639 ff.

China; . . . all American bankers, capitalists, railroad contractors, builders, and engineers, mining experts and operatives, manufacturers and machinists, missionaries and physicians," the whole Open Door complement, would be kept out of China.[58]

American diplomats kept up a steady pressure as well on the State Department for a restoration of good feelings. Rockhill in China, Huntington Wilson in Japan, and Root once established as secretary of state demanded congressional changes in the law so that all Chinese nonlaborers might enjoy full benefit of an eastward opening door. For his own part the president intended to "do justice" and was "taking a stiffer tone with [his] own people than any President has ever yet taken."[59] In addition to dispatching Taft, Roosevelt made public pronouncements in opposition to exaggerated fears of a yellow peril, issued instructions to enforce the exclusion laws without harshness and appointed another committee with Jeremiah Jenks as chairman to investigate the whole operation of the Bureau of Immigration.[60]

At the same time as they warned of the dangers of the boycott, Americans in China advised that the railroad building plans of the American China Development Company were in even more serious danger. Aware that major control of the company had fallen into foreign, mostly Belgian hands, Chinese led by the Director General of Railways Sheng Hsuanhuai threatened and in fact gave notification of a planned revocation and buying-back of the original concession for a Canton-Hankow railway. Just as in the boycott, the death notice of

58. Seth Low to Roosevelt, Nov. 23, 1905, TRP, series 1, box 100; Everett Walters, *Joseph Benson Foraker: An Uncompromising Republican* (Columbus: Ohio State University Press, 1948), pp. 189–90. Roosevelt to Taft, Sept. 2, 4, 1905, TRP, series 2, vol. 57; Y. C. Wang, "Free Enterprise in China: The Case of a Cigarette Concern," *Pacific Historical Review*, XXIX (Nov. 1960), 395. *Nation*, LXXXII (Jan. 1, 1906), 28. Charles Chaille-Long, "Why China Boycotts Us," *World Today*, X (March 1906), 309–14, quotes James J. Hill. Foster wrote in *Atlantic Monthly*, XCVII (Jan. 1906), 127.

59. Phillips, *Ventures in Diplomacy*, p. 27; Rockhill to the State Department, June 17, Aug. 4, Aug. 26, 1905, Dispatches, vols. 127–28; Huntington Wilson Papers, Sept. 1905, Ursinus College Library, Collegeville, Pa.; Root to Roosevelt, Nov. 24, 1905, TRP, box 100, and Roosevelt to Rockhill, Aug. 22, 1905, series 2, vol. 57, also TRP.

60. Roosevelt to Taft, Sept. 2, 4, 1905, TRP, series 2, vol. 57; Roosevelt to Henry Cabot Lodge, May 15, 1905, series 2, vol. 55; Roosevelt memo, Feb. 24, 1906, also TRP, series 2, vol. 61. *Journal of the American Asiatic Association*, V (July 1905), 174–75.

the company was taken as a sign of growing Chinese hostility and a threat to all the golden dreams of the Open Door.[61]

Roosevelt and Senator Henry Cabot Lodge agreed that commercial interests in the Orient were in great danger. Jenks warned of the risk a discrediting of the company would prove to be. Rockhill urged meeting Chinese objections by increasing American or Chinese control of the company. To do this, in January the House of Morgan had purchased twelve hundred shares of the company from King Leopold of Belgium. Roosevelt now had to forestall the sale of this remaining American interest back to China as well as convince the Chinese that American control did in fact exist.

Still practicing his profitable role as legal advisor to Morgan and before moving to the State Department, Root urged sale of the shares to China. Roosevelt assured the banker, "In every honorable way the Government will stand by you and will do all that in its power lies to see that you suffer no wrong whatever from the Chinese or any other power in this matter."[62] In January, Morgan had asked John Hay for just such an endorsement. Now despite Roosevelt's statement of close Washington–Wall Street cooperation, the banker accepted a six and three-quarter million dollar indemnity for sale of the concession when it seemed clear that the Chinese were serious in their determination to cancel. Roosevelt's anti-Chinese attitudes were thus strengthened by Chinese "duplicity" in this matter. Although he was informed the railway plan might have been saved if Morgan was willing to take only a modest profit, Roosevelt could not blame the banker for pulling out. "The risk is too great for them to go on," he wrote Rockhill in late August. The Chinese, he informed the minister, rank just behind the Russians in arrogance and insincerity.[63]

61. Braisted, "United States and the American China Development Company," Conger to Hay, June 10, 1904, Nov. 15, 1904, Dispatches, vols. 125–26.

62. Roosevelt to J. P. Morgan, July 18, Aug. 17, 1905, TRP, series 2, vol. 57; Jenks wrote for the *North American Review*, CLXXI (Oct. 1905), 518–29; Rockhill to the State Department, June 2, 1905, Dispatches, vol. 127; Philip Jessup, *Elihu Root* (New York: Dodd, Mead, 1938), I, 433, and Root note, Sept. 22, 1905, Root Papers, box 185, LC. Also see Charles Whittier to Hay, March 3, 1905, Hay Papers, box 17.

63. Roosevelt to Rockhill, Aug. 29, 1905, TRP, series 2, vol. 57. Also Jeremiah Jenks to Roosevelt, Nov. 23, 1905, TRP, box 100. See also State Department Numerical File 1576/1–3 for a review of the situation.

As the president wrote, his daughter's party approached China. Among its ranks was E. H. Harriman with a most important mission resulting directly from the American China Development Company failure. As a last-minute compromise while negotiating with Morgan, China had promised Americans first preference on the financing of the sale to China of a Manchurian railway from Port Arthur to Harbin, currently owned by Japan but under negotiation at the end of the Russo-Japanese War. With Harriman already interested in building a worldwide transportation network to link his American railway and Atlantic and Pacific steamers with a Eurasian railway, opportunity emerged from failure. The beginning of a still grander plan to give Americans a foothold in the Far East was of even more importance than the failure of the Canton-Hankow business in bringing Harriman along on these adventures in wonderland.[64]

Harriman's interest in Manchuria, a much-desired territory for the extension of American influence, is a fitting illustration of the total situation in 1905. Exaggerated fears of a yellow peril had produced a crisis in confidence with a commercial boycott as the primary result. Yet, the dream of China as a market for American goods and ideas had not been shattered. In fact, to many on the scene, this show of solidarity among the Chinese indicated that reform of the empire was underway and needed only more American-inspired progress to become a real awakening.[65] This increased Chinese awareness in their own affairs demanded a more attentive response, thus the many personal and official representatives of American business, government, and reform in the Far East.

Another lack of confidence, this one in the ownership of the American China Development Company and its relations with the American government, doomed the long-planned Canton-Hankow railway link. Here again, past failure was vastly overshadowed by new projects, thus also explaining the importance of Harriman's visit in the autumn of 1905.

64. F. B. Loomis to Roosevelt, Aug. 29, 1905, TRP, series 1, box 96, and Lloyd Griscom to Roosevelt, Sept. 21, 1905, TRP, series 1, box 97. Consult George Kennan, *E. H. Harriman* (Boston: Houghton Mifflin, 1922).

65. Rockhill to the State Department, Aug. 26, 1905, Dispatches, vol. 128, and files of Huntington Wilson for Sept. 1905, H. Wilson Papers.

New Perspectives—Foreign and Domestic

While China remained then a veritable wonderland for American adventures, two developments, seen really for the first time in 1905, would cause a change in the tactics, if not the almost universally accepted goals, of American policy in the Far East. Japan's victory over Russia and the acquisition of Korea at the Portsmouth Conference completely reversed the international power balance. The great Russian menace feared by Mahan and Brooks Adams, the danger of a landed, reactionary, non–Anglo-Saxon power dominating Chinese and especially Manchurian affairs was swiftly and dramatically replaced by the sudden succession of Japan. In the summer of 1905, Secretary of War Taft had stopped in Japan for secret discussions with Count Katsura. He would return again to both China and Japan in 1907. The readjustment made necessary by the realization that the once friendly and docile Japan had become a seagoing, progressive, yet oriental empire began gradually in 1905. It would become one of the two prime factors causing a rethinking of American tactics toward China.[66]

Of equal significance after 1905 was the feeling that American efforts had gone astray not because of policy errors, but because of a lack of definition in the organization and administration of such policy. For all the historical honors heaped on Roosevelt for the realism of his diplomacy, American thinking about China in this period had been as vague as it was promising. A part of the suggested answer would be a general reorganization of the machinery of both the State Department at home and the consular service abroad, resulting in the creation of a Far Eastern division within the department in 1906. Those like Huntington Wilson, Rockhill, and Root, who suffered

66. On attitudes during and after the war see, Winston B. Thorson, "American Public Opinion and the Portsmouth Peace Conference," *American Historical Review*, LIII (April 1948), 439–64. There is a lively historical debate on the nature of the Taft-Katsura meeting in 1905. Tyler Dennett, "President Roosevelt's Secret Pact With Japan," *Current History*, XXI (1924–25), 15–21, argues that it was secret and unplanned. John T. Pratt in a letter in *Pacific Affairs*, XVIII (Dec. 1945), 369–74, asserts it was not secret, and Raymond Esthus, "The Taft-Katsura Agreement-Reality or Myth," *Journal of Modern History*, XXXI (March 1959), 46–51, is sure it was not even a pact but a consistent piece of American diplomacy which did not even succeed. On Harriman's dealings with Katsura see Richard T. Chang, "The Failure of the Katsura-Harriman Agreement," *Journal of Asian Studies*, XXI (Nov. 1961), 65–76.

through the trial of 1905, sought to apply the lessons of that year as they understood them.[67]

These administrative changes fit into a larger pattern of reform of the means by which Americans sought widely accepted goals. Efforts to rationalize the industrial system and make it more efficient were under way at home and would become important enough to be characteristic of the period as a whole. So too the lesson of 1905 in China was that changes were necessary to make the means by which the door was to be opened both more efficient and therefore, it was felt, more successful. The struggle between the conflicting nature of such changes—whether they should consist of more strenuous independent anti-Japanese American efforts or a mutual cooperation with others in the Far East—would be the second factor directing the shape of America's future in China after 1905.

The wonderland of China remained intact after 1905. The fact that it did, despite the trying conditions making Alice's adventures necessary, is perhaps the most important legacy of that year. Having suffered through boycotts and concession cancellations, the myth of the golden door would stay untarnished for many years to come. The struggle to wrench it open would continue as well. New international and domestic perspectives would see to it that the process of opening the door would never seem as simple or disorganized as it had in the first five years after John Hay officially declared it under way.

67. See Secretary of Commerce and Labor James R. Garfield to George Kennan, July 1, 1905, Kennan Papers, box 2, and Huntington Wilson to Willard Straight, March 23, 1908, Willard Straight Papers, Cornell University Library, Ithaca, New York. On reorganization of the State Department see Huntington Wilson, *Adventures of an Ex-Diplomat* (Boston: B. Humphries, 1945), ch. 25. For reform of the consular service see the very limited discussion by Donald Dozer, "Secretary of State Elihu Root and Consular Reorganization," *Mississippi Valley Historical Review*, XXIX (Dec. 1942), 339–50 and the more successful recent Thomas G. Paterson, "American Businessmen and Consular Service Reform, 1890's to 1906," *Business History Review*, XL (Spring 1966), 77–97.

2

✿

The Dynamic Duo
Competition and Cooperation

"SINCE I came to Peking," journalist Frederick McCormick wrote in 1908, "I have seen a great change in the Japanese government policy. The diplomatic," McCormick observed, "had taken up with other views," which, he supposed, "are those of the military." Japan's adoption of a more belligerent tone following its success against Russia in 1905 was a change which other Americans in China, many of them journalists, thought they recognized as well. What was needed they felt was an aggressive and competitive American response to this supposed Japanese challenge. Yet as early as 1909 many of these same Americans would be applauding or at least accepting deep United States involvement in an international, cooperative banking group whose leaders at least, "had no objection to Japanese participation."[1]

In an effort to open the China door after 1905, United States policy was the subject of a developing tactical debate. Stated in static extremes the alternative directions considered were a fiercely competitive, independent posture or an efficient, cooperative, rationalized position. Neither alternative questioned the goals of the Open Door or the capitalist economic philosophy. Each mirrored similar stands within the domestic political and economic order and rejected the laissez faire con-

1. Frederick McCormick to Willard Straight, Feb. 21, 1908, Willard Straight Papers (hereafter cited as StrP), Cornell University Library; Ithaca, N. Y.; and Straight to Augustus Jay, Dec. 19, 1909, also in StrP.

31

cept of a limited government role in reaching commonly shared goals.

Tension between competitive and cooperative international alternatives served as the setting for the evolution of American policy in China after 1905. The dynamic growth of such policy was not, however, an attempt to fully realize either alternative as much as it was an effort to structure some acceptable compromise between them. Immediately after 1905, excited and unexpected fears of Japan heavily weighted such compromise on the side of an aggressive, competitive role for the United States. As the positive advantages of cooperation began to displace, though not dispel, anti-Japanese attitudes after 1907, compromise solutions moved closer to international combination than to independence. At most, even by 1909, such solutions sought to attain the best of both possible worlds by cooperating with certain "responsible" or "well-positioned" powers but not with the feared Japanese.

Cooperation designed to thwart one very important uninvited guest was seen eventually by staunch cooperationists as just as dangerous as no cooperation at all. Though an undercurrent at first, this argument for combination even with Japan in the Far East came to the fore by 1911. The classic debate of the presidential campaign of 1912, often viewed as a domestic battle between competition, compromise, and cooperation, must be observed as a similar struggle in the shaping of foreign policy. The seemingly inconsistent nature of American policy in China also must be explained therefore as the staggered-step, compromise victory of the cooperative system over a tenacious competitive tradition.

When even the successful cooperationists overstepped the bounds of an acceptable compromise, in this case by joining hands with the Japanese, they were forced to take several giant steps back in 1913. From there a new cycle of compromise leaning closer and closer to cooperation was launched again, this time greatly facilitated by the emergency organization needed after America entered world war in 1917. Though fundamental goals, as represented in John Hay's famous notes, were never questioned or reviewed throughout the period and beyond, competition and cooperation continued to supply the tension just as compromise provided the direction of American policy in China.

American Journalism in Asia

While the rising sun of Japan dominated the horizon after success against Russia, the war also enabled American journalists in China to bask in another illumination, the bright spotlight of the American press. Annexation of the Philippines and the Boxer uprising had caused American newspapers, magazines, and wire services to dispatch reporters to Manila and Peking. It was not until the Russo-Japanese War that these individual correspondents became a semipermanent group often dominating headlines at home.[2] McCormick, for example, had been in China for the Associated Press since 1901. During the war he first received real recognition covering the Russian side. Also describing heroic Russian nurses or the explosive nature of Japanese firepower were reporters such as Frederick Palmer of *Collier's*, Tom Millard of the *New York Herald*, and Martin Egan of the Associated Press.[3]

Certainly part of the intensity of the American press coverage of the war reflected the highly successful nature of the journalism of the day. Defined critically by Theodore Roosevelt in 1906 as "muckraking," American magazines of the day featured sensational stories and equally sensational circulations. Yet by Roosevelt's own admission in the same year, China was the real storm center of world interest. It was natural, therefore, that both during and after the war, the Far East would become a target for the magazines.[4] Alongside such typically titled muckraker pieces as "The Reign of Boodle and the Rape of the Ballot in St. Louis" and "The Armour-Refrigerator Car Company Exposed," B. O. Flower's *Arena* magazine for 1905 included an article on "Our Policy Toward China." The less sensationalist *Independent* revealed the same interest in the Orient by leading off a 1910 issue with a double-barreled attack on "What Is the Matter with Milwaukee?" by socialist Victor L. Berger and "The Present Situation in China," as reported by a former American consul.[5]

2. Lloyd Griscom, *Diplomatically Speaking* (Boston: Little, Brown, 1940), p. 245.

3. Ralph Paine, *Roads of Adventure* (Boston: Houghton Mifflin, 1922), pp. 308 ff. For a contemporary example see *Cosmopolitan*, XXXIX (Sept. 1905). An excellent place to start a study of journalists and the Russo-Japanese War would be in the Martin Egan Papers, held privately by Egan's widow in New York.

4. Its superficial nature not withstanding, Louis Filler's *Crusaders for American Liberalism* (New York: Harcourt, Brace, 1939) is filled with useful information on a subject too little studied until very recently. Roosevelt's muckraker speech is dated April 14, 1906. On his characterization of China see Theodore Roosevelt to W. W. Rockhill, August 6, 1906, Theodore Roosevelt Papers (hereafter cited as TRP), series 2, vol. 65, LC.

5. *Arena*, XXXIII (Jan.–June, 1905). *Independent*, LXVIII (April 21, 1910), 840–46.

Perhaps the classic example of this "China muckraking" appeared in the widely read *Success* for 1907 and 1908. Following up on his own work as well as that of Samuel Hopkins Adams, Edward Bok, and Upton Sinclair into the evils of the domestic drug and meat-packing industries, Samuel Merwin traced a similar Chinese menace in a book titled *Drugging a Nation: The Story of China and the Opium Curse.*[6] To the muckraker, domestic evils and corruption prevented the distribution of much of America's wealth and blessings at home. Similarly in China, Merwin perceived, opium blocked the door to the successful spread of Western civilization. Clarifying this comparison, Merwin asked his reform-minded readers to "try and imagine a self-made politician outwitting and beating down the traditions of Tammany Hall in New York City." To understand why reforms lagged in China, he advised multiplying the troubles of the New Yorker by "a thousand or two." China was a land of paradox where women wore socks and men wore stockings and where names were reversed so that Uncle Sam became Sam Uncle. The reason for all this was the notorious opium den which Merwin exposed much as Upton Sinclair did when he cried out against conditions in the meat-packing plants in *The Jungle*. Dim light, thick blue haze, and sickish fumes made breathing a difficult effort. By implication, at least, they also made the goals of the Open Door more remote.

The analogy between the work of Sinclair and Merwin can be carried several steps further. *The Jungle* created a storm of protest resulting in pressure for the Pure Food and Drug Act of 1906. Merwin's muckraking preceded the call for an international opium conference begun in 1909. It must also be noted that in each case, as in similar efforts at reform elsewhere, the hard lobbying work was done not by the magazines but by missionary C. H. Brent and especially Harvey Wiley of the Department of Agriculture's Bureau of Chemistry, whose domestic but not international influence has been studied.[7]

The interest of the American press in Chinese affairs after 1905

---

6. See Merwin's articles in *Success*, X–XI (Oct. 1907–April 1908). These were then combined in Samuel Merwin, *Drugging a Nation—The Story of China and the Opium Curse* (New York: Fleming H. Revell, 1908).

7. Filler, *Crusaders*, pp. 144–70; Upton Sinclair, *The Jungle* (New York: Doubleday, Page, 1906). On the opium question see State Dept. Numerical File (hereafter cited as SDNF) 774, especially: Harvey Wiley to Robert Bacon, March 27, November 5, 1908, and Elihu Root to Senator Nelson Aldrich, January 9, 1909, National Archives (hereafter cited as NA).

indicates much more than just a successful variation of muckraking, oriental style. Important in reporting and thereby forming American attitudes toward the Far East, American observers in Asia were enormously influenced themselves by the ease with which Japan dispatched the formerly highly feared Russians. No man symbolized or indeed shaped this changing attitude as well as did Willard Straight. Barely into his twenties, Straight understood and held firmly to the trade, investment, and reform goals of the Open Door upon his arrival in China in 1901. As his biographer, colleague, and friend Herbert Croly summarized, Straight knew that the Open Door had "become a matter of building railroads, tapping natural resources, founding industries and of seeking those changes in Chinese political and social organization which would equip it to stand the strain of modern industrialism."[8] He had learned this at the hands of Jeremiah Jenks whom Straight remembered in a note reminiscing to a Cornell classmate about the "good old days when the possibilities of a trip around the world with one Jenks had some attraction."[9] Along with the knowledge of political economy learned from Jenks, Straight possessed artistic talents worthy of a professional. Such a combination enabled him to seek to "remodel Asia" in much the way Ernest Fenellosa had preached an "oriental renaissance." His plans were not all aesthetic, for he pursued as well some of the "romance that had gone with the sea trade in colonial times."[10]

While he did serve briefly as a war correspondent, the Russo-Japanese conflict was hardly necessary to kindle Straight's or America's ambitions for China. Yet to reach those goals, Straight was the first to realize the long road ahead. His sense of the requisite hard work was matched only by his sense of humor as he wrote in 1908 that though he was sick, he was certain it was not grippe, for "grippe there is none in Manchuria, nor is the 'Door' sufficiently 'Open' as yet to permit the passage of too dangerous draughts."[11]

Aware of the muckraking success at home, Straight seized upon

8. Herbert Croly, *Willard Straight* (New York: Macmillan, 1925), p. xiii.

9. Straight to Henry Schoelkopf, August 15, 1904, StrP, box 38.

10. Consult Martin Egan's memorial to Straight in the *New York Evening Post*, Oct. 4, 1924, found in the Egan Papers. Also Robert Moore Collins's remembrance quoted in Croly, *Straight*, pp. 554–55. For his own analysis see Straight to Mabel Boardman, Nov. 30, 1907, Mabel Boardman Papers, Library of Congress (hereafter cited as LC), and Straight, "Diary," May 12, 1907, StrP.

11. Straight to E. H. Harriman, February 16, 1908, StrP.

the obvious lesson of the widespread American press coverage of the war and sought to perpetuate a permanent publicity program. Fielding what they were sure was a great team, Straight and another American, George Marvin, put such a plan into operation in 1908. Working with McCormick, Egan, and Millard, as well as the English J. O. P. Bland of the *New York Times* and Joe Ohl of the *New York Herald*, Straight's scheme called for an American-Chinese news bureau to compile vast amounts of material to be released to the many different channels wanting such news—the China coast papers, foreign correspondents, and the Chinese vernacular press. In this way the geopolitical dreams of communication cables, once realized, would be guaranteed news as interpreted by a select group of American reporters. The idea of controlling the wire services of the Orient with American interpreted news was taken up by others as well. Edwin and Charles Denby, sons of the former minister to China, toyed with the idea of a "Pacific Era" magazine. Perhaps most important would be the foundation for the later work of the World War I Creel committee on public information.[12]

Straight's position as war correspondent had been just a way station for him on his move within the American foreign service to Korea and his post in Manchuria. To this new Manchurian assignment he took the active support of E. H. Harriman, who was then planning to develop a worldwide transportation system. This association with the railroad magnate was probably the most important consequence of the crises of 1905 for Straight. A Manchurian railway outlet was the key to the Harriman plan. Straight's work in behalf of securing such a link earned him a featured place in future investment schemes and a career with the House of Morgan and not the State Department.[13]

An Aggressive, Anti-Japanese Attitude

The significance of Straight's ambitions after 1905, however, lies in the assumptions inherent within them and not in their originality. The Far East had an organized news service before, but it had been con-

12. George Marvin to Straight, April 16, 1908, and George Marvin's summary dated February, 1922 both in StrP. Also Edwin Denby to Root, Oct. 17, 1906, Elihu Root Papers, Box 187, LC.

13. An interesting review of the Harriman plan as written by a contemporary is George Kennan's piece in *Asia*, XVII (June 1917), 271–76.

trolled by the Reuters news agency which reflected England's alliance with Japan in its reports after 1902. There were Manchurian railways before as well, but they too were in foreign hands, either the Russian Chinese Eastern or the Japanese South Manchurian. Before and even during most of the Russo-Japanese War, American sympathy rested almost universally with the Japanese. Russians, to use Theodore Roosevelt's adjectives, were "corrupt, tricky and inefficient," while the interests of "rejuvenated, civilized and efficient" Japan "harmonized" so well with those of the United States.[14] Young diplomats arriving in the Far East were informed that "Japan's success means the open door."[15]

Dissent from this pro-Japanese attitude was punishable in official circles by ostracism. In Korea, American missionary minister Dr. Horace Allen warned as early as 1900 that Japan's military strength might swallow Manchuria. Called home for a 1903 confrontation with Roosevelt, Allen tried to make the point that the United States might one day have to cross swords with Japan. He got nowhere with the president whom Allen claimed "seemed anxious to see a fight between Japan and Russia." Finally in late 1905 after the death of his friend John Hay, the unfavorable personal observations of Alice Roosevelt and Taft, and the acquisition of Korea by Japan at the Portsmouth conference, Allen was recalled from Seoul.[16]

Without an official position, Allen suddenly found himself with great moral support. His belief that Japan was "crowding us out of Korea and Manchuria" and would be a "thorn in the flesh of our Asiatic trade" was echoed in State Department reports from Lloyd Griscom in Tokyo and in public statements like that of Iowa congressman John

14. Roosevelt to Rockhill, Aug. 29, 1905, TRP, series 2, vol. 57; Roosevelt to Griscom, July 27, 1905, TRP, series 2, vol. 57; Roosevelt to Kennan, May 6, 1905, TRP, series 2, vol. 55. Roosevelt, "Two Americas," in *The Strenuous Life: Essays and Addresses* (New York: Century, 1902), p. 231. John Foster's view of American-Japanese harmony can be found in *National Geographic*, XV (Dec. 1904), 463–78.

15. Henry Fletcher to his father, May 4, 1904, Henry Fletcher Papers, box 2, LC.

16. Horace Allen to Senator J. Sloat Fassett, Nov. 3, 1900, Horace Allen Papers, box 2, press copy book 6, New York Public Library (hereafter cited as NYPL), Manuscripts Division; Allen note, Feb. 26, 1904, Allen Papers, box 3, press copy book 7; Rockhill to Allen, June 30, 1904, Allen Papers, box 4, container 5; Allen to Dr. Scranton, Dec. 8, 1905. Also Fred Harvey Harrington, *God, Mammon and the Japanese: Dr. Horace N. Allen and Korean-American Relations, 1884–1905* (Madison: University of Wisconsin Press, 1944), pp. 314–18.

Hull who was sure that "Japanese commercial expansionism will aim to control . . . the development of the new order of things in the East."[17] Before a Senate committee, Bishop James Bashford, Methodist missionary, admitted that the Japanese were "crowding us very hard in China."[18] In October 1904, *The Outlook* had dispatched world traveler and reporter George Kennan to bring back a "broad, intelligent, impartial and human view of the great conflict." Less than a year later Kennan received urgent letters from his editors wondering, "if she [Japan] is going to dominate . . . China and Chinese civilization?" and questioning the result of what they were sure were "social forces at work of profound importance to the whole civilized world."[19]

These first anti-Japanese impressions grew stronger in the next several years. By May 1907, Straight, not wishing to be an "alarmist," still could not see "any evidence that the Japanese in this part of the world are willing to play the game fairly." A year later he observed that every Japanese effort was "directed toward blocking the affairs by other foreigners in China." Finally early in 1909 he committed himself to McCormick's position that the former befriended Japanese were "China's most imminent enemy."[20]

Directly related to this growing hostility was the realization by Americans in China that such a new threat must be met by an aggressive and totally independent American role in the Far East, such as that envisaged by Straight's publicity and railroad dreams. With the growing dread of Japan after 1905, it was argued that in pursuit of the goals of the Open Door the United States must be the dominant factor in the Far East or no factor at all. The road to the truly open door required not only the development of a new China as had been recognized since 1900, but the growth as well of a powerful "American policy" or "New America" in the Pacific.[21]

17. See Allen lecture before the Naval War College, dated 1906, Allen Papers, box 3, press copy book 9. Hull's comments appear in the *Journal of the American Asiatic Association,* V (April 1905), 66. Griscom to Roosevelt, Sept. 21, 1905, TRP, series 1, box 97.

18. *Journal of the American Asiatic Association,* VI (June 1906), 143–49.

19. Lawrence Abbott to George Kennan, Oct. 1904, George Kennan Papers, box 2, and Abbott to Kennan, Aug. 8, 1905, Kennan Papers, box 3, LC.

20. Straight to Rockhill, May 8, 1907, SDNF 551/621; Straight memo, Feb. 25, 1908, StrP, and Straight to State Department, SDNF 2413/239A.

21. B. L. Putnam Weale (pseud.), *The Truce in the East and its Aftermath* (New York: Macmillan, 1907), pp. 414–16. Arthur Smith, *China and America*

So Horace Allen could defend his position, "I am not anti-Japanese, I am not pro-Russian. I am American all through." Straight also added to the rhetoric of this independent role by emphasizing the unique position of America as the principal exponent of the Open Door policy yet without "political ambitions" in China. Stressing the similarly uinque qualities of America, independence and individualism, Straight called for a double-time march. Tom Millard, a reporter every bit as imbued with the same spirit, defined this competition as one of "felicitous aggressiveness."[22] By this technique the United States would insure the lead in China, even against Japan, a country far better qualified, geographically, culturally, or racially. This independent American position may be seen as a blend, historically, of the Open Door with the equally traditional expansionist enthusiasm often labeled Manifest Destiny. Speaking before the National Association of Manufacturers in May 1909, S. D. Scudder of the International Banking Corporation made this explicit. "You have completed the home task," Scudder began exuding the confidence of such an expansion. Now, while America's destiny remained the same, the scene had shifted. "The door stands open before us by a miracle," he went on; "to our right the southland bids us come in through Puerto Rico. A little further along to our left, Hawaii and the Philippines ask us to enter the Far East." "The world," Scudder concluded, "is ours."[23]

An independent American role in China was then not an intended departure from the original John Hay notes. The secretary himself had often spoken in terms of "acting independently" and not being a partner to any "scheme of concerted action."[24] Still, the emphasis after

Today (New York: Fleming H. Revell, 1907). Frederick McCormick, "Has the War Eliminated America From the Far East," *Outlook,* LXXXIV (Oct. 6, 1906), 318–24.

22. See Horace Allen lectures, 1906, Allen Papers, box 3, press copy book 9. Straight to Mabel Boardman, Nov. 30, 1907, Boardman Papers; Straight to Root, Dec. 2, 1907, SDNF 2413/97–99; Straight to Root, Dec. 30, 1907, StrP, Box 3; Straight to Henry Schoelkopf, Nov. 25, 1910, StrP. Tom Millard's opinions appeared in many places; see *New York Times,* June 21, 1908, found in William E. Griffis Papers, Rutgers University Library, New Brunswick, N. J.

23. Far Eastern Division to William Phillips, May 1909, SDNF 788/219–22 and *Journal of the American Asiatic Association,* IX (June 1909), 135.

24. John Hay to Roosevelt, April 25, 1903, quoted in A. E. Campbell, "Great Britain and the United States in the Far East, 1895–1903," *Historical Journal,* I (1958), 174–75. See Roy V. Magers, "John Hay and American Traditions in China," *Social Science,* IV (1929), 299–311.

1905 rested much more on an aggressive and anti-Japanese competitive independence than it did on Hay's earlier calls designed for the "protection of American rights." As Charles Forcey points out, making the necessary link between domestic and diplomatic developments, the older independence represented a kind of nineteenth century laissez faire Open Door while the new role asserted the power and money of the twentieth-century American government.[25]

W. W. Rockhill's "Old China" Versus Willard Straight's "New China"

Nowhere may this contrast be seen more clearly than in the ironic fate of W. W. Rockhill. The chief American architect of the Open Door notes, Rockhill, though minister to China between 1905 and 1909, painfully gave up his place as the director of that policy's implementation to Willard Straight. The relationship between these two men is highly illustrative. Both felt that Far Eastern affairs should be directed by those experienced on the scene and not left to traveling dignitaries like Secretary Taft or the president's daughter. Interestingly, both described the famous visit of 1905 in almost identical language. Straight commented ten days after the departure of Alice's party that they had been an "irresponsible gang." Rockhill used almost the same phrase in depicting them as a "pack of irresponsible men and women."[26] Somehow Straight was able to hide his attitude and to impress all present, especially Harriman, who would take him into his confidence and employ. In Peking, Rockhill, already reprimanded by Roosevelt for his tiffs with various missionaries, had a complete falling out with several in the party, especially Harriman. Criticized for his arbitrary naming of the Americans to receive an imperial audience, the minister "deliberately deceived and misrepresented" Harriman, on what the railroad magnate admitted was an "unimportant matter."[27]

Rockhill and Harriman did not disagree on the fundamental American trade, investment, and reform goals in China. Only months before the visit of Alice's party, Rockhill had stressed the need to guard "our

25. Charles Forcey, The Crossroads of Liberalism: Croly, Weyl, Lippmann and the Progressive Era, 1900–1925 (New York: Oxford University Press, 1961), p. 171.
26. Straight to Schoelkopf, Oct. 10, 1905, StrP. Paul Varg, Open Door Diplomat: The Life of W. W. Rockhill (Urbana: University of Illinois Press, 1952), p. 72.
27. Varg, Open Door Diplomat, p. 41; Roosevelt to Rockhill, May 18, 1905, TRP, series 2, vol. 55; Harriman to Root, November 25, 1905, Root Papers, box 41.

interests here." Nor may it be argued that the minister failed to see an independent role for the United States in China. At the outbreak of war in 1904 he had observed, "the United States is the only power which . . . can step in and help on a settlement."[28] It is true that Rockhill was quite miffed at Harriman and other financial interests for the bad feeling bred by the American China Development Company fiasco. The real answer to the Rockhill-Harriman feud seems to lie, however, in the difference of opinion over the danger of a Japanese thrust into China and Manchuria and the need for an aggressive American response to such a challenge.

While Harriman's protégé, Willard Straight, warned of Japan's unwillingness to play the game fairly, Rockhill reassured Washington that the "Japanese have not the necessary capital to develop either Manchuria or Korea." To the young consul in Mukden, Rockhill admonished, "At all events you should freely confer with the Japanese consul general and ascertain his views on all questions in which our respective governments are mutually interested." Rockhill further implored Straight that the Open Door "is the oft-repeated declaration of the Japanese government."[29]

Rockhill feared Straight's personal ambitions as well as his attitude toward Japan. George Marvin put it directly when he wrote to Straight in the spring of 1908. "As for R.—look out," Marvin began in the shorthand which characterized the friendly letters between the two and their close associate Henry Fletcher, second in command to Rockhill in Peking. Marvin clarified his blunt declaration, "He is determined to deny to the consul general any credit for initiative and to oppose certain measures because they have originated in Manchuria." Thus Straight was forewarned against the real meaning of the concluding thought appearing frequently in dispatches from Rockhill to the effect that before committing himself he "should submit the matter to this Legation and await further instructions."[30]

Differences over Japanese motives and Straight's ambitions were

28. Rockhill to State Department, June 2, 1905, U.S. Dept. of State Dispatches (hereafter cited at Dispatches), vol. 127, NA. Rockhill to Charles R. Crane, March 9, 1904, Charles R. Crane Papers, held privately by John O. Crane, Institute for Current World Affairs, New York.

29. On Rockhill and Straight see the extensive correspondence in SDNF 551 and 788, especially: Rockhill to Root, Oct. 11, 1906, 551/427 and Rockhill to Straight, Dec. 31, 1906, 788/504.

30. Marvin to Straight, April 16, 1908, StrP.

heightened and crystallized by the two men's split over how aggressively the goals of the Open Door should be pursued. In the colorful Marvin-Straight correspondence where almost everyone took on a descriptive name, William Woodville Rockhill became "William Woodpile." The image of an inactive and scholarly Rockhill came through clearly as well in the more widely adopted nickname of "old Buddha." Even Marvin would admit later that Rockhill was "one of the two or three most noted sinologues of his time." After 1905 this was, however, a liability to those who tired of "awaiting further instructions."[31] Dispatches from Rockhill were filled with mixed hope and despair for Chinese political and economic reform and in them can be found the first real discussion of important future Chinese progressives like Yuan Shih-kai.[32] While Rockhill mused, Straight and Marvin, as well as two of Rockhill's own young assistants at Peking, Henry Fletcher and William Phillips, were at work with these very men, Yuan and especially Tang Shao-yi, in an effort to rush reforms and the hoped-for subsequent American advances into action. Rockhill could write Root that "for the time being we may be satisfied to watch developments in Manchuria," but Marvin was doubtful that he (Rockhill) "will be of much help to the Celestial Eagle situation."[33]

Noting this attitude in his biography, Paul Varg has stressed Rockhill's scholarly opposition to such aggressive action. Though less friendly to be sure, George Marvin came closer to the real cause. By Marvin's definition, Rockhill was a reactionary. *Traditionalist* would have been a kinder word, yet Marvin's observation is to the point, "His heart was in old China. He was an acknowledged master of the old diplomacy of forms and laissez-faire."[34]

When even Theodore Roosevelt recognized a potential danger from Japan after the California school crisis of 1906–07 and dispatched the American battle fleet on its famous world cruise, Marvin's sense that

31. Ibid.; Varg, *Open Door Diplomat*. Marvin's recollections, Feb. 1922, in StrP. Rockhill's "scholarly" personality was observed by one of his assistants at Peking; see William Phillips, *Ventures in Diplomacy* (Boston: Beacon Press, 1952), p. 18.

32. For example, see Rockhill to Root, Jan. 24, 1907, SDNF 1518/27–30; April 24, 1907, 1787/593, and Oct. 31, 1908, 778/1033.

33. Rockhill to Root, Aug. 8, 1908, SDNF 551/683, and Marvin to Straight, April 16, 1908, StrP.

34. Varg, *Open Door Diplomat*, ch. 13, and Marvin's 1922 summary, StrP.

Rockhill would be of little help was verified. Roosevelt's naval big stick in the Orient was an example to one observer that the "United States is the one power which . . . can at the present moment give all the help that is needed." Yet Rockhill opposed the coming of the fleet to China feeling it would be misunderstood by China as a sign of America's position and intentions. Given the constant diplomatic reiteration of America's absolute reluctance to fight in the Far East and equally frequent defense of the Open Door as a policy designed to keep the peace, there was relevance to Rockhill's criticism. At the time, however, it was Rockhill and not China who misunderstood the new, aggressive American posture which could make good use of such a show of strength. Commenting to Straight on the minister's opposition to the fleet, Frederick McCormick threw up his hands at Rockhill's more reserved position, "He seems to want to stop the progress of the world and to hang up the diplomatic fiddle and bow and let things soak for good."[35]

Such a view had been bypassed by the fearful reaction to the outcome of the Russo-Japanese War. Finally, even Rockhill came to sense this as his own estimate of Japan sagged. By 1909 he was speaking out in terms of the "menace" of Japan often enough to salvage an important diplomatic post in St. Petersburg. His place in Peking could be better filled, it was felt, by a man of the new not the old, an advocate of a forceful and not a laissez faire attitude in China.[36]

On the most important independent American step in China after 1905, the use of the Boxer indemnity to bring Chinese students to America, Rockhill and Straight both could support the plan in principle, though differing widely again on its anti-Japanese implications and aggressive implementation. No other action so embodied the very essence of the Open Door goals than this educational "act of international friendship." While a long debate has taken place as to the clever

35. B. L. Putnam Weale (pseud.), "What the American Fleet Could Do for China," *North American Review*, CLXXXVIII (Oct. 1908), 481–494. McCormick to Straight, April 24, 1908, StrP. For traditional views of the coming of the fleet see A. Whitney Griswold, *The Far Eastern Policy of the United States* (New York: Harcourt, Brace, 1938), pp. 127 ff, and Thomas A. Bailey, "The World Cruises of the American Battleship Fleet, 1907–09," *Pacific Historical Review*, I (Dec. 1932), 389–424, in which Bailey allows an overemphasis on the typically Rooseveltian nature of the action to blind him to other motives behind the decision to send or, for that matter, oppose the fleet's coming to China.

36. Rockhill to Philander Knox, April 13, 1909, SDNF 5767/36–37.

creator, American or Chinese, of this plan, the spark could have come from almost any fertile imagination, so obvious were the benefits. As Walter Hines Page wrote in a *World's Work* editorial, "if we desire the good will, the trade and an intellectual influence in China, there is no other way to get these things quite so directly as by welcoming and training the men who a few decades hence will exert a strong influence in governmental, educational, financial and industrial ways."[37]

Even before 1905, educator Gilbert Reid, missionary Arthur Smith, economist Jeremiah Jenks, and minister Edward Conger had all stressed pieces of the jigsaw puzzle finally put together by Elihu Root in June 1907, approved by Roosevelt that December, and finally enacted by Congress the following May.[38] Most overlooked in discussions of the origin of the indemnity question is the way an educational use fit so well with the growing anti-Japanese feeling of the post–1905 period. Following the war, a rash of reports warning that Chinese students were being taken to Japan appeared in diplomatic channels as well as from reformers at home and in China, like Seth Low and the YMCA's Fletcher Brockman. Some eight thousand future influential Chinese being guided through their studies in Tokyo stirred increased fears that the "great octopus" would sweep all opportunity in China before an American drive could really get started.[39]

The original American share of $24 million of the $333 million indemnity was estimated by Root to be $11 million above the already generously calculated damages suffered by Americans during the rebellion. Rockhill's great fear was that the surplus would, in fact, be remitted to China where it would just go back into the treasury, to be squandered by the empress dowager. Heeding this warning, the amount beyond the total damages was canceled while the balance was

37. *World's Work*, XII (June 1906), 7594.

38. Carroll B. Malone, "The First Remission of the Boxer Indemnity," *American Historical Review*, XXXII (Oct. 1926), 48–64. Edwin Conger to John Hay, October 1, 1901, Dispatches, vol. 114.

39. See Straight's letter in the *Nation*, LXXXI (Aug. 31, 1905), 179–81. Note in the Huntington Wilson Papers dated Sept. 1905, Ursinus College Library, Collegeville, Pa. Seth Low to Roosevelt, Nov. 23, 1905, TRP, series 1, box 100. Fletcher Brockman report dated 1906 in the John R. Mott Papers, FA910, Yale Divinity School Library, New Haven, Conn. Straight to H. Wilson, March 3, 1908, SDNF 1518/123–27.

not remitted but rather retained by the United States for the education of Chinese boys in America.[40]

Beyond this procedural proposal based on his knowledge of old China, Rockhill had few specific plans for the way in which the money and the education could be utilized. Tang Shao-yi, himself a Columbia graduate, and a "corker," to use Willard Straight's terminology, had more specific ideas. Sensing Rockhill's lack of aggressiveness and new imagination, Tang told Straight that rather than "disturbing dynamics and moral philosophy in prize packages," Americans should work to really strengthen China.[41] He would have preferred to use the money for railways or a Manchurian bank to be jointly controlled by China and America, but the recent fiasco of the American China Development Company made such financial plans impossible. There was the older plan of Jenks to use the indemnity to stabilize China's currency but by its creator's own definition that would be more expensive and not as popular as an educational use. If it must be education at first, Tang and Straight still had much more aggressive ideas for America. As George Marvin noted, this was to be no traditional concession but a decisive step "in the building of new China" and the grasping of "opportunities and possibilities which are theirs and ours."[42]

Such opportunity was represented in the American-educated Chinese, mostly alumni of Cornell, Pennsylvania, Columbia, California, Yale, and Illinois universities, who were already occupying positions in the Chinese foreign office as well as in the banking, engineering, mining, and agricultural fields. A majority of these students concentrated on engineering and commerce, fields which Marvin described

40. For Root's survey of the indemnity dated Feb. 1907 see SDNF 2413/12–120. For Rockhill's worry see Rockhill to Root, Aug. 6, 1907, SDNF 2413/79. The same idea was presented earlier in a letter from Franklin Matthews to Roosevelt, Sept. 22, 1905, TRP, series 1, box 98.

41. On Tang Shao-yi's plans and attitudes see Straight to Fletcher, Jan. 10, 1908, Fletcher Papers, box 2.

42. Charles Vevier, "The Open Door: An Idea in Action, 1906–13," *Pacific Historical Review*, XXIV (Feb. 1955), 49–62. Jeremiah Jenks to Root, Oct. 13, 1905, Root Papers, box 41; Jenks to William Howard Taft, July 1, 1905, William Howard Taft Papers, General Correspondence, series 3, box 106. Marvin wrote a general letter supporting the plan, e.g., Marvin to Roger Merriam of Harvard University, 1908, StrP, box 38. Marvin also wrote a series of articles for *Outlook:* See "An Act of International Friendship," "The American Spirit in Chinese Education," and "Tang Shao-yi," all vol. XC, Nov. 14, Nov. 28, and Dec. 5, 1908.

as "what is best in our history and institutions."[43] There was little reason to doubt, as one YMCA official noted, "the tremendous importance
of reaching these men who are leaving for our shores while they are in
the impressionable stage of student life."

Perhaps the two most important of these impressionable students
turned out to be philosopher Hu Shih, Cornell class of 1912 and
Columbia Ph.D., and diplomat V. K. Wellington Koo, Yale undergrad-
uate and Columbia Ph.D., 1912. While Americans congratulated themselves on the humanitarian nature of the Open Door, Koo wrote to
John R. Mott of the YMCA on how much he was taken with social customs in the United States. Although upset that Americans proved less
religious than as depicted by missionaries, the future Chinese delegate
to the Versailles peace conference praised Americans for their "respect
for women, simplicity of manners, home dinners and teas, athletic con-
tests, outdoor excursions, and benefit performances" which "always
win the admiration of Chinese students."[44]

The educational use of the indemnity had an aggressive as well as a
humanitarian side. George Marvin, noting this, called on Americans
to look ahead ten or twenty years not only to a new China but to a new
America, whose destiny, once other markets were oversupplied, might
very well lie completely in the Pacific. "There must be an awakening,"
Marvin concluded, using the familiar image of the sleeping Chinese.
Yet significantly, he did not stop there. This awakening must come, he
explained, "in America as well as in China." Rarely characterized as
lazy, Americans were now being told that pre-1905 attitudes toward the
Orient would allow a dangerous and expansionist Japan to catch a
relaxed America falling into a costly slumber.[45]

43. Marvin, in "An Act of International Friendship," and "The American Spirit
in Chinese Education," lists the statistics on Chinese students. Schools attended:
Cornell–22, Pennsylvania–12, Columbia–5, California–5, Yale–5, Illinois–5. Fields:
Railway engineering–19, commerce–16, mechanical engineering–13, mining engineering–9, arts–6, agriculture–2, and military science–2.

44. Young Men's Christian Association, World Service Papers, 1907, Folder a
(1906–1908), YMCA National Headquarters Library, New York. New York Times,
Oct. 16, 1910. V. K. Wellington Koo to John R. Mott, Jan. 18, 1911, John R.
Mott Papers, B519.

45. Marvin, "The American Spirit in Chinese Education."

The Roosevelt Administration's Uncertain Response

In the discussions over the use of the indemnity, Jeremiah Jenks reported that President Roosevelt had "modified his view substantially."[46] While this is an apt phrase to describe evolving American attitudes toward the Far East in the period, it is particularly useful to an understanding of the role of Roosevelt and Secretary of State Elihu Root after 1905. Roosevelt's overt friendliness to Japan and his interest in an Anglo-American entente moving him still closer to the interests of Japan, England's ally in the Far East, often camouflage the modification taking place between 1905 and 1909 even in the president's mind.[47]

During and after the Portsmouth meetings, Roosevelt staunchly defended his role in preserving the "integrity of the Chinese Empire" and his faith that Japan's "policy is the policy to which we are already committed." Similarly, Elihu Root was "much gratified" by the peace treaty and wished only that "poor Hay could have lived to see these guarantees established for the doctrines he advocated so long and so earnestly."[48] Such complacency stirred real fears. Back from Korea, Horace Allen, who had felt the menacing winds from Japan even before 1905, observed that the State Department was too far away to pick up these warning signals. "It is a great thing having you and Charles Denby at hand from the East," he wrote to Huntington Wilson in 1906, "for there has seemed to be a lack of knowledge of that quarter in the Department at times."[49] The presence of such anti-Japanese advisors as Denby and Wilson at secondary level positions

46. Jenks to Root, Oct. 13, 1905, Root Papers, box 41.
47. On the Anglo-American nature of policy see Howard K. Beale, *Theodore Roosevelt and the Rise of America to World Power* (Baltimore: Johns Hopkins Press, 1956), p. 158; A. E. Campbell, "Great Britain and the United States in the Far East," cited earlier, and Luella Hall, "The Abortive German-American-Chinese Entente of 1907–08," *Journal of Modern History*, I (June 1929), 219–35. For a contemporary view see the work of Archibald Colquhoun, especially *Overland to China* (New York: Harpers and Brothers, 1900). For an example of a recent work suffering from a pro-Japanese assessment of the administration see Richard Leopold, *Elihu Root and the Conservative Tradition* (Boston: Little, Brown, 1954), pp. 59–62.
48. Roosevelt to the Emperor of China, Sept. 9, 1905, TRP, series 2, vol. 58; Roosevelt to Senator Henry Cabot Lodge, June 16, 1905, TRP, series 2, vol. 56; and Root to Lord James Bryce, Sept. 27, 1905, Root Papers, box 185.
49. Allen to Huntington Wilson, July 9, 1906, Allen Papers.

in the State Department and the crisis stirred by San Francisco school board rulings against Japanese children contributed to a growing doubt, even in the White House, about Japan and the future of the Open Door. In 1905 Roosevelt had written to Henry Cabot Lodge that Japan would probably never "look toward" the American-controlled Philippines. Two years later he was referring to these same islands as the Achilles' heel which made the "Japanese situation dangerous."[50]

The president certainly continued to hold firm to the goals of the Open Door policy. Even if he viewed the Chinese unfavorably, Roosevelt never really questioned the assumption that "untrammeled intercourse" would result in "incalculable benefit to the world in general and to the peoples of the East in particular." Near the end of his second term he was still calling for conservation measures in China and a furthering of the "progress now being made in the introduction of Labor-saving devices, with consequent industrial evolution." In fact, the goals of the Open Door paralleled closely Roosevelt's domestic philosophy of ameliorating social ills before they bred revolution. As he put the domestic and diplomatic link so well, "Here at home we believe that the remedy for popular discontent is not repression but justice and education. Similarly, the best way to avoid possible peril, commercial or military, for the great Chinese people, is by behaving righteously toward them."[51]

As his doubts if not fears of Japan increased, the president's own unique brand of personal aggressiveness matched the mood of those openly hostile to Japan. Showing, as if any proof were needed, that he was no "old Buddha," Roosevelt ordered the world voyage of the American fleet. With the Panama Canal and an ever-larger part in European power politics already behind him, Roosevelt was struck by the way the fleet magnificently symbolized Mahan's two-ocean America. The president and his circle of fashionable friends, known as the Tennis Cabinet, including young William Phillips back from his apprenticeship at Peking, could not have failed to see the contrast between the "white fleet" and the hundred-year-old Chinese vessel, Whang Ho, only the second junk to visit American waters, which coin-

---

50. Roosevelt to Lodge, June 16, 1905, TRP, series 2, vol. 56, and Roosevelt to Taft, Aug. 21, 1907, TRP, series 2, vol. 74.

51. Roosevelt to the Emperor of China, Sept. 9, 1905, TRP, series 2, vol. 58. See the president's message to Congress on conservation dated Dec. 8, 1908, reprinted in *National Geographic*, XX (Jan. 1909), 18–29.

cidentally limped into Boston harbor in June 1908. While Roosevelt may have been motivated by larger international designs and a militarist leaning, the sending of the battleships played right into the hands of those who specifically favored an aggressive American push into the Far East.[52] On the indemnity, Roosevelt was neither the creator nor even a strong supporter of the plan to bring Chinese students to America. His assent by 1907, however, did make possible in much the same way the efforts and the success of this uniquely American response to a Japanese challenge.[53]

Now that Washington was performing so much better in early 1908 as the leader of an anti-Japanese American drive in China, Willard Straight felt it time to solidify this position by bringing Tang Shao-yi to a face-to-face confrontation with Roosevelt and Root. Very much aware and in sympathy with the plans of Harriman and Straight to blanket Manchuria and the world with American railways, Tang journeyed under the guise of an official thank you for the indemnity plan. The more important purpose of his extended three-month stay in America was to press for still further commitment of the United States to an active, independent role especially in support of railway investment and the proposed Manchurian bank.[54]

With Tang's Washington arrival set for December 2, the State Department suddenly exploded much of the advance work done by Straight by detonating what Americans in China would regard as a most untimely and unfortunate bombshell: the diplomatic exchange of notes between Tokyo and Washington, known to history as the Root-Takahira Agreement of November 30, 1908.

While explanations of this mutual pledge to defend the status quo

52. William Phillips wrote of the Tennis Cabinet's meetings in Rock Creek Park and at the H Street home of Henry Adams; see Phillip's *Ventures in Diplomacy,* pp. 34–39. Consult also Oscar Straus, *Under Four Administrations: From Cleveland to Taft* (Boston: Houghton Mifflin, 1922), p. 338. On the voyage of the Whang Ho see the *Boston Globe,* June 28, 1908, in the Griffis Papers. Also Roosevelt to Taft, Aug. 21, 1907, TRP, series 2, vol. 74.

53. Roosevelt to Rockhill, Feb. 27, 1907, TRP, series 2, vol. 71, and Harold Isaacs, *Scratches on Our Minds: American Images of China and India.* (New York: John Day, 1958), pp. 144–45.

54. See a series of notes from Straight to Fletcher dated Jan. 16, Feb. 6, March 11, and March 17, 1908, all in Fletcher Papers, box 2. Also Rockhill to Root, July 20, 1908, SDNF 2413/140 and Phillips to Alvey Adee, Sept. 9, 1908, SDNF 2413/146–48. Vevier, "The Open Door," 49–62.

in the Pacific have been attempted in terms of Roosevelt's pro-Japanese realpolitik in protecting the Philippines by giving Japan a free hand in Manchuria, such an analysis has serious drawbacks.[55] There is little evidence to support the view that the president or the secretary of state feared an immediate Japanese move against the Philippines, especially since the Gentlemen's Agreement of 1907 had substantially cooled the school crisis situation. Certainly Roosevelt's sentiment toward Japan had seriously weakened enough since 1905 that this agreement cannot be viewed as another restatement of the Open Door as participated in by both countries as recently as the Taft-Katsura interchange of 1905.

Shocked by the Root-Takahira notes, Willard Straight sadly reported China would now be ready to listen to Germany, England, Russia, and France as well as America, since the United States like these other powers had allied itself verbally with Japan's interests. A student of political economy as taught by Jeremiah Jenks, Straight should have realized such a blow to America's independent hopes would be forthcoming. Having defeated or at least witnessed the demise of Rockhill's brand of laissez faire diplomacy, Straight's plans for a competitive role were now opposed by those, like Roosevelt and Root, who favored a milder, more highly controlled and regulated cooperation. With the country more involved in the political affairs of the world, some Americans favored giving up the pretense of isolation or independence and adopting a framework in which all could share without the struggle requisite for a complete, competitive triumph. A nineteenth-century flirtation with laissez faire in America's domestic economic development was replaced by an active governmental role in opening the doors of opportunity. The well-studied conflict between those who sought such opportunity through rekindled competition, or trust-busting, and those who went after similar ends by increased cooperation or a rationalization of the capitalist economy was then being

---

55. For such traditional views see: Thomas A. Bailey, "The Root-Takahira Agreement of 1908," *Pacific Historical Review*, IX (1940), 19–35, and Griswold, *Far Eastern Policy*, pp. 128–32. A somewhat broader though still basically traditional view can be found in Jessie Ashworth Miller's "The United States and Chinese Territorial Integrity, 1908," in *Essays in History and International Relations in Honor of George H. Blakeslee*, ed. Dwight E. Lee and George E. McReynolds (Worcester: Clark University Publications, 1949), pp. 233–56.

mirrored in the independent versus cooperative approaches toward the universally desired Open Door in China.[56]

While Elihu Root exchanged notes with Ambassador Takahira, others in the State Department were negotiating an arrangement for equal protection of American and Japanese trademarks in China and Korea. The seemingly unrelated and universally ignored quantities of State Department correspondence on this trademark question indicate as much about the motivation of the Root-Takahira agreements as all the volumes devoted to realpolitik. As chief State Department clerk Wilbur Carr wrote to the engineering editor of *The American Machinist* only three months before the exchange of the more famous notes, it was imperative that Americans and Japanese register their trademarks with each other. Japan employed a system with categories based on original registration of the article while the United States had adopted a classification determined by a product's actual usage. If no convention was made on these varying systems, conflicts, piracy, and chaos would result. The trademark controversy revealed the relevance of what Louis Galambos calls the "Associative ideology" to an understanding of the Root-Takahira Agreement. By this term he means something familiar to students of corporate capitalism, a "new gospel" replacing the "individualistic, competitive concepts with an ideal of rationalized, cooperative behavior; it made stability a key goal of economc activity."[57]

To be sure, an antitrust free enterprise tradition, often strongest among small businessmen, remained at home and abroad and raised doubt as Howard K. Beale has observed, "to what extent could the idea of close cooperation be sold to the American people?" Still the

56. Croly, *Willard Straight,* p. 276. Straight to State Department, SDNF 2413/239A. For Jenks's interest in such questions see Jeremiah Jenks and W. E. Clark, *The Trust Problem* (Garden City: Doubleday, Page, 1900). This basic work in the field appeared in many later revised editions. On the transition from laissez faire to something which he labels neo-mercantilism see William A. Williams, *The Contours of American History* (Cleveland: World, 1960), pp. 320–90. On the conflict within the industrial system see the work of Louis Galambos, "The Trade Association Movement in Cotton Textiles, 1900–1935," *Explorations in Entrepreneurial History,* 2d ser., II (Fall 1964), 31–55, and his *Competition and Cooperation* (Baltimore: Johns Hopkins Press, 1966).

57. Root to Rockhill, June 13, 1907, SDNF 406/52–54; Wilbur Carr to the Engineering Editor of the *American Machinist,* Aug. 7, 1908, SDNF 406/209. Galambos, "The Trade Association Movement," p. 48.

belief spread and was strengthened by the Root-Takahira exchange that the key to the Open Door rested in the phrase that "competition is war, and war is hell." Roosevelt stressed the importance of stability, embracing order, predictability, and most of all efficiency, in his message greeting Tang Shao-yi. In words to be heard again from other presidents about other areas, Roosevelt called for a square deal in China. "It is to the advantage, and not to the disadvantage, of other nations," he began for the consumption of America's potential rivals, "when any nation becomes stable and prosperous, able to keep the peace within its own borders, and strong enough not to invite aggression from without."[58]

The Promise of International Efficiency

A real split existed as to how to reach the goal of "commercial equality" in China even before the official announcement of such a policy in 1899. Tyler Dennett, a leading early twentieth-century student of Far Eastern affairs, has defined the real issue of China policy, not as whether there should be an Open Door, but whether "the United States should follow an isolated or cooperative policy to make sure of the open door."[59] While Dennett correctly traces the roots of such a split all the way back through the nineteenth century, it became far more significant after 1900 with the actual statement of the Hay notes and the similar division at home in responding to a rapidly developing economic order. As early as the campaign of 1900, the candidacy of William Jennings Bryan and the issue of annexation of the Philippines caused antitrust sympathizers to attack the "basic issue" of the "concentration of commerce" or the trust, in both domestic and foreign policy. The link was made quite pointedly when magazine writers picked up Twain's criticism of missionaries, labeling that group the "Blessings-of-Civilization Trust."[60]

58. Beale, *Theodore Roosevelt*, p. 158; Harold Faulkner, *The Decline of Laissez-Faire, 1897–1917* (New York: Rinehart, 1951), pp. 172–75. Roosevelt greeting, December 2, 1908, SDNF 2413/226a.

59. Tyler Dennett, *Americans in Eastern Asia* (New York: Macmillan, 1922), pp. vi–vii.

60. *Arena*, XXIV (July 1900). See also the George McClellan Jr. Papers, container 11, LC. Paul Varg, *Missionaries, Chinese and Diplomats: The American Protestant Missionary Movement in China, 1890–1952* (Princeton: Princeton University Press, 1958), pp. 48–49. Also the very interesting Harold Baron, "Anti-Imperialism and the Democrats," *Science and Society*, XXI (Summer 1957), 222–39.

Not all observers of the close tie between the consolidation of industry at home and possible cooperation toward an Open Door abroad were critical. Following up on his brother's idea that the "trend of political organisms" was toward combination, concentration, and centralization, Henry Adams observed perceptively in his *Education* that Secretary Hay's Eastern policy had grasped the "instinct of what might be named McKinleyism; the system of combinations, consolidations, trusts, realized at home and realizable abroad." What Adams had in mind was an Atlantic system, a pet objective as well of Admiral Mahan. To reach the highest goal, the "rational process and efficiency of action," inherent in centralization, Mahan had proposed such an Anglo-Saxon cooperation to oppose Russia.[61]

Charles Conant, who had summarized the goals of the Open Door so well in his *United States in the Orient,* also provided an enlightening discussion of the tension between competition and cooperation.[62] By no means an advocate of governmental hands-off or laissez faire, Conant was still deeply imbued with a free-trade kind of competition in the "struggle for commercial supremacy." Yet even in the United States, which he styled a "competitive, progressive democracy," there were lessons to be learned from absolutism, the opposite philosophy of government. These were especially "consolidation of kindred interests, unity of purpose and efficiency in action," best represented by America's greatest rival in 1900, Russia, which Conant then defined in American terms as "the greatest trust in the world." Competitive democracy could become destructive, and when it did it must learn the lesson of absolutism and impose trust companies to limit production. When such destructive competition became international, the principle of concentration must be applied by national trusts to estab-

---

61. See Henry Adams, *The Education of Henry Adams: An Autobiography* (Boston: Houghton Mifflin, 1918), pp. 423–24; interestingly *The Education* was written in 1905, though not published until later. See also the very perceptive analysis in Robert Osgood, *Ideals and Self-Interest in America's Foreign Relations: The Great Transformation of the Twentieth Century* (Chicago: University of Chicago Press, 1953), pp. 64–65. Also Charles Vevier, "Brooks Adams and the Ambivalence of American Foreign Policy," *World Affairs Quarterly,* XXX (April 1959), 11; Walter LaFeber, *The New Empire* (Ithaca: Cornell University Press, 1963), p. 84. On Mahan see *The Problem of Asia* (Boston: Little, Brown, 1900), pp. 18, 46, 123. Also Cushing Strout, *The American Image of the Old World* (New York: Harper & Row, 1963), p. 155.

62. Charles Conant, *The United States in the Orient* (Boston: Houghton Mifflin, 1900), passim.

lish commissions rather than spheres of influence and to organize the industry, capital, and transportation of the world for greater efficiency. Association and cooperation had to replace free play so that a "union of men" would be substituted for "men acting alone."

Still, Conant clung to the competitive tradition of Adam Smith's capitalism. Combination, he concluded would eventually serve to stifle competition and thus threaten efficiency. Regulation must be kept, therefore, to its narrowest limits so as to work the delicate balance between absolutism and competitive democracy. In this way, Conant felt, the Anglo-Saxon function of spreading democracy and efficient laborsaving methods of production to less advanced people would be best served.

In the first years of the century the delicate balance symbolized by the voluntary cooperation of the Open Door notes had been successful or at least not seriously challenged. Domestically Robert Wiebe depicts the "easy years" before 1907 as a kind of prologue or first act. For Wiebe the panic of 1907 is the turning point; the end of this first act and the coming of uncertainty, crisis, and climax, all the attributes of good drama and serious political and economic problems. Similarly, 1907 is a useful divider in the debate over Open Door tactics. With an older, laissez faire approach defeated, conflict and resultant efforts at compromise between a competitive and cooperative role for America in China would develop just as they did at home on banking, commercial, and railroad questions.[63]

Supporters of an independent or competitive role did not need an economic panic to convince them of their position. In China, they were ever more wary of Japanese designs. In the United States, they were equally afraid of the encroachments of the trust. The panic of 1907 did, however, convince these large business interests that some kind of systematic cooperation or consolidation must replace cutthroat competition at home and abroad so as to prevent further disruptions and instability.

Drawing on the lesson of 1907, Judge E. H. Gary of United States Steel, later a most interested visitor to the Far East, felt the need for a "utilization of our opportunities . . . a closer cooperation, a better understanding, a complete confidence, a full and free interchange of ideas and information." Jacob Schiff of the banking house of Kuhn, Loeb and Company, greatly concerned with investment possibilities

63. Robert Wiebe, *Businessmen and Reform: A Study of the Progressive Movement* (Cambridge: Harvard University Press, 1962), ch. 3–4.

in China, wrote in 1907 that it was time for "America and Europe to work hand in hand to avoid playing one against the other." Perhaps the most widely read statement of the need for cooperation, efficiency, and a new nationalism both at home and abroad came shortly after the panic of 1907 with the publication of Herbert Croly's *Promise of American Life*.[64] In his tenth chapter Croly turned to what he termed "a national foreign policy." Certain that there were essential American interests in China perhaps second only to the need for a "stable American international organization," Croly warned that discipline and experience would be needed to deal with the dangers involved. Yet it was worth the risk since, as Roosevelt had already hinted in his call for a Chinese square deal, the need to develop a valid foreign policy would remove the possibility of an irresponsible or revolutionary attitude developing at home. Concentrating efforts not on the old western frontier, but on the new horizon of an "international, economic, technical and political efficiency" would actually aid the similar "work of internal reconstruction and amelioration" in the United States as well.

The New York *Journal of Commerce* summarized the ideas of Gary, Schiff, and Croly when it specifically called for "some common plan of action among the foreign powers by which China may be given all the financial aid she requires in return for an honest . . . execution of treaty obligations."[65] Such a plan would begin to be elaborated with the development of the 1909 banking consortium to finance railway construction. This international conception grew out of the desire of Harriman and Tang Shao-yi for Chinese and Manchurian railways. In that light, it is not surprising to find Willard Straight deeply involved in the consortium operation. Especially after Harriman's death in 1909, the ambitious young American could easily see that the immediate future rested with the powerful financial interests like Schiff and the House of Morgan who formed the core of the American group entering into an English, French, and German plan to finance railways in central and southern China. The group was concerned with

64. Speech of E. H. Gary, Sept. 11, 1908, "Addresses and Statements," (collected and bound by the Museum of the Peaceful Arts, 8 vols., 1927, found in NYPL). Jacob Schiff to General James Wilson, March 13, 1907, James Wilson Papers, box 13, LC. Herbert Croly, *The Promise of American Life* (New York: Macmillan, 1909), pp. 308–10.

65. *New York Journal of Commerce*, July 21, 1909, Knox Scrapbooks, vol. 24, Knox Papers, LC.

the rationalized cooperation inherent in such a consortium. For all his efforts in its behalf, Straight, at least at first, was still more involved in the possibility of American control of the whole show. While he toned down his anti-Japanese declarations and recognized that his new superiors "have no objection to Japanese participation," Straight remained resolute in the belief that America need guard its independence. This "isolation," as Straight called it, was all the more vital as "signs of disagreement among our tripartite friends" became more pronounced.[66]

Alternative Solutions

The consortium, designed to allow combination with the West European powers but not Japan, was a form of compromise or limited partnership developed out of the tension between competitive and cooperative attempts to achieve the goals of the Open Door. Another compromise also emerged briefly after 1905. This alternative, favored by the competitive, anti-Japanese forces would have barred cooperation with any of the consortium powers but allowed the United States to seek a friendship of necessity with Russia, long felt, (at least before 1905) to be America's chief rival in the Far East. Those favoring competition, such as Horace Allen and the soon-to-be well-known Chicago industrialist Charles Crane, thought it possible to work safely with the defeated though still geographically well-placed Russians in order to block Japan as well as England, France, or Germany.

After the Russo-Japanese War, mining and railway expert John Hays Hammond reflected sadly on America's inability to develop a working relationship with Russia. "Had it been possible for our capitalists and captains of industry to have cooperated with Russia in the development of her possessions in Siberia and other parts of the eastern empire," Hammond observed, those areas "would have afforded a very remunerative field of investment for American capital." Even more significantly, he mourned that if only such cooperation had been achieved, "we," and not the Japanese, "would have the initiative in the development of the resources of Manchuria, Korea and China . . .

66. Straight to H. Wilson, May 10, 1908, StrP, box 3; Straight to H. Wilson, Aug. 3, 1909, StrP; Straight to State Department, March 11, 1909, SDNF 1518/271; and Straight to Augustus Jay, Dec. 19, 1909, StrP.

together with much of the trade that would naturally follow our operations in these countries."[67]

Although the logic of cooperation could be seen in such statements, calls for a marriage of convenience with Russia were designed, as Willard Straight desired, to help America compete not cooperate. With the widespread acceptance by Straight and Hammond of the broader though still anti-Japanese consortium cooperation, plans for a Russian rapprochement were pushed only by those committed to a basically independent American role. Locked out of this mutual entrance, Russia made any chance of an American partnership more remote by joining hands in 1907 and again in 1910 with its former enemy, Japan.[68]

Partly as a result of this rise of two enemy camps, the European consortium and the Russo-Japanese, Straight's close friend Henry Fletcher concluded, perhaps for the first time anywhere, that a limited compromise between a cooperative approach and an anti-Japanese independent role was destined to fail.[69] Writing to Root, Fletcher observed that a purely independent answer was untenable. Every individual success, he remarked (sounding like a domestic defender of business consolidation), would be blocked by a temporary coalition of rivals. International groups were fine, he continued, but only if they were truly cooperative. Fletcher, sharing post–1905 fears of Japan, was convinced that "no important railway concession may be secured in Manchuria without Japan's approval." Because of this fear, or as he put it, "in view of Japan's position here," and not out of any lingering sympathy for the Japanese, Fletcher favored full cooperation as the only answer. Japan's opposition, he assured Root, "can be removed and her support secured only by an allotment of any concession sought by the syndicate of pooled interests." Anti-Japanese sentiment, in one man's opinion, had come full circle in just three years. In 1905 the "easy cooperation" inherent in Hay's Open Door

67. Harrington, *God, Mammon and the Japanese*, pp. 315–16; Rockhill to Allen, June 30, 1904, Allen Papers, box 4, container 5; Charles Crane to *New York Times*, Aug. 1, 1903, Charles R. Crane Papers. John Hays Hammond, "American Commercial Interests in the Far East," *Annals of the American Academy of Political and Social Science*, XXVI (1905), 85–88. This article was also published under the title "The Menace of Japan's Success," in *World's Work*, X (June 1905), 6273–75.

68. See Griswold, *Far Eastern Policy*, pp. 156–57, and Croly, *Willard Straight*, ch. 9–10, on Straight, competition, and Russia.

69. Fletcher to Root, Feb. 28, 1908, SDNF 5315/73–74.

notes had been bypassed by a threat recognized in Japan. By 1908 that very threat made a truly independent role impossible and served as a strong argument for a reluctant but necessary full cooperation.

Surely only a minority accepted Fletcher's logic in 1908. Some like Tom Millard and Charles Crane would seek to maintain an almost unswerving independent course. Others, especially in the State Department, favored the compromise of anti-Japanese cooperation with the European powers as a means of resolving domestic and international pressures.

Willard Straight had still another answer. "If you love me," he wrote in 1908, "vote for Taft."[70] The dominant figure of Roosevelt was finally to be replaced and Straight was sure that William Howard Taft was the right man. Returning to the Orient in 1907, Taft met with Straight in Vladivostok. Both men were impressed with each other. Though close to the president and to Root, Taft had already taken a far more anti-Japanese position than either. Writing from the Orient, Taft stated the impression that Japan was determined to secure trade through "undue privileges." In agreement with this sentiment, Straight anxiously informed the traveling secretary of war that independent American action was essential since the Chinese so greatly relied on the United States "particularly in regard to the Manchurian situation."[71]

While in the Far East, Taft also spoke out for what could be interpreted as such an independent American position. Noting that Americans had rushed through the door fast enough that in Shanghai "American woman meant prostitute" and in going to visit the red light district one said he was "going to America," Taft strongly supported a United States court for China under Missouri Judge Lebbeus Wilfley. Very much in keeping with the Open Door goal of reform so that "China could take her place among the progressive nations," the Court also stood as an example of what Americans alone could accomplish.[72] Taft also used his influence with Mabel Boardman of the Red

70. Straight to Schoelkopf, March 22, 1908, StrP.

71. Taft to Root, Oct. 10, 1907, Taft Papers, box 146; Straight to Taft, Sept. 15, 1907, Taft Papers, series 3, box 145.

72. On the court see Taft to Root, Oct. 10, 1907, Taft Papers, box 146, and the comments of Lebbeus Wilfley, *Journal of the American Asiatic Association*, VIII (March 1908), 69–71.

Cross to provide American famine relief for China. This idea originated with Louis Klopsch, publisher of the missionary *Christian Herald* as well as the popular *Success*, which was at this time "muckraking China" in Samuel Merwin's opium exposé. Publicizing the philanthropic side of the Open Door, this kind of famine relief aid would be used again after 1907 as another sign of America's intent and ability.[73]

The election of William Howard Taft was seen by Straight as essential for the achievement of the goals of American policy in China, hopefully through an aggressively independent approach. Forces interested in the opportunity for domestic and international cooperation or dollar diplomacy, as it would come to be known, also looked favorably on Taft's candidacy. Both "competitors" and "cooperators" felt a Taft administration would provide a continuation and probably an improvement. Conflicting methods of reaching the unchallenged goals of the Open Door were to be reconciled by Taft, the experienced, "all-things-to-all-men" in the Far East. Similarly on the domestic front, hopes were high among the former Roosevelt faithful. In both areas, Taft was not the epitome of all things but rather a compromise at best. From the very first his administration's efforts to resolve the competitive-cooperative tension would serve only to increase the split they sought to heal. Nowhere may the continued development of this breach be seen more clearly than in the controversy over appointing a minister to replace Rockhill in the pivotal Peking position.

73. Consult the papers of the American National Red Cross at their headquarters in Washington, especially file N.H. 404, Oct. 1937. See also James F. Rodgers to Robert Bacon, April 18, 1907, file 898.5, 1906–07. On Klopsch see file 898.5/02 at the Red Cross Library; Also Frank Luther Mott's "The Magazine Called *Success*, 1896–1928," *Journalism Quarterly,* XXXIV (Winter 1957), 46–50.

3

Our Man in Peking
"The Very Sad Case of Mr. Crane"

UPON hearing that her friend Charles R. Crane had been appointed minister to China in the summer of 1909, Ida Tarbell, muckraker extraordinary, saluted the new diplomat. "I shall watch your work with the sincerest interest and I shall now make my long planned visit to China! Indeed you need not be surprised if the whole *American* crowd moves bodily to Peking!" she warned. Two months later Miss Tarbell again wrote Crane. This time she sympathized for his sudden recall and resignation just prior to his departure for China. This humiliation was the Taft administration's last straw, she declared.[1]

The presidency of William Howard Taft has been generally described as an "ordeal" or as "troubled."[2] The years 1909–1913 have the makings of good tragedy. The plot revolves around a series of crises during

1. Ida Tarbell to Charles Crane, Aug. 2, 1909, Charles R. Crane Papers, held privately by John O. Crane, Institute for Current World Affairs, New York; and Charles R. Crane, "Memoirs," p. 150, also in the Crane Papers. I would like to thank Charles Crane's son, John O. Crane, for permission to use his father's papers and his own most informative recollections.

2. These two characterizations appear respectively in such different interpretations as Gabriel Kolko, *The Triumph of Conservatism: A Reinterpretation of American History, 1900–1916* (New York: Free Press, 1963), p. 159, and George Mowry, *The Era of Theodore Roosevelt, 1900–1912* (New York: Harper & Brothers, 1958), ch. 12.

which a group of journalists and midwestern congressmen become convinced that the hand-picked choice of their hero, Theodore Roosevelt, is an imposter. Assuming Taft to be their leader in the fight to oust Speaker of the House Joe Cannon, to achieve a lower tariff, and to defend the principle of conservation, these self-labeled insurgents find the president moving instead toward their arch-enemy Senator Nelson Aldrich. With Taft suddenly too conservative and judicial rather than progressive and political in outlook, opposition within the Republican party looks first to Wisconsin's Robert La Follette but eventually to Roosevelt for leadership. This would set the stage for the Armageddon of 1912 and the ultimate sacrifice of Taft by the former president's Bull Moose cohorts. Although this progressive alienation from Taft is usually based on the well-known domestic squabbles, diplomatic questions are mentioned in connection with tariff debates and the general renunciations of Taft's dollar diplomacy friendship with Wall Street and the trusts.[3]

Somewhere in the characterization of the Taft years as interim, inconsistent, and ambiguous, the appointment and subsequent recall of Crane had been dropped. While Arthur Dunn's 1922 survey of the period listed the "Crane affair" along with the Cannon, conservation, and tariff eipisodes, Kenneth Hechler's 1940 treatment, *Insurgency*, omits any mention of foreign policy in ranking the causes of progressive disenchantment with Taft.[4]

An analysis of the embarrassing diplomatic scene in the summer of 1909 shows that the Taft years, though a personal failure as usually depicted, actually foreshadow a deeper division to be seen again especially in the election of 1912. A great part of the sound and fury coming from the insurgent camp was merely that: vocal, opportunistic criticism inspired by the realization that Taft was not and could not be Roosevelt or anything like him. Still the administration and a part of its opposition differed on more than political or personal issues. In basic agreement as to ends, they had different concepts on how to respond to a developing industrial order. The State Department under

3. For a typical presentation see Robert Osgood, *Ideals and Self-Interest in America's Foreign Relations: The Great Transformation of the Twentieth Century* (Chicago: University of Chicago Press, 1953), pp. 102–03.

4. See Arthur W. Dunn, *From Harrison to Harding* (New York: G. P. Putnam's Sons, 1922), II, and Kenneth Hechler, *Insurgency* (New York: Columbia University Press, 1940), p. 17.

Philander Knox was moving, hesitantly to be sure, toward a limited cooperation with other powers in the development of China as a market for goods, money, and ideas. This paralleled a similar trend in the rationalization of the domestic economy toward subtle yet powerful forms of industrial coordination as in the trade association. Just as this movement met antitrust sentiment at home, so it encountered resistance from defenders of a highly competitive and independent American role abroad. In the course of a speaking tour in the summer of 1909, which in itself raised some doubts as to his diplomacy, Charles Crane seemed to be impressed by these independents and not the cooperationists whose influence was felt in Washington. An examination of his brief career deserves more attention than it has received. Not only did it add fuel to the insurgent anti-Taft fire but it illustrated a basic split among policy makers, both domestic and foreign.

Taft's Victory

Although no mention is generally made of China policy as an issue in the campaign of 1908, both Taft and William Jennings Bryan had visited China and had definite ideas on the subject. The 1908 Republican campaign textbook included a chapter entitled "The Statesmanship of William Howard Taft in the Orient."[5] This was one area in which Taft was supposed to surpass his peace-prizewinning predecessor. Experienced as governor general of the Philippines, the then secretary of war had qualified as Roosevelt's personal emissary to the Far East in 1905 and 1907. Speaking in Shanghai in October 1907, Taft had declared his desire to fashion "a policy in the Pacific that will last this country for a generation, maybe a century." This Taft doctrine mixed John Hay's Open Door with Roosevelt's reform record at home and "encouraged the empire to take long steps in administrative and governmental reform, the development of the resources of China and the improvement of the welfare of the people." As so often proved to be the case, Taft's program did not match his plea. Seeking a progress "in many directions that lead to greater national efficiency," he proposed less than basic steps such as the reform of the consular service,

---

5. Edgar A. Horning, "Campaign Issues in the Presidential Election of 1908," *Indiana Magazine of History,* LIV (Sept. 1958), 237–64, mentions every possible domestic issue but ignores foreign policy; *Journal of the American Asiatic Association,* VIII (Oct. 1908), 268.

a United States court for China, and a dignified government building for Shanghai.[6]

For his part, Bryan had published a book on his Far Eastern impressions entitled *Letters to a Chinese Official*. Sounding surprisingly like avowed expansionist Brooks Adams's *Law of Civilization and Decay*, the perennial Democratic candidate predicted the eventual victory of "progressive civilization," an amalgam of Christianity and laborsaving machinery. The Pacific was to Bryan what Palestine had been to Jesus nineteen centuries earlier. While Taft saw much to praise in China, Bryan was highly critical of a civilization that was overrated and a people without a mission.[7] This negative impression of China made it impossible for even Bishop James Bashford to support Bryan, despite their personal friendship. On the other hand Bashford found Taft to be the best candidate he had met. The commercial American Asiatic Association matched this missionary enthusiasm for Taft who would make "a very intelligent and influential advocate." "A vote for right against wrong" was the analysis of Jeremiah Jenks, Cornell political scientist and advisor on Chinese affairs.[8]

After the Republican victory, the *New York Herald* summarized the feeling about the new administration: "President Taft is personally familiar with the issues involved in the Eastern question, and this knowledge will assure a progressive and enlightened American policy in China."[9] Complementing Taft's familiarity was the growing interest of Wall Street bankers in China and Manchuria as fields for investment. The simultaneous appearance of the Taft and Wall Street interest ensured that "enlightened American policy" would be the pursuit of "proper and progressive business."[10] A new corps of diplomats,

6. Ibid., VII (Dec. 1907), 326; *New York Times*, Oct. 9, 1907.

7. William Jennings Bryan, *Letters to a Chinese Official: Being a Western View of Eastern Civilization* (New York: McClure, Phillips, 1906). The essay was in answer to the earlier *Letters from a Chinese Official: Being an Eastern View of Western Civilization* (New York: McClure, Phillips, 1903). Bryan and others were fooled in believing that the author was truly Chinese. The anonymous writer was the English Platonist and pacifist G. L. Dickinson.

8. James Bashford, "Diary," XXVII, 18–30, Bashford Papers, Missionary Research Library, Union Theological Seminary, New York; *Journal of the American Asiatic Association*, VIII (Nov. 1908), 289–90; Jeremiah Jenks to William Howard Taft, Nov. 4, 1908, Taft Papers, Library of Congress (hereafter cited as LC).

9. *New York Herald*, July 17, 1909.

10. Huntington Wilson to W. W. Rockhill, State Dept. Numerical File (hereafter cited as SDNF) 551/118a, National Archives (hereafter cited as NA).

including Willard Straight and Assistant Secretaries of State William Phillips and Huntington Wilson, had been preparing for just such a happy set of circumstances. As early as 1907 Straight foresaw Taft as a leader in the undertaking of America's "commercial and industrial responsibilities." This is "precisely the movement for which we have been praying," Phillips wrote in 1908. With Taft as president this vision was about to be fulfilled, or so it seemed, in the person of Willard Straight and the instrument of the banking consortium. After serving as chief agent for railroad magnate E. H. Harriman's proposed financial invasion of the previously Japanese and Russian controlled Manchurian railways, Straight worked in early 1909 as the direct link between the promising Washington and Wall Street interest in the Far East. Harriman had sought Manchurian railroads as part of the chain he hoped to stretch around the world. Straight now served as agent of a newly formed American banking group in Peking which sought to encircle China, not the world, with Western, and in Straight's plans, American railways. A group of British, French, and German bankers had recently turned their attention back to building a system of railways south and west from Hankow, the so-called Hukuang Railways. The movement envisaged by Straight and Phillips was the development of an American group headed by J. P. Morgan and Company to join this banking consortium. To this end and to the profits in trade sure to follow, Taft and Knox gave open support. When Phillips drafted memos advocating the introduction of the methods and improvements known to progressive America in China as a means of securing Eastern markets, Knox approved. Privately the secretary assured his new team, "We don't propose to furnish all this altruism and get none of the trade."[11]

Hiring

One major question mark remained. Convinced that W. W. Rockhill, ironically the leading creative force behind the original Open Door

11. William Phillips to Willard Straight, Sept. 9, 1908, Straight Papers (hereafter cited as StrP), Cornell University Library, Ithaca, N. Y.: Straight to Mabel Boardman, Nov. 30, 1907, Boardman Papers, LC; Philander Knox memo, May 10, 1909, and letter to the Senate, July 28, 1909, Knox Papers, LC. For general description of the workings of the consortium see Frederick V. Field's *American Participation in the China Consortiums* (Chicago: University of Chicago Press, 1931) and Charles Vevier, *The United States and China, 1906–1913: A Study of Finance and Diplomacy* (New Brunswick: Rutgers University Press, 1955).

notes, was not aggressive enough in search of American economic interests, Taft sought a new face to suit "the most diplomatic position that I have to fill." What was needed was "a man on the ground who realizes the necessity and has the force and pluck and experience to take advantage of the opportunity."[12] Taft could not have imagined how difficult it would be to get one there.

The president's stated first choice, like so many of his early, hasty, and politically motivated actions, had to offend all interested parties. The young men in the State Department, the insurgents in the Congress, and the Chinese could not be happy with the offer to Charles Fulton, a Republican and former Oregon senator. Even though Taft was probably only paying a political debt knowing that the bid would be refused by Fulton, the appointment was strikingly unattractive. A fifty-six-year-old anticonservationist, Fulton had voted in favor of the restriction on immigration from the Orient.[13]

After Fulton declined, China hand Jenks applied, but the administration turned in the direction indicated by the *Cincinnati Times-Star* when it spoke of the "new field for the young men who have graduated from our technical schools and colleges, for China, besides planning great railways is about to undertake vast waterway projects, too."[14] One attractive possibility appeared to be John Hays Hammond, consulting engineer for Harriman's Union Pacific Railway and an expert on the selection of profitable mining districts. Another such potential minister able to "deal with the problem of developing natural resources and industry" was Frederick Delano, consulting engineer for the Chicago West Side Elevated Railway and former manager of the Chicago, Burlington and Quincy.[15] When both refused, the spotlight narrowed on another Chicagoan, Charles Crane. Heir to his father's large plumbing company, lifelong oriental and Russian traveler, and past president of the reform Chicago Municipal Voters League, Crane seemed

12. Taft to Rollo Ogden, April 21, 1909, Taft Papers, Presidential Series 8, vol. III.

13. See Mowry, *Era of Theodore Roosevelt*, p. 215; *Collier's*, XLIII (April 24, 1909), 10; Taft to Tom Millard, April 13, 1909, Taft Papers, series 3, box 246.

14. Taft to Jenks, April 28, 1909, Taft Papers, Presidential Series 8, vol. III; *Literary Digest*, XXIX (July 3, 1909), 4.

15. John Hays Hammond, *The Autobiography of John Hays Hammond* (New York: Farrar and Rinehart, 1935), II, 487, 544–45. H. Wilson to Taft, June 14, 1909, H. Wilson Papers, Ursinus College Library, Collegeville, Pa.; *Who's Who in America*, 1908–1909 (Chicago: A. N. Marquis, 1908).

uniquely qualified.[16] A man of much apparent "pluck, force and experience," the new minister to China would typify, it was hoped, the hustling, "shirt-sleeve" American businessman with whom many sought to replace the older, trained diplomat.[17] Mr. Dooley approved of this idea, "Me own idee is that we oughtn't to sind anny ambassadures abroad f'r a long time. 'Tis on'y wanst in awhile that something comes up between this counthry an' another that can't be settled be th' agent iv Armour an' Comp'ny or th' corrisponint iv th' Assocyated Press."[18] If Willard Straight's brief tenure with the AP during the Russo-Japanese War counts, then it appeared early in the summer of 1909 that Mr. Dooley's plan would come true, substituting Crane for the Armour Company.

The new minister would later say that Taft indicated he wanted the public excited over the China opportunity. "Speak it out red hot," was the phrase the president used. True to this instruction, Crane's acceptance statement was the first of many "red hot" speeches he would be accused of making. After paying homage to Taft's 1907 Shanghai address and the Monroe-type doctrine expressed there, the hustling businessman-progressive explored the new China frontier. "China is now the focus of the world's greatest international problem," Crane began. "I can think of no nation in whose progress, prosperity and security the United States has greater interest." This interest he defined as the commercial opportunity and immense field for American enterprise found in China's great industrial expansion. As to his own role, Crane was frank, summarizing it as "securing and maintaining a foothold there."[19]

The appointment drew support from Crane's wide circle of friends.

16. Detailed biographical material on Crane is scarce. See Leo J. Bocage, "The Public Career of Charles R. Crane," (Ph.D. diss., Fordham University, 1962) and the brief sketch by Donald M. Brodie in the *Dictionary of American Biography*, XXII, Supp. Two, 128–130. Crane's interesting if somewhat rambling "Memoirs" are under publication negotiation and presently may be read only in typescript form.

17. For examples of this thinking see James H. Wilson, Aug. 2, 1909, J. Wilson Papers, box 16, LC, and *New York Herald*, Sept. 19, 1909.

18. *American Magazine*, LXVI (June 1908), 111. In his dissertation cited above, Bocage does, coincidentally, make mention of Crane's association with the Armour Company.

19. Crane, "Memoirs," p. 142; Crane, "Letters, 1869–1919," pp. 276–77, Crane Papers; and Knox Papers, box 4.

The Independent stressed the approval of those interested in Chinese trade, railways, and education.[20] Willard Straight saluted the new minister from London where he was negotiating American entrance into the consortium. Wisconsin sociologist E. A. Ross rejoiced in the "wise action." Lillian Wald congratulated Crane from her Henry Street Settlement and remarked how she had "always been deeply interested in China and the Chinese."[21] From the editorial offices of the *American Magazine* came the approval of Ida Tarbell and Lincoln Steffens. Steffens in particular wanted to hear of the new financial method. Jokingly he assured Crane, "I'll promise not to ask you to make China increase her debt so that I may share in her, but I am otherwise interested."

Many approved with the hope that their own special reform interest would be applied in China now that one of their own was in charge. Crane, they reasoned, was to be free of all political debt, except of course to his friends. "He is a reformer," Norman Hapgood and *Collier's* announced hopefully.[22] David Fairchild of the Department of Agriculture thought Crane should give special consideration to experimental plants in what was the world's richest field for new cultivation. An educator named H. Strong felt confident that Crane's industrial experience would help him realize that only more and more Western education could save China. Success in Strong's terms would come only when they "shall have substituted mechanics for Confucius."

Unqualified support came from *La Follette's Magazine* with reformers like Steffens and Jane Addams as well as Wisconsin professors Ross, John R. Commons, and foreign relations expert Paul Reinsch on the editorial board. The magazine, in its first year of publication, found Crane the best of all possibilities, "a linguist and a traveller who understands the Oriental mind, an experienced businessman on a large scale and most fortunate of all a rare type of businessman who has been at the heart of many of the most important reform movements in this country." Sounding much like a State Department memo as prepared by Phillips or Huntington Wilson, *La Follette's* felt Crane would foster "the interests of the United States in the world trade that will grow out of China's awakening."[23]

20. *Independent*, LXVII (July 22, 1909), 210–11.
21. By far the best source for the approval of the appointment is the collection of congratulatory notes received by Crane, July 17–August 25, 1909, Crane Papers.
22. See *Outlook*, XCII (July 31, 1909), 772–73, and *Collier's*, XLIII (July 31, 1909), 7.
23. *La Follette's Magazine*, I (July 31, 1909), 3–4.

Firing

Belated August congratulations began to reveal an interesting new tone. With the honeymoon between Taft and the reformers clearly over, the Crane appointment was not just another good administration move but a saving grace. One such note was struck by the mother of Roosevelt's conservationist Gifford Pinchot. In her letter of August 5, Mary Pinchot applauded the Crane selection for which she could "forgive the administration what I consider its grievous mistakes."

On the day Mrs. Pinchot wrote, Taft made his most grievous mistake. Aware that his refusal to join in the drive to unseat Speaker Cannon and his frequent meetings with Aldrich had convinced the low tariff insurgents that he was consorting with anti-Roosevelt, reactionary forces, Taft signed the high Payne-Aldrich tariff. He believed it would be accepted and hoped he "would be able during the coming year to carry through the rest of his program and thus insure the success of his presidency with the people."[24]

The people, at least those on La Follette's, were not so sure, as Edgar Eugene Robinson stated in his attack on the tariff in the August 28 issue. By mid-September Taft responded to such criticism with a speaking tour, the most important stop being Winona, Minnesota. As George Mowry notes, after the Winona address, criticism of the administration reached a new, final, and clearly public form. As Taft drew the lines, he was a "middle-of-the-road progressive" and his foes were extreme and conspiratorial.[25] Yet before the president's words were even reported, still another schism appeared when Collier's opened its big guns on Taft for defending Secretary of the Interior Richard Ballinger in his feud with Gifford Pinchot over the secretary's decision to reopen western water-power lands to public sale.[26]

Ida Tarbell's August warning that the whole American crowd might move to Peking suddenly seemed more serious than humorous. In September 1909 the only Open Door in the government for anti-Taft

24. Taft to his brother Horace, June 27, 1909, Boardman Papers; Stanley Solvick, "William Howard Taft and the Payne-Aldrich Tariff," Mississippi Valley Historical Review, L (Dec. 1963), 442.

25. See Henry Stimson, "Diary," vol. II, Stimson Papers, Yale University Library, New Haven, Conn.; Taft to his brother Horace, June 27, 1909, Boardman Papers.

26. La Follette's Magazine, I (Aug. 28, 1909), 9; Collier's, XLIII (Sept. 18, 1909), 11. See also Mowry, Era of Theodore Roosevelt, pp. 249, 254.

forces was Charles R. Crane's. The new minister's door was in fact too open, or so some in the State Department felt. The wrong people were seen entering, and the wrong statements came out. Crane's unusually strong pro-Russian and anti-Japanese attitudes were known in Washington as early as 1902.[27] With these sentiments more and more common after Japan consolidated its 1905 victory over Russia in Manchuria, a man in Peking with Russian connections could be a useful asset.[28] It soon became clear, however, that Crane planned to take with him journalists like Straight's friend George Marvin and the maverick China hand Tom Millard. Both were violently anti-Japanese: Marvin had been in the employ of the Chinese as a publicist in 1908 and Millard had been a member of his staff.

Ironically, given the growing resentment of Taft's ties to Aldrich and the trusts, Crane's friend Marvin was now known to be too close and too proud of his contacts with Straight and the House of Morgan. Millard had been among the first to warn of Japan in what he called the New Far East of the post Russo-Japanese War period.[29] Realizing that the new minister could become allied if only by implication with blatant financial or diplomatic positions which the department was not willing to publicly advocate, Assistant Secretary of State Wilson suggested Crane be warned to "refrain from utterances and action of any kind which might color to such imputations," and to "avoid any personal associations which might be taken as an indication of a partisan influence as regards the relations of Japan and China."[30]

Worried about just such associations, Knox arranged a July luncheon for Crane to make new friends among the Wall Street hierarchy. Crane

27. John Hay to Theodore Roosevelt, May 1, 1902, Hay Papers, LC. Hay mentions Crane's belief in Russia's exceptional position in northern China.

28. Straight to E. H. Harriman, Aug. 2, 1909, StrP.

29. George Marvin to Straight, April 16, 1908, StrP; Tom Millard to Taft, Dec. 10, 1908, Taft Papers, series 3, box 220; Millard to James Wilson, Sept. 10, 1906, and July 29, 1909, J. Wilson Papers. Also see Millard's *The New Far East* (New York: Charles Scribner's Sons, 1906). Millard is one of several journalists who need more study in terms of the implementation of the Open Door. Until his death in 1942, he wrote books and articles, edited several papers including *The China Press* (1911) and *Millard's Review* (1917), and served as advisor to China most importantly at the Versailles Peace Conference.

30. See Marvin to H. Wilson, July 8, 1909, SDNF 5315/344; Alvey Adee to Crane, Sept. 29, 1909, and H. Wilson to Knox, Sept. 30, 1909, both in the Knox Papers, box 4.

later claimed his relationship or lack of one with Wall Street had bothered Knox from the beginning. From all reports, however, this meeting of the Chicago Municipal Voters' League with Morgan's Henry P. Davison, Mortimer Schiff of Kuhn, Loeb and Company, and Thomas Lamont then of the First National Bank went without a hitch. The bankers' man, Willard Straight, complimented Huntington Wilson on the "splendid appointment."[31]

Armed with firsthand consortium information, Crane continued to follow Taft's edict to "speak it out red hot," even using that phrase in remarks before the Illinois Manufacturers' Association. With E. Carleton Baker, a clerk in the Far Eastern Division already collecting Crane's "red hots," Millard proposed further publicity by using the annual dinner of the Asiatic Association as a giant gala send-off for Crane. Secretary Knox opposed the idea of seating the president or himself on a dais to honor a minister prior to his even having begun his service. Agreeing with Millard that unity of purpose was vital in China matters, Knox still cautioned, "If we sky rocket it now, we will fail to live up to expectations we have aided in creating."[32]

Even without such notable guests, the Crane-Millard skyrockets blazed brighter than ever at the September 20 New York dinner attended by important and interested bankers, journalists, industrialists, and public officials including Attorney General George W. Wickersham. Baker's book of "Cranisms" got two noteworthy additions. The minister, a former Democrat, compared Taft to "old Uncle Grover" and explained the consortium as "the new form of hold-up which the State Department has recently been so successfully engaged in—of forcing money on China." The New York Herald, deeply interested in China and an administration supporter, omitted that "hold-up" sentence from its extensive coverage of the evening.[33]

Although Huntington Wilson later recalled that his "hair stood on end" at the term "hold-up," Crane had received no formal instructions

31. Crane, "Memoirs," pp. 142–43; Straight to H. Wilson, Aug. 3, 1909, SDNF 5315/470–72.

32. E. Carleton Baker's collection is found in the Knox Papers, box 4, the best, though by no means the only, source for developments between August and October concerning Crane. In that box can also be found: Millard to Knox, Aug 12, 1909, and Knox to Millard, Aug. 23, 1909, both discussing the dinner.

33. Again, Knox Papers, box 4, and Journal of the American Asiatic Association, IX (Oct. 1909), 261–65, which reprinted the entire text.

from Wilson or the department to correct his frequent slips of the tongue. With his scheduled departure fast approaching, Crane called at the State Department in the week following the banquet. No one was there to meet him. Taft had advised him to see Knox but the secretary was at his Valley Forge home. Wilson was ill and soon to be hospitalized with an emergency appendectomy. Approaching the venerable second Assistant Secretary Alvey Adee, Crane was met with the usual exhibition of the latest in family pictures and the idea to drop by the newly created Far Eastern Division. On duty that day was none other than Baker, soon to have Straight's old job as consul in Mukden, Manchuria, and presently absorbed in the details of a Sino-Japanese crisis over the Antung-Mukden railway.[34]

In 1905 China had agreed to have Japan operate and maintain a 188.7-mile line from Antung to Mukden, the terminus of their larger Japanese South Manchurian railway. A war-caused lack of funds had delayed work and brought into question the legitimacy of the original option granted by China. With the railroad would go the right to mines in the area and the choice of a terminal site in Mukden. Having these advantages the Japanese could control Manchurian mines and entrance into Mukden and thus onto the South Manchurian railway. Henry Fletcher, American chargé in Peking, spoke out against such Japanese monopolization. A close confidant of both Straight and Marvin, Fletcher was then asked if violations of the Open Door were threatened. While his answer of September 23 was indefinite, the possibility of a protest to Japan existed within the department when Crane visited.[35]

For all the absence of detailed instructions, Crane did learn at least of this currently hot item. When he later met one of his old newspaper cronies, Sumner Curtis of the *Chicago Record Herald,* the minister "spoke it out red hot" and mentioned that formal protest was imminent. Although such a decision was not officially reached until mid-October, the leak certainly forced the issue.

With Crane on his way to San Francisco and an October 5 sailing and Taft still touring the West, Wilson and Knox suddenly took the

34. Huntington Wilson's summary, dated April 8, 1910, can be found in his papers at Ursinus College. See also the important Taft to Knox, Oct. 24, 1909, Knox Papers, bound vol. IX. Details of Crane's visit were prepared by Baker for Crane's friend and Far Eastern communications expert Walter S. Rogers. Dated 1917, this report appears in the Crane Papers, appendix 3.

35. See SDNF 5767/48–140.

initiative. Hearing of the Antung-Mukden leak in the September 27 *Chicago Record Herald,* Wilson's first comment was simply, "Isn't that man impossible?"[36] Learning that Crane had definitely been the source of the story, State Department counsellor Henry Hoyt advised his recall for careful examination and possible reassignment to Chile. Both Crane and Taft learned that such action had been taken in a telegram from Knox on October 3. Although the minister and the president met for a hastily arranged breakfast following the news, neither knew the grounds for the recall. In fact, as long as Curtis refused to reveal his informant, Knox could not announce the reason for the action and Crane's only knowledge could come from the educated guesses of the reporters who met him at each stop on his trip back to Washington.

Taft at first hoped revocation of the appointment could be avoided. Eight days after learning of the action he compromised once again. "What ever you shall decide in the Crane case," he assured Knox, "I shall abide by."[37] From the time of the confrontation between the minister and the secretary in Knox's apartment, the versions of the story vary significantly. Knox reported that after being confronted with the leaked protest, Crane agreed to resign. On the contrary, Crane remembered no such acquiescence but merely Knox's claims of indiscretion. In any event, there reached a point as E. Carleton Baker reports when Crane asked point blank whether he had the secretary's confidence. Knox's blunt reply sealed the minister's doom. "Well if you put it that way," he told Crane, "you haven't."[38]

Controversy

In China, Willard Straight noted in his diary that the recall aroused considerable discussion and feared it would have a most unfortunate effect on Chinese leaders.[39] This was nothing compared with the unfortunate effect on Crane's influential friends following his denial of guilt in a resignation statement on October 12. Something less than the

36. See Wilson's review of the incident, April 8, 1910, H. Wilson Papers. Step by step evolution of the recall decision can be traced only in the Knox Papers, box 4.

37. Taft to Knox, Oct. 3, 1909, Knox Papers, bound vol. VIII, and Taft to Knox, Oct. 11, 1909, Taft Papers, Presidential Letterbooks.

38. See E. Carleton Baker's report of the crucial meeting in the Knox Papers, box 4.

39. Straight, "Diary," StrP, box 2.

direct insult of a personal friend and reformer would have aroused the anti-Taft insurgents and journalists. Even those not involved could see what was coming "on the heels of the Ballinger-Pinchot and Cannon controversies, the fight of the house insurgents and the senate progressives." *The Independent* was sure it could make out the same pattern as appeared "quite emphatically enough in the case of Secretary Ballinger. But the end of this case is not yet, any more than we have the end of the so-called Ballinger-Pinchot disturbance. Mr. Crane has friends. . . ."[40] Fifty of these Chicago friends signed a protest linking Crane's supposed indiscretions to Taft's 1907 Shanghai doctrine. Lillian Wald "lamented the serious loss," and other New York reformers agreed with the member of the *America Magazine's* editorial board who wrote to Ray Stannard Baker, "Isn't it rotten about Crane?"[41]

Finley Peter Dunne speaking in his own voice and not that of Mr. Dooley hoped the incident served to stress the failure of the State Department's legal minds who did not bother to consult the president and worse did not share Crane's alliance "with a great variety of progressive people and interests." Concluding in the inevitable lighter mood, Mr. Dooley's sidekick evaluated Wilson and Adee as diplomats worthy of any European country except Great Britain, Germany, France, Russia, Spain, Portugal, Italy, Austria, Turkey, and the Balkan states.[42]

The incident's political significance was expressed in a letter to *The Nation* from J. Laurence Laughlin, a Chicago friend of Roosevelt.[43] Laughlin found that "in this part of the world it is already clear that the Administration, and not Mr. Crane had suffered." He warned prophetically, "A few more Winona speeches, a few more deferences of the Aldrich-Cannon combination, a few more such bulls by the State Department, and the next House of Reprseentatives ought to pass into the control of the opposition."

Despite all criticism, perhaps once more because he felt compelled to support an act of his administration under fire, Taft stood behind the

40. *Cleveland Plain Dealer*, Oct. 14, 1909, in Knox Papers, box 3, and *Independent*, LXVII (Oct. 21, 1909), 942.

41. Once again for the attitude of Crane's friends see the Crane Papers and Crane, "Memoirs," p. 150. Also unsigned letter on *American Magazine* editorial office letterhead to Ray Stannard Baker, Oct. 14, 1909, R. S. Baker Papers, series 2, container 92, LC.

42. *American Magazine*, LXIX (Jan. 1910), 429–32.

43. *Nation*, LXXXIX (Nov. 4, 1909), 429.

decision. Even some of his closest friends, like Mabel Boardman of the Red Cross, were "exceedingly indignant at the most unfortunate incident." Still the president was sure Crane had come to his post with preconceptions of policy and had strong streaks of vanity and conceit. Besides, Taft declared, he had advised Crane to speak only within the public declarations of the State Department.[44]

To the insurgents this episode took its place as part of a great conspiracy. Once again Taft had not been faithful to his word, this time as expressed in Shanghai, during the 1908 campaign, and as recently as his "red hot" instructions to Crane. Impressions were widespread that the penalty outweighed the crime, that there was much of the story undisclosed, and that the whole business smelled of intrigue.[45] Even if proof was not handy, the charge that powers greater than the president or the secretary of state had been responsible was a winning political gambit. Given the ire between both sides by the fall of 1909 the mileage to be gotten from the Crane incident probably explains in great part why so many not directly concerned with America's position in the Far East got so upset.

There were two obvious villains, the Japanese and the "interests." Crane's long-standing anti-Japanese attitudes, his support of Russia in 1905, and the nature of the leak blamed for the ouster gave credence to a possible Japanese dissatisfaction with the choice. The "interests" were a perennial enemy of the insurgents. *La Follette's* argued that Crane would not bend his knee to Wall Street and the story in the Chicago paper was a mere camouflage.[46] *Collier's* raised the shadow of secret night guests at Knox's Valley Forge retreat. Though unidentified, the mysterious visitors were implied to be partners in the China loan whose unpublicized trip caused the sending of the recall telegram the next day.[47]

Tom Millard, his cauldron bubbling, mixed the two together into a most distasteful potion of exotic demons. It was the "Japs and the Jews," Millard told Crane. Certain for several years that "somebody

44. Mabel Boardman to Frank B. Tracy, Oct. 2, 1911, Boardman Papers; Taft to Knox, Oct. 24, 1909, Knox Papers, bound vol. IX.

45. See *Journal of the American Asiatic Association,* IX (Nov. 1909), 289; "The Very Sad Case of Mr. Crane," in *Harper's Weekly,* LIII (Oct. 23, 1909), 4; and *Chicago Record-Herald,* Oct. 13, 1909, found in StrP.

46. *La Follette's Magazine,* I (Oct. 23, 1909), 3.

47. Norman Hapgood to Crane, Oct. 20, 1909, Crane Papers; *Collier's,* XLIV (Nov. 6, 1909), 9.

will have to lick the Japs," Millard saw a conspiracy headed in America by the German Jewish banker Jacob Schiff, head of Kuhn, Loeb and a friend of Japan, especially since its war with Russia in 1905. Crane's support of Russia in that conflict had convinced Schiff, or so Millard reasoned, that the new minister was sympathetic with that country's anti-Jewish pogroms. Remembering after the fact that Schiff had refused to see him before his departure despite Lillian Wald's urgings, Crane wrote in his memoirs that opposition to his appointment on Wall Street had determined his future long before any alleged indiscretions. Millard added that news of the decision to withdraw the appointment was in fact known in Japan several days before it was in the United States. According to his analysis, Schiff and the Japanese forced the State Department to "make an ass of itself, and stultify its Eastern policy."[48]

Seemingly untroubled by such characterization the department did little to elaborate its reasons in the matter. Huntington Wilson wrote in 1910 that Crane's penchant for "perpetrating indiscretions" and his constant reference to Taft's careless "red hot" instruction were the prime factors. Even this limited explanation was not published until Wilson's autobiography appeared much later.[49] Some magazines willingly accepted and defended the recall. *The Nation* thought Crane indiscreet and blamed the whole episode on "Red Hot Diplomacy." *The Outlook*, with which Roosevelt would soon be associated, believed the department's version, questioning only the consequences of such action on American-Japanese relations.[50]

Interpretation

Who can be believed? Was it conspiracy or indiscretion? The general conspiracy argument, used so well by muckrakers like Upton Sinclair,

48. Millard to Crane, Oct. 25, 1909, and Crane to Millard, Nov. 26, 1909, both in Crane Papers; Crane, "Memoirs," p. 151. The absence of the whole department hierarchy on the day of Crane's visit and the idea that this was so arranged to "set him up" to see Baker and then be fed the material for a leak and a recall seems implied in much of the conspiracy reasoning although it is never stated baldly enough to be cited as such.

49. H. Wilson's version, April 8, 1910, H. Wilson Papers; Wilson's *Adventures of an Ex-Diplomat* (Boston: B. Humphries, 1945) is an example of the kind of autobiography that attempts to whitewash a whole career, which was in this case one of endless frustrations after 1913.

50. *Nation*, LXXXIX (Oct. 21, 1909), 372; *Outlook*, XCIII (Oct. 23, 1909), 357.

is attractive because it is as difficult to dismiss as to prove. Especially useful in explaining any mishaps in America's "unwanted" role as a world power, the conspiracy method of proof was adopted by Taft and Knox as well as the insurgents. Late in his term Taft confided that his presidency had been blocked at every turn by an alliance of Perkins, Munsey, Pinchot, Crane, La Follette, Brandeis, Beveridge, Cummins, TR, the Senate progressives, and the magazines. Knox explained the appointment of Crane's Chicago friend Walter Fisher as secretary of the interior to replace Ballinger on the basis of his being a member of the "Roosevelt conservancy" and "Crane" teams.[51]

Even accepting, as was probably the case, that Schiff and the Japanese were upset at the new minister and his statements, the conspiracy argument is predicated on unsubstantiated assumptions: first, that Knox and Wilson were pro-Japanese enough to let Tokyo make their decisions and second, that Schiff would or could so influence Washington let alone his Wall Street peers.[52] Surely the evidence indicates that at least Wilson shared the rapidly growing distrust of Japan common among young diplomats like Straight. The close ties among George Marvin, the House of Morgan, and Crane, in addition to Straight's hearty approval of the choice, show a strong segment of Wall Street not anxious for a recall despite the sentiments of Schiff. Finally, if such influential "interests"—be they Japanese, Jews, or otherwise—were so against Crane, how had he been appointed in the first place?[53]

The conspiracy argument takes the obvious and well-placed opponents, distorts their motives, and imbues them with all persuasive

51. See Knox Papers, box 3. Also Taft to Boardman, Dec. 24, 1911, Boardman Papers. Taft was at least correct in predicting the forces which would defeat him in 1912. Among those not directly involved in this incident were: George Perkins of United States Steel and the Progressive party in 1912; Frank Munsey, industrialist, magazine publisher, and also Bull Mooser; Louis D. Brandeis, lawyer, advisor to Woodrow Wilson, and later justice of the Supreme Court; and finally the two midwestern Alberts, Senators Beveridge and Cummins of Indiana and Iowa respectively.

52. *Japan Chronicle,* Aug. 19, 1909, in SDNF 551/404.

53. Bocage, "The Public Career of Charles R. Crane," relies on the State Department's pro-Japanese feelings for explanation. For a more careful analysis of the shift away from this earlier attitude toward the anti-Japanese sentiments of Straight and Wilson see Raymond Esthus, "The Changing Concept of the Open Door Policy, 1899–1910," *Mississippi Valley Historical Review,* XLVI (Dec. 1959), 435–54.

powers. Still, the grain of truth in this reasoning does destroy the State Department line as well. Given the already deteriorating Taft position in his party, it is unlikely a leading Republican like Knox would risk the inevitable storm unless he feared something far more than an over-garrulous minister. It is equally doubtful that sufficient motivation can be found in the variously stated personal arguments that Knox's legalistic, nondiplomatic training or his irritation at not being consulted while Taft made the original choice were responsible.[54] The pivotal question is whether there was some possible reason capable of persuading the secretary to court political disaster in order to eliminate Crane.

Willard Straight liked to think of his role in the Far East as part of the game. Put somewhat more diplomatically, there was no denying that Wall Street and Washington were playing for big stakes. China and Manchuria were undergoing "enormous internal development" and American manufacturers and merchants were hoping to reap countless opportunities. In the summer of 1909, the game was participation in Chinese and Manchurian railway building. Although all parties to the Crane incident sought to win not lose, they felt it vitally important how the game was played.[55]

Throughout the consortium negotiations, delicacy if not absolute secrecy was the goal. With a blackout impossible and widespread rumors in the press, Straight warned this would have to be a "careful game" and cautioned that he had "discussed it with no one."[56] Secretary Knox feared that Crane and especially Millard could destroy the whole project or at least set the wrong tone. Much as George Marvin approved of the appointment, he worried that the "long winded" Crane would create feelings of apprehension with Millard at his side. Others felt the same about Marvin's association with Crane.[57]

---

54. Explanations based on Knox's personality and training can be found in Dunne's Jan. 1910 *American* piece and in Laughlin's Nov. 4 letter to *Nation*. (See notes 42 and 43.)

55. Straight to H. Wilson, Sept. 25, 1909, StrP; Knox to the Senate, July 28, 1909, Knox Papers, bound vol. VIII; and H. Wilson to Henry Fletcher, June 19, 1909, StrP. Charles Vevier's *The United States and China* is a meticulous monograph on this whole topic.

56. Straight to H. Wilson, Aug. 3, 1909, SDNF 5315/470–72, and Straight to Jacob Schiff, Sept. 19, 1909, StrP. For speculation by even a nonsensationalist journal see *Outlook*, XLII (July 3, 1909), 535.

57. Marvin to Fletcher, Aug. 20, 1909, and Dec. 21, 1909, both in the Henry P. Fletcher Papers, box 2, LC.

Given such background a charge of indiscretion seems sincere. The alleged leak of a proposed protest to Japan can be seen as a cover for the bigger slips the department imagined Crane making in Peking. Extensive coverage of the minister's actions by his reporter friends made the situation even more untenable. The very delicacy of the consortium forced Knox and Wilson to silence their real anxieties and thus expose their action to charges of all sorts of dire conspiracy.

The choice of William J. Calhoun as Crane's successor reflected this desire for what one paper termed the "golden basis of silence." A lawyer with brief diplomatic experience as special envoy to Cuba and Venezuela, Calhoun had important Chicago and insurgent credentials. Besides pacifying the critics, Calhoun was picked to "soft-pedal for a while," as Straight noted.[58]

Still, it is doubtful that Knox would have risked exposure to insurgent journalists at home, just to eliminate similar diplomatic overexposure abroad. Compounding Crane's possible indiscretions was the probability that as minister he would try his hand at personal policy making.

Though most of his insurgent supporters certainly did not have such well-conceived plans for implementing the Open Door, inherent in all the debate over Crane was the fear in the State Department that Millard's brash words were signs of a desire to "commit the new regime to an aggressive, swashbuckling course which [was] the reverse of the game Crane ought to play."[59] Himself just a generation removed from the great fortune-builders of the late nineteenth century, Crane listened attentively when Millard pressed, as he and others had since 1906, for a truly independent American policy in the Far East. Millard's reasoning was consistent: "If it is not colored in the interests of China and America," he had written to Taft, "it will be colored in the interest of China and some other western power. It is high time we should interest ourselves, as Americans, in these methods of influencing international affairs."[60]

On the other side, Knox, who had successfully broken up the Northern Securities rail combination while attorney general in 1902,

58. *Detroit Free Press*, Dec. 7, 1909, in Knox Scrapbooks, vol. XXIV, Knox Papers; Taft to William Calhoun, Dec. 26, 1909, Taft Papers, series 8, vol. X; *Journal of the American Asiatic Association*, IX (Jan. 1910), 357; and Straight to unidentified correspondent, April 17, 1910, StrP.

59. Marvin to Fletcher, Aug. 20, 1909, Fletcher Papers, box 2.

60. Millard to Crane, Oct. 25, Crane Papers; Millard to Taft, Dec. 10, 1908, Taft Papers, series 3, box 220.

was being asked to institute a kind of international trust. It is clear that what pressures came from the "interests" were towards the elimination of destructive competition in the world economy, just as they sought to reduce it at home. As usual Willard Straight put it best. Showing that a man deeply concerned with the need for an independent American role could feel the pressure and tension for rationalization as well, he wrote in 1908: "The policy of mutual cooperation and division of the profits as opposed to the old system of single efforts versus combined opposition would hasten the time when China would be seamed with wealth-producing and opportunity-giving railways." Always the noble advocate, Knox advised American diplomats that the government "regards full and frank cooperation as best calculated to maintain the Open Door."[61]

Despite this cooperative logic, the long tradition of American detachment from European politics, the growing hostility to Japan and a strong antitrust sentiment gave the argument for an independent policy deep patriotic and economic roots. Even with the pressures he felt for cooperation, Straight stressed the need to "guard our isolation." Coming from a self-professed imperialist, the use of the term *isolation* has real meaning, certainly not noninvolvement but rather the preservation of just such an independent sphere of action.[62]

Strong manufacturing distrust of the banking community added more economic weight to the case against the cooperation inherent in a banking consortium arrangement. Millard's publisher George Bronson Rea pestered the State Department with questions of how much benefit American manufacturers would derive from participation in loans if they did not also share in supplying standards, material, and engineers for the railways.[63]

---

61. Straight memo, Feb. 25, 1908, StrP.

62. Straight to H. Wilson, Aug. 3, 1909, SDNF 5315/470–72. Straight's proud imperialist admission can be found in a letter to Mabel Boardman, Nov. 30, 1907, Boardman Papers.

63. Rea, publisher of *The Far Eastern Review*, is another old China hand who merits attention; he later served as aide to Dr. Sun Yat-sen. See note of Amos Wilder (Shanghai consul) to Knox, Jan. 4, 1910, SDNF 5315/777. That division within business interests can be used to revolutionize the understanding of even a well-studied field, see the work of two Civil War and Reconstruction historians: Robert P. Sharkey, *Money, Class and Party* (Baltimore: Johns Hopkins Press, 1959), and Irwin Unger, *The Greenback Era* (Princeton: Princeton University Press, 1964).

It is this tactical split which the recall of Crane most dramatically reveals. As Raymond Esthus has shown, 1909 was a turning point in the elaboration of the Open Door. Esthus depicts a radical shift from what he defines as John Hay's realistic, commercial Open Door to Philander Knox's moralistic and financial one. While correct in emphasizing the role played by Straight and Wilson and tracing their increasingly anti-Japanese attitudes, Esthus is too concerned with the eventual outcome of the game. All the players in 1909 had the same goals in sight. All had been trained in the increasingly anti-Japanese rules. No artificial conflicts as to ends need be created when the real split apparent among those directly involved in developing America's role in China was a tactical one.[64]

Crane's fitting into a cooperative framework, however limited, seemed doubtful. In particular the thought of his ultimately sitting still for a Japanese share was incredible. Certainly Knox, Wilson, and Straight gagged as well at the thought of such cooperation with Japan as Schiff desired.[65] Though such a partnership with Japan would be resisted to the last, the crucial decision to begin moving in the direction of a compromise limited cooperation, with the European powers at least, was made in the summer and fall of 1909. While Crane's speech-making proclivities may have been painful to bear, his style of playing the game would surely have been fatal to State Department plans. Such plans called for a move toward voluntary cooperation as a solution for economic problems, Crane would never yield in his hope for independent American action.[66]

Legacy

The whole episode rings with the inconsistency and lack of leadership or communication characterizing so much of the Taft administra-

64. Esthus, "Changing Concept of the Open Door." For a different view, placing Knox's financial policies in reference to the Hay doctrine, see William A. Williams, *The Tragedy of American Diplomacy*, rev. ed. (New York: Dell Publishing Co., 1962), p. 68.

65. Knox to Phillips, Oct. 6, 1909, Knox Papers, bound vol. IX; Straight to Augustus Jay (minister to Japan), Dec. 19, 1909, StrP.

66. Crane did become minister at the end of Woodrow Wilson's second term. See Crane to Secretary of State Bainbridge Colby, March 23, 1921, U.S. Department of State Decimal File 793.94/1170, in which he is still calling for such "independent American action."

tion. In all the discussion of conflicting policy positions, sight must not be lost of the fact that the excitement, if not the real significance, of the Crane recall stems from the use made of it by anti-Taft forces only at most indirectly concerned with America's program and position in China. In this sense the whole episode ranks with the Cannon, Ballinger-Pinchot, and tariff questions in the agonizing insurgent realization that Taft was not Roosevelt. The implied and unanswerable assumption is that had Roosevelt still been in charge, Knox and Wilson, Crane and Millard, even Schiff and the Japanese would not have been able to control the situation as the various interpretations of the incident argue they did.[67]

Although the Crane affair markedly reveals once again the enigma of William Howard Taft, it unfortunately does not explain it. Even in the Far East, an area of his supposed expertise, Taft's whole conduct of the search for the right man in the pivotal Peking position was paradoxical. After stressing the importance of the post, he offered it to a clearly unqualified man, Senator Fulton. After making a universally approved choice in Crane, Taft had allowed Crane to be executed right before his eyes. Certainly by switching so radically from seeming insurgent to staunch conservative on every contested point, Taft aggravated the problems facing his administration.

It must be asked, however, whether these problems were in fact solvable at that time, even by Roosevelt. A real split over tactics to be used to cope with the rapidly expanding opportunity in China was at the core of the Crane feud with the State Department. It was magnified by the political tensions of the post-Roosevelt period. A similar situation existed on a broader scale as the election of 1912 loomed closer. A basic difference of opinion on how to order the new industrial society would become intensified by the politics and personalities of Taft, Roosevelt, and Woodrow Wilson.

Examination of this usually ignored Crane incident reveals a question of foreign policy helping to play a key role in the split between Taft and the group of journalists, municipal reformers, congressional

67. Two later magazine reviews of the episode in the perspective of more Taft-insurgent difficulties and the reappearance of the shadow of Roosevelt on the political horizon are especially interesting: see Mark Sullivan's piece in *Collier's*, XLIV (Jan. 8, 1910), 9; and Ray Stannard Baker's "The Measure of Taft," *American Magazine*, LXX (July 1910), 336.

insurgents, and businessmen who would leave the ranks of the Republican party to support either Roosevelt or Wilson in 1912. The traditional explanations of conspiracy or Taft's personal failure fall short in showing how such a disastrous political mistake could have been made. The implication is of course that the oft-studied domestic crises of the troubled Taft years deserve similar reexamination.[68]

68. The work of Kolko, *The Triumph of Conservatism*, Robert Wiebe, *Businessmen and Reform: A Study of the Progressive Movement* (Cambridge: Harvard University Press, 1962), and Samuel Hays, *Conservation and the Gospel of Efficiency: The Progressive Conservation Movement, 1890–1920* (Cambridge: Harvard University Press, 1959) provide such a reexamination.

4

War and Peace

Toward 1912 and Beyond

MINING and railroad expert John Hays Hammond, having successfully bypassed the controversy that befell Charles Crane by declining
a Taft bid to be minister to China in 1909, returned to a career that
had already earned him the designation of the highest salaried man
in the world. In 1911, Hammond took time out from his profitable
ventures to address the American Peace Congress in Baltimore. The
title of his speech was a "Businessman's Interest in Peace," but his
talk was really about the future of China.[1] A firm believer in the Open
Door policy, Hammond called upon the great nations of the world to
"neutralize China" after the fashion of Belgium and Switzerland. The
world could insure thereby a perpetually open market for resources
and trade. While there was little original in a neutralization plan,
Secretary of State Philander Knox having designed an earlier such
scheme for Manchurian railways, the Hammond proposal indicates a
larger relationship between American actions in the Far East and the
questions of war and peace and the domestic economy.

1. John Hays Hammond, *The Autobiography of John Hays Hammond* (New
York: Farrar and Rinehart, 1935), II, 487, 544, 674. *Current Literature*, XLIV
(June 1908), 606–08, and John Hays Hammond, "The Business Man's Interest in
Peace—Why Not Neutralize China?" *Maryland Quarterly*, Maryland Peace Society,
Nov. 1911, found in the New York Public Library (hereafter cited as NYPL).

The "Peace and Cooperation" Movement

That the Open Door was a policy necessitating and hopefully preserving peace was as much an accepted fact to John Hay's contemporaries as it is a forgotten one to Americans several Asian wars later. Americans "will not fight" for Manchuria's commerce or China's integrity, Hay had observed. Every succeeding secretary of state echoed similar sentiments either in the flat declaration of Knox that "it is not presumed that the United States would ever resort to war" or the more excited exhortation of Robert Lansing in 1914 that "it would be quixotic in the extreme to allow the question . . . to entangle the United States in international difficulties."[2]

It was not then visionary or spiritual pacifism which brought Hammond, industrialist Andrew Carnegie, or George Perkins of United States Steel to the forefront of the American peace movement in the early twentieth century. Rather it might be said that such a movement was more Pacific than it was pacific in orientation; more concerned with successfully securing the business aims of the Open Door than in faithfully following the tenets of a warless society. War was an "insensate waste of life and revenues." Peace and only peace allowed the Open Door to operate to American advantage.

In William Howard Taft's inaugural address this logic was clearly at work, though it is often dismissed as dollar diplomacy or the concept of government as a servant to business. "Our international policy is always to promote peace," the former secretary of war noted. Within a peaceful framework, lasting reforms could be achieved. A modern China free from war would "secure at the same time freedom from alarm on the part of those pursuing proper and progressive business methods."[3]

The chain connecting the Open Door and the peace movement had

2. John Hay to Theodore Roosevelt, April 25, 28, 1903, John Hay Papers, Library of Congress (hereafter cited as LC); Philander Knox memo, Sept. 19, 1910, Philander Knox Papers, LC, bound vol. 11, and Robert Lansing to Paul Reinsch, Nov. 4, 1914, State Dept. Decimal File (hereafter cited as SDDF) 763.71/192, published in *Papers Relating to the Foreign Relations of the United States* (Washington: Government Printing Office, 1928), Supp., p. 190. Much of this discussion of the "new" peace movement is based on my talks with Michael Lutzker, who is presently at work on what he calls this "practical" pacifism of the period. Though our conclusions are somewhat different, I am indebted to his insight and research on these materials.

3. State Department Numerical File (hereafter cited as SDNF) 551/118a, National Archives (hereafter cited as NA). A marked copy of the speech was sent by Huntington Wilson to W. W. Rockhill.

another link. Remembering and fearing a "yellow peril," John Hays Hammond concluded his call for neutralization by stressing the need to pacify and modernize China so as to prevent the rise of a hostile Chinese military menace in the future. His whole address stemmed from the immediate fear that money which could go towards Chinese economic development might be misspent on an army and navy. Such fears were reported as well by another American, University of Chicago geologist T. C. Chamberlain, who sensed that great infusions of American reform in China could make the difference between a future of benevolence and one of aggression, between the victory of the scientist and that of the soldier.[4]

With different perspective both Hammond and Chamberlain arrived at the same answers: peace, education, and, most of all, cooperation. The move to neutralize and pacify China, in fact, the very tie between the peace movement and the Open Door was an outgrowth of the broad aim to rationalize and make more efficient America's domestic and international affairs. War to Hammond was a waste, a debt, a closing of markets. He defined peace, on the other hand, as the obtaining of minimum cost by the elimination of unnecessary operating expenses. To the scientist Chamberlain, war was rivalry while peace, education, and efficiency were cooperation to produce profitable intercourse. Making his most telling point in a book of many, Tyler Dennett emphasized this conclusion that cooperation meant peace. The opposite path—an independent, competitive or "isolated" role—was "essentially belligerent and inevitably led to a pitting of the United States against not one but all of the powers and against the Asiatic states as well."[5]

The pressure for cooperation in the Far East, victorious in the Crane episode was reinforced after 1909 by support from influential members of the American peace movement. An examination of the ranks of the Red Cross China Famine Relief Committee is highly illustrative. Avowed peace men such as Columbia University President Nicholas Murray Butler, former Secretary of Commerce Oscar Straus, industrialists Carnegie, Perkins, and Cleveland Dodge, and editor

---

4. T. C. Chamberlain, "China's Educational Problem," *Independent*, LXIX (Sept. 22, 1910), 646–49. The same issue contains two other pieces: "The Leadership of the New Peace Movement in America," by Rev. Frederick Lynch and "After Cannonism What?" by Congressman Victor Murdock.

5. Tyler Dennett, *Americans in Eastern Asia* (New York: Macmillan, 1922), pp. vi–vii.

Oswald Garrison Villard were joined on the committee by consortium bankers Jacob Schiff and J. P. Morgan, Jr., and by old China hands like Seth Low and John Foord of the American Asiatic Association, John R. Mott of the YMCA, and Melville Stone of the Associated Press.[6] While not proving any definite interlocking directorate among advocates of peace, cooperation, and the Open Door, such evidence does support the logic of Hammond's arguments favoring all three.

Though stronger than ever after 1909, forces favoring a cooperative strategy in reaching the commercial, investment, and reform goals of the Open Door in China still faced the problem of Japan and the persistence of a competitive tradition. Some such as Crane and Tom Millard refused to admit the possibility of any solution save American economic war against Japan. Even more troubling, however, were those like Henry Fletcher and eventually Theodore Roosevelt who challenged the logic of cooperation designed to thwart rather than to accept Japanese interests in China. Such limited cooperation, the compromise position of Knox and Huntington Wilson developed during the Crane incident, produced continued support of consortium loan efforts and plans to neutralize Russian and Japanese railway holdings in Manchuria. More significantly such compromise failed, as Roosevelt would point out, to reduce the conflict between more extreme cooperative or competitive ideas for American policy. Given financial and philosophical pressures for combination, further efforts at compromise under Taft moved closer to the fully cooperative position. Reflecting the back and forth nature of policy created by the cooperative-competitive tension, such Taft administration measures were opposed and in fact reversed by the victory of Woodrow Wilson and his many pro-competition supporters. The election of 1912 must be seen then not only as a crucial confrontation between Roosevelt, Taft, and Wilson but between the forces of cooperation, compromise, and competition for a dominant voice in the constantly evolving struggle to control American foreign and domestic policy.

Maintaining an Independent Tradition

Not yet finding their new champion in Woodrow Wilson, adherents

6. See the papers of the China Famine Relief Committee, file 898.5, Central China Famine, 1910–1912, in American National Red Cross Library, Washington, D.C.

of an aggressive independent role in China held the weakest position in the continuing debate over Open Door tactics after the recall of their spokesman Charles Crane. Clearly the House of Morgan recognized the persistence of a competitive tradition in suggesting that "it will be unwise not to maintain in China at least the idea of independent negotiations."[7] The very thought that a Wall Street bank greatly concerned with efficiency and cooperation had to keep up such a front indicated the lack of any real effective pressure for competition. With an enthusiasm about opportunity in China surpassed only by a fear of Japan, advocates of an independent role such as Millard and George Bronson Rea certainly attempted to stir up such pressure. Anti–Wall Street in orientation, their suggestions were hardly as original as they were impassioned.

Returning to the lesson of 1905, Millard sought a permanent publicity campaign to include daily, weekly, and monthly publications as well as an annual yearbook of China. The 1911 founding of the *China Press* as the first totally American-subsidized paper in China was the only visible result of such an effort. In direct conflict with the British-owned *North China Daily News*, the Millard paper was financed logically enough by Charles Crane. In the same way Crane served as angel to other efforts to establish American news outlets by John B. Powell and Ben Fleischer in Shanghai and Tokyo.[8]

Writing frequently in private and public, Rea's sales pitch remained the same as well. An engineer by trade, Rea complained that the consortium was designed to benefit American bankers and to harm American manufacturers. The lack of uniform standards on the railroads financed by the international bankers, the corruption among purchasing agents, and most especially the use of British rolling stock convinced Rea and the locomotive interests he represented that cooperation violated the spirit of the Open Door doctrine.[9] For a while he

7. J. P. Morgan memo, November 7, 1910, William Howard Taft Papers, series no. 2, box 102, LC.

8. The Philander Knox Scrapbooks, especially vol. 24, are an excellent source of newspaper clippings revealing much about the period. On the Millard plan see the *Memphis News*, July 7, 1909. Also Tom Millard to Gen. James H. Wilson, Feb. 17, 1911, James Wilson Papers, box 16, LC. See also John B. Powell, *My Twenty Five Years in China* (New York: Macmillan, 1945), p. 10.

9. George Bronson Rea to Amos Wilder, Sept. 19, 1911, SDDF 893.77/1181. *Far Eastern Review*, XLIV (Nov. 1911), 609–11. Huntington Wilson to R. S.

toyed with the idea of eliminating bankers and allowing China a free hand in the construction of its railways. Such a plan would allow for cheaper work since expensive consortium labor and credit charges would be removed. The goal of this program was of course the right to supply the heavy equipment needed. Not only could Americans then work independently but there would be created a double demand. If railways cost approximately half as much to build, twice as many could be begun.[10]

Whatever its intent, such a plan smacking of "China for the Chinese" ran counter to the whole idea that goals at home or abroad could be reached by anything but positive American governmental action, whether competitive or cooperative. Dismissing the Rea idea in a letter to *The Outlook,* Assistant Secretary of State Huntington Wilson could "hardly believe that you mean China shall be left entirely alone and no attempt made to advise her." Graphically drawing the domestic analogy, Wilson reprimanded those who favored such a plan: "as well leave the slum to manage its own santitation and thus infect the whole city."[11]

Both Millard and Rea, finding little success in other schemes, came to support a totally American attempt to finance railway construction. The instrument they selected was the moribund American China Investment and Construction Company sponsored by George Macy and A. W. Bash and represented by F. G. Cloud, a kind of latter-day Willard Straight, who in fact had held Straight's old position as consul

---

Miller, April 16, 1912, SDDF 121.56/2, and Rea to Woodrow Wilson, March 26, 1913, SDDF 893.77/1263. As stated in the discussion of the reasons behind the Crane dismissal (ch. 3, note 63) the business community, often depicted as a monolithic unit, had within it deep divisions. In China in the early twentieth century one very basic such split between manufacturers and bankers, between those who would supply goods and those who would supply money, served as an economic conflict most significant in the shaping of competitive and cooperative strategies. Further research is essential to determine more meaningfully the secondary-level problems of non-Wall Street banks (which were probably closer to the manufacturer's position) and large industrial firms (certainly more in sympathy with the consolidation desired by Wall Street banks).

10. On the Rea plan see *Journal of the American Asiatic Association,* X (Feb. 1910), 1–2.

11. Huntington Wilson to *Outlook,* Jan. 19, 1910, Huntington Wilson Papers, Ursinus College, Collegeville, Pa. See *The Progressives and the Slums* by Roy Lubove (Pittsburgh: University of Pittsburgh Press, 1962).

in Mukden, Manchuria. Violently anti-Japanese and feeling that Tokyo would and had used financial fraud and opium smuggling to gain preferential and unfair advantages, this "rival group" sought to finance an independent American loan to China.[12]

Though such competition was found inexcusable by members of the consortium group, the independent position won an important convert. Arriving in Peking as a cooperationist, Crane's replacement "Quiet man" William Calhoun was soon convinced that Russia and especially Japan would not be fair to China. "Cooperation is only valuable," the minister observed, "when the powers interested are fair to each other and fair to China." If all are not fair, "cooperation is impracticable if not impossible." So converted Calhoun wondered why the Bash-Cloud group was not deserving of the same support as the consortium. Nowhere was the independent versus cooperationist split drawn more clearly than in the State Department response to Calhoun. The minister already was aware that "we have gone too far in assisting the group to warrant another course." More significantly, he was also informed that such international participation in loans as made possible by the consortium was in harmony with the policy of the department and tended to insure the essential cooperation of the other powers.[13]

Some other independent actions did continue after 1909 much as they had before. Practicing its own unique brand of missionary social work the YMCA further developed American technical education lessons given in the vernacular.[14] American efforts at river conservation, begun as early as 1906 and more successful later under Woodrow Wilson,

12. Tom Millard, "Blundering in the Far East," *American,* LXX (July 1910), 413–25. Willard Straight to E. H. Harriman, July 12, 1909, Willard Straight Papers (hereafter cited as StrP), box 4, Cornell University Library, Ithaca, N. Y.; *New York Times,* Nov. 27, 1909; for the origins of the "Rival group" see several State Department files in particular; SDNF 788/916, SDNF 5315/320–21, SDDF 893.51/138. For the anti-Japanese feeling of the Bash-Cloud people see E. Carleton Baker to Knox, July 22, 1911, SDDF 693.001/143, and William Calhoun to Knox, Jan. 11, 1911, SDDF 693.003/383.

13. Knox to Calhoun, Oct. 6, 1910, and Calhoun to Knox, Oct. 12, 1910, SDDF 893.51/138, 150. Calhoun to Knox, April 3, 1911, SDDF 158.931/149; Calhoun to Knox, June 11, 1912, SDDF 893.51/981. Also Straight to Henry Fletcher, Dec. 11, 1910, StrP.

14. George Lerrigo to Fletcher Brockman, Jan. 14, 1911, YMCA file x970.4, designated Lerrigo Correspondence, YMCA National Headquarters Library, New York.

did manage to establish important foundations in the years before 1912. Projects on the Whangpoo, Liao, and Hwai rivers were perhaps the fullest blend of America's Open Door goals. They provided, it was believed, improved commercial channels, increased investment opportunities, and immediate conservation reform. More specifically this work came to involve the Standard Oil Company, the largest importer of goods in ocean steamers, an American corps of engineers under the direction of one C. D. Jameson, and the American National Red Cross or more directly, its head Mabel T. Boardman, the second female lead in the famous adventures of Alice Roosevelt in wonderland.[15] In her correspondence with John D. Rockefeller, Jr., Miss Boardman stressed the independent motivation behind the conservancy plans. Russia and Japan were taking advantage of the situation as it existed. American reforms were necessary to improve the quality of China's rivers to receive oceangoing vessels bringing Red Cross relief as well as oil. Rather than an engineering firm, Miss Boardman concluded, it would be "easier for us to offer to assist," since all would be "more ready to believe that an engineer sent by the American Red Cross has no other motive than an altruistic one."[16]

Despite such plans, hopes for an independent American role in China after 1909 often ended like the career of agriculturalist E. C. Parker. After spending several years trying to accomplish something for American trade, Parker declined reappointment to a Manchurian post.[17] The consortium loan negotiations, he reported, restricted his aggressive and competitive endeavors too greatly. As the House of Morgan noted, an outright competitive position was more a tradition than a viable alternative as long as those moving toward international cooperation controlled American policy. As such, it did serve as a check on cooperation. It must never be forgotten, Bishop James Bashford wrote, that "the United States, even alone if need be, should insist upon fair dealing." After all, he observed, was not that also the case at home where the government had learned to insist upon

15. On Standard Oil's role see C. McCaslin to William Kent, consul at Newchwang, Feb. 8, 1911, SDDF 893.811/42. For Jameson see Mabel Boardman to Taft, Oct. 14, 1912, SDDF 893.811/75.

16. Mabel Boardman to John D. Rockefeller, Jr., June 5, 1911, and Boardman to Starr J. Murphy, June 30, 1911, Red Cross file 898.5/2, Hwai River Conservancy, 1911–1914, Finances and Accounts, Red Cross Library.

17. E. T. Williams to Knox, Sept. 29, 1911, SDDF 893.01A/1, 3.

fair dealing "between great combinations of capital upon the one side and the laboring masses upon the other."[18]

An Evolving Administrative Logic

Such combinations and the cooperation inherent in them were, however, much more than just a preserved tradition after 1909. The words of Bashford are again instructive. Individualism was a partial, one-sided development. The "organization of capital into trusts and labor into unions," the China missionary pointed out, "are reversions from our nineteenth century conception of individual freedom."[19] The new century was by contrast one of organization, professionalization, or "economy and efficiency," as a Taft commission was aptly titled. Frederick W. Taylor's scientific management, described by Samuel Haber as the gospel of efficiency and the secular Great Awakening, was perhaps best expressed by the non industrial statement of the 1910 World Missionary Conference that "waste of energy in competition and ill-adjusted efforts are always foolish; in China today they are especially so."[20]

To eliminate such waste Americans interested in an efficiently opening door tried several important repairs. Some took part in a September 1909 discussion of China and the Far East held under the aegis of historian George Blakeslee at Clark University.[21] Sensing that the sessions produced no understanding between Millard's call for a distinctive American policy and Straight's picture of the present situation in Manchuria, one of those present, John Foord, began an even broader effort to reshape his American Asiatic Association. Foord sought to develop an organization, much like domestic trade associations, to act as an agency to study, for East and West, "the possibilities

18. See James Bashford's report "The True Policy of the United States in the Far East," p. 19, found in the Knox Papers, box 12.

19. Bashford, "Chinese Guilds," *Survey*, XXIII (Jan. 1, 1910), 481–84.

20. Samuel Haber, *Efficiency and Uplift: Scientific Management in the Progressive Era, 1890–1920* (Chicago: University of Chicago Press, 1964), p. 113. E. D. H. Klyce, "Scientific Management and the Moral Law," *Outlook*, XCIX (Nov. 18, 1911), 659–63. World Missionary Conference, *Report of Commission III: Education in Relation to the Christianization of National Life* (New York: Fleming H. Revell, 1910), pp. 111–12.

21. George H. Blakeslee, ed., *China and the Far East* (New York: Thomas Y. Crowell, 1910). *Outlook*, XCIII (Sept. 11, 1909), 52–53.

of helpful cooperation in beneficial enterprises for the advantage of both."[22] Consul Julean Arnold linked the need for such cooperation to the success of the American businessman when he advised those interested in China to apply "the same intelligent consideration, the same spirit of enterprise and progressiveness which characterizes him at home."[23]

While many of these programs and ideas clearly maintained a competitive instinct while advocating efficiency and cooperation, the State Department, especially Assistant Secretary Huntington Wilson, came more and more to place its emphasis on the rationalized capitalist system and not the free enterprise competitive tradition. Wilson liked to think that his "pet hobby," the creation of a Far Eastern division, had turned the department into a machine capable of coordinating financial, industrial, social, and commercial knowledge for the use of the businessman that Arnold had addressed. Convinced that domestic politics and not further diplomacy were in his future, Huntington Wilson had a consistent philosophy if not a successful career ahead. Flirting for a while with the eugenics movement to improve the race, he explained that individualism had run riot. What was needed, Wilson argued, was an "era of economic efficiency and social justice, through a wisely measured paternalism and centralization." Such centralization would allow for cooperation and thus efficiency. Making the vital connection between cooperation and China, Huntington Wilson observed, "We have problems of combination at home, but if there is a field where all the efficiency of combination may be availed of with large benefit and no possible detriment to the nation, it is in the foreign field."[24]

22. See *Journal of the American Asiatic Association*, XII (April 1912), 68–69, and XIII (May 1913), 109. The association did begin publishing a much more general and sweeping periodical entitled *Asia* in 1917.

23. Julean Arnold, "Advancement of American Trade Interests in China," *Overland Monthly*, LVII (May 1911), 467–68.

24. Though Wilson's autobiography is very weak there is much material in Huntington Wilson, *The Peril of Hifalutin* (New York: Duffield, 1918), p. 175. See also Wilson's speeches of 1912 as collected in his papers at Ursinus College, especially Nov. 1, 1912, in Jasper County, Missouri. Consult the 1913 confidential file in the Wilson papers as well. In the Taft Papers see Wilson's Oct. 18, 1912 speech in Chicago and a letter dated Sept. 6, 1911 to Charles Hilles, both in Presidential Series, no. 2, box 40.

Although he preferred to speak of such policy as the "New Diplomacy," Huntington Wilson stood ready to do battle with those who criticized Taft's support of the use of American capital in the development of China as dollar diplomacy. It was rather, he insisted, a policy designed to keep the peace and achieve prosperity. America's increasingly cooperative view was a "practical business-like policy for a practical business nation."[25]

The next step after the consortium for those holding such a view was the plan to neutralize all Manchurian railways. In mid-December 1909, Secretary of State Knox proposed that China purchase Russia's Chinese Eastern and Japan's South Manchurian railways and allow for joint administration of them by the powers. While the anti-Japanese vibrations of the day rang out loud and clear from this effort to internationalize Manchurian, meaning in good part Japanese railroads, the roots of the neutralization idea as in John Hays Hammond's later plan rested in the deep-seated pressure for cooperation and efficiency. The melody if not the intensity of the whole plan was tuned to the symphony of efficiency Wilson sought to compose. Neutralization and concomitant efforts at currency and trade reform would facilitate cooperation. They would remove the railroads of Manchuria and the commerce of China from European politics and place them under "economic, scientific and impartial administration."[26]

In the Darwinian language of the day, Huntington Wilson spoke of the "evolution" of efficiency. No word better described the process by which Philander Knox became a champion of cooperation. In 1907 before a Yale University Law School audience, Knox warned against "abnormal conditions" such as monopolies, preferential service, and rebates able to "destroy the normal operations of commerce." Even

25. Charles Vevier, "The Progressives and Dollar Diplomacy," (Master's thesis, University of Wisconsin, 1949), p. 88. Taft's second annual message is an excellent example of Wilson's thinking in action; see the Knox Papers, bound vol. 9. Also Wilson's Nov. 1, 1912, Missouri speech and the 1913 confidential file, both in the Huntington Wilson Papers.

26. See the Knox letters of Dec. 14, 15, 1909, explaining the plan, in SDNF 5315/617. Also H. Wilson to W. W. Rockhill, Dec. 23, 1909, and State Department Aide-Memoirs, Dec. 1909, both in SDNF 5315/665. Paul H. Clyde, *United States Policy Toward China: Diplomatic and Public Documents, 1839–1939* (Durham: Duke University Press, 1940), p. 245. On cooperation to reform China's currency and trade see William Phillips to the Far Eastern Division, May 1909, SDNF 788/219–22.

during the Crane uproar, the secretary remained reluctant to announce the support of his department for international monopolies and pre-divided equal shares. Impressed by the logic of efficiency, influenced by powerful forces pressing for consolidation at home and interested in opening the doors of China and the world to the expansion of American trade, Knox moved quite easily into an alliance with an already established international monopoly. The support of the well-positioned members of the peace movement, like Hammond, was the final step in the evolutionary process. By 1912 Knox was firmly committed "to unite in sympathetic and practical cooperation" for peaceful development. "Where nations invest their capital," he wrote for the *Saturday Evening Post,* "there they are intent upon preserving peace and promoting the development of the natural resources and prosperity of the people."[27]

A portion of the American press responded favorably to the Knox neutralization plan and the cooperation it would promote. The *New York Journal of Commerce* optimistically reported that a China revising her currency and tariff positions was on the way to "honesty and efficiency in the Occidental sense." Other editorials reflecting the post-1905 "yellow peril" fears of Japan in China, supported the neutralization idea as a militant policy designed to prevent the Koreanization of Manchuria.[28] With such a threat in mind themselves the Japanese reacted by affirming their own little cooperative arrangement outside the four-power consortium. On July 4, 1910, Japan and Russia signed a treaty guaranteeing each other's interest in Manchuria.[29] What Henry Fletcher had shown as early as 1908, the inherent flaw of a limited cooperation working against rather than with Japan, was now evident. Hardly as independent and aggressively anti-Japanese as Crane or

27. Huntington Wilson speech, Oct. 18, 1912, Taft Papers, Presidential Series, no. 2, box 40; Knox's Yale speech may be found in the Knox Papers, box 8; Knox to Phillips, Oct. 6, 1909, Knox Papers, bound vol. 9; *Pittsburgh Dispatch,* Nov. 14, 1909, Knox Scrapbook, vol. 26; Calhoun to Knox, Oct. 1, 1910, SDDF 893.51/198 and *Saturday Evening Post,* CLXXXIV (March 9, 1912), 43.

28. See the Knox Scrapbooks for the *New York Journal of Commerce,* and others such as *Duluth New Tribune,* Jan. 30, 1910, *Wall Street Summary,* March 16, 1910, and the *Hempstead Republican* and *San Francisco Evening Post and Globe* for sample opinion from diverse sections of the country.

29. *New York Times,* July 17, 1910. Also the Knox Papers, vol. 5, for diplomatic reports of the treaty.

Millard would have liked, the State Department compromise of cooperation to thwart competition had managed within five years to drive former enemies into each other's arms and thus block efforts to make the Open Door more efficient.

It was to this problem that Theodore Roosevelt addressed himself in December of 1910. Often interpreted as a rejection of the Open Door or an admission of Japan's preponderant position in Manchuria, the former president's well-known advice to Taft was neither.[30] Having returned from his African safari to find the political feud between the congressional insurgents and the president, Roosevelt sought to define, however vaguely, his own stand on the issues of the day, not the least of them the future of the Far East. Never a Japan-baiter or advocate of competition, the former president was now in addition reinforced by his recently acquired knowledge of Herbert Croly's *Promise of American Life*. Foreshadowing the 1912 campaign, the Roosevelt remarks may be seen then as the first statement of the new nationalism on the Open Door.[31]

Roosevelt felt as he later expressed in his *Autobiography* that a policy designed to cooperate without Japan was "most mistaken and ill-advised . . . combining irritation and inefficiency."[32] It was this inefficiency that irked him as well in the 1910 letter to Taft. "The Open Door policy in China was an excellent thing," Roosevelt began. The past tense has led many later readers to conclude that at least in his mind, it was over. The very next phrase dispels that idea. "I hope it will be a good thing in the future," he continued, "so far as it can be maintained by general diplomatic agreement." Total cooperation or "general agreement" was the means to perpetuate the Open Door, as indeed Roosevelt so desired. Lacking such combination the Open

30. Theodore Roosevelt to Taft, Dec. 22, 1910, Knox Papers, bound vol. 12; for a traditional treatment see A. Whitney Griswold, *The Far Eastern Policy of the United States* (New Haven: Yale University Press, 1938), p. 132.

31. On the Croly-Roosevelt relationship see Eric Goldman, *Rendezvous With Destiny* (New York: Alfred A. Knopf, 1952), ch. 9, especially pp. 188–89. See also the more developed treatment in Charles Forcey's *The Crossroads of Liberalism: Croly, Weyl, Lippmann and the Progressive Era, 1900–1925* (New York: Oxford University Press, 1961).

32. Theodore Roosevelt, *Theodore Roosevelt: An Autobiography* (New York: Macmillan, 1916), p. 414. Roosevelt maintained his views still later as well; see his *Japan's Part*, a pamphlet published by J. B. Millet in 1918.

Door "completely disappears as soon as a powerful nation determines
to disregard it, and is willing to run the risk of war rather than forego
its intention."

Substitute Japan for "powerful nation" and the situation in 1910 is
clear. Without an agreement with Japan, the hopes of the peace movement for cooperation would disappear. Limited cooperation as a compromise produced the same result as a totally competitive posture,
namely, inefficiency, or in John Hays Hammond's terms, war. Although
Roosevelt, hardly a military novice, thought war with Japan unfeasible
since it would require a fleet like England's and an army like Germany's, others were willing to take the chance rather than cooperate.

The extreme independent, anti-Japanese belligerence came in
Homer Lea's 1909 *The Valor of Ignorance*.[33] Anxious to arouse the
Chinese to the very military expenditures that Hammond so feared,
the frail, crippled Lea divided his tortured hours between writing, plot-
ting the rise of an antiimperialist Chinese army, and searching the
coast of his native California for the spot of the anticipated Japanese
attack. The unique task of twentieth-century America, Lea reasoned,
was to overthrow the laissez faire tradition that had lasted too long and
"to spread abroad over the earth the principles of its constitutions or
the equity of its laws." While such words reached Sun Yat-sen, whose
revolutionary forces were guided by Lea until his death in 1912, they
failed to stir many Americans. Lea's message fell on deaf ears, particularly in a state department gradually accepting not war but the other
end of Roosevelt's spectrum, cooperation, even including Japan.

Minister William Calhoun might "rather see the groups dissolved,
and the Americans eliminated therefrom, than to submit to the spolia-
tion of China by Russia and Japan," but consuls and businessmen
within his domain spoke more and more of trying "to systematically
seek to secure the cooperation of the higher Japanese business inter-

---

33. Roosevelt to Taft, Dec. 22, 1910, Knox Papers, bound vol. 12; Homer Lea,
The Valor of Ignorance (New York: Harper & Brothers, 1909, 1942.) Interestingly
enough, while the 1909 edition had an introduction by Gen. Adna Chafee famed
for the Boxer campaign, the 1942 wartime republication of the suddenly relevant
anti-Japanese book had a foreword by Claire Booth Luce praising Lea for his
"accurate" forecast. See also John P. Mallan, "Roosevelt, Brooks Adams and
Homer Lea: The Warrior Critique of the Business Civilization," *American
Quarterly*, VIII (Fall 1956), 216–30.

ests."[34] Knox might try to explain the four-power consortium and neutralization as efforts to keep the peace and thus really benefit Japan's commerce and industry but at the same time he inquired from those on the scene what price Japan and Russia would settle for should their partnership be sought.[35] The State Department might even use Jeremiah Jenks to convince Roosevelt and his fellow editors of *The Outlook* that no war with Japan was possible since neither side would attack. They might even persuade themselves in the department that "Jenks seems to have had some luck with the council of the universe" and that the "spirit and attitude of the Board, including the Contributing Editor, had been quite materially modified."[36]

Yet really it was the State Department which was having its ideas so modified or developed toward the very position Roosevelt had taken. Japan, as Henry Fletcher continued to report, had an excellent, efficient sales operation in China with one firm in control of selling, engineering, shipping, and banking. The United States, on the other hand, had to go through mill owners, brokers, China trade firms, native selling agents, and local merchants just to market its cotton.[37] With so far to go to be truly efficient, the United States made what the cooperationists had come to see as the necessary next step by taking the lead in late 1911 in seeking the admission of Japan and Russia to the consortium. On June 20, 1912, cooperation won its greatest victory thus far as the four-power group became six.[38]

This triumph or transition to a fuller cooperation was best represented and expressed again in the thinking of Willard Straight.[39]

34. Calhoun to Knox, June 11, 1912, SDDF 893.51/981; Thomas Sammons to Knox, Nov. 17, 1910, SDDF 693.001/142.

35. Knox to Minister O'Brien (Tokyo), Jan. 20, 1910, SDNF 5315/690; Knox to Minister Schuyler (Tokyo), Dec. 2, 1910, SDDF 893.51/222. Huntington Wilson to Knox, Jan. 20, 1910, H. Wilson Papers.

36. Jeremiah Jenks to R. S. Miller, Dec. 29, 1910, and Miller to Taft, Dec. 30, 1910, both in the Taft Papers, series 2, case file 40, box 326. See Jenks's later piece for *The Outlook*, "The Japanese in Manchuria," XCVII (March 11, 1911), 549–54.

37. R. Wesschoeft (Shanghai) to Henry Fletcher, Oct. 12, 1909, Fletcher Papers, box 2, LC.

38. See Griswold, *Far Eastern Policy*, p. 171.

39. Straight's correspondence as always was voluminous on this question. The change in his thinking is taken from these sample letters: Straight to E. H. Harriman, Sept. 6, 1909, StrP; Straight to Henry Davison, Jan. 16, 1911, Feb. 6, 1911,

Suspicious and jealous of even his European partners, especially the Germans, Straight was still harping throughout 1910 on the need to isolate Japan and Russia. Although he was willing to cooperate with the Europeans in order to make Japan and Russia afraid to act, Straight's emphasis remained on the "game for America and the Americans." By January 1911, however, the gap between the independent position of a George Bronson Rea and Straight's own cooperative stance was too visible to go unnoticed. Reaffirming the almost universal nature of the Open Door goals, Straight cut to the heart of the matter when he informed Rea that "we are probably in disagreement as to the form rather than as to the substance."

Such disagreement grew even though Straight resisted to the last the notion that "our position would be improved by cooperation with Japan in China." However, by December 1911 he was temporarily resigned to abandoning any hope of an independent American role and to "admit to a participation in all Chinese business our Russian and Japanese friends." Like the whole argument for cooperation, Straight had come a long way from the 1906 exchanges with W. W. Rockhill. Suddenly Straight was sure that "Japan's policy is not as militant as it once was." He even added in March 1912 an explanation of his actions in the light of the new agreement: "No one will be more pleased than myself if we may all be able to cooperate . . . with a fair field to all. That is all I have ever asked." Before a missionary group a year later, the banker's man put the final touches on his new found philosophy. Success, meaning the involvement of American manufacturers, bankers, and reformers in China, could only be reached through cooperation between the State Department and Wall Street and between America and the rest of the world. Rather than face the certain defeat by united political opposition, Straight finally agreed with his friend Henry Fletcher's 1908 assessment that he must "coop-

---

StrP; Straight to J. P. Morgan, Nov. 16, 1910, SDDF 893.51/220; Straight to Edward Bowditch, Feb. 23, 1911; Straight to George Bronson Rea, Jan. 11, 1911; Straight to Jacob Schiff, March 5, 1911; Straight to Henry Schoelkopf, Dec. 18, 1911; and Straight to Henry Bonar, March 13, 1912, the last five all in StrP. See also Straight's six-page letter to missionary Arthur Brown, Feb. 18, 1913, in the Goucher Papers of the Missionary Research Library, Union Thelogical Seminary, New York. Finally also in StrP see his review, "The Politics of Chinese Finance," an address he gave before the East Asiatic Society of Boston, May 2, 1913.

erate with other interested nations . . . despite even their possible failure to adopt an attitude as friendly to China as our own."

It would be tempting to attribute the temporary victory of coopera- tion over fears of Japan to external and simultaneous events, especially the Russo-Japanese treaty of 1910 or the later Chinese Revolution of 1911–12. To do so, however, is to carelessly ignore the domestic pressures leading in the cooperative direction. America's action was shaped more by the way events at home and abroad seemed to fit into a developing cooperative logic than by necessities of international politics based on events not even firmly understood in the United States. Though mere coincidence is not explanation, it needs to be pointed out that just three days before Straight accepted the need for full participation in the loan negotiations, Henry L. Stimson, later to play a key role in the development of American Far Eastern policy, addressed the New York Republican Club. "We recognize frankly," Stimson concluded in a discussion of the domestic economy, "that a large amount of combination on the part of our industries is economi- cally necessary and beneficial."[40]

The Chinese Revolution of 1911

Itself the beginning of cataclysmic change in Asia and the world, the Chinese revolution of 1911 at first reinforced the State Department's and America's preconceived ideas about the future. Within the depart- ment an additional opportunity was felt, as Huntington Wilson announced, "to emphasize the principle of concerted action by applying it to the question of recognition." After inquiries to the five consortium partners as to whether or not to immediately recognize the new Chinese republic proved "uniformly unfavorable to present action," Secretary of State Knox reassured Wilson "for the time being I am disposed to let the matter stand where it is."[41]

40. Straight to Schoelkopf, Dec. 18, 1911, StrP; Henry L. Stimson's address is found in the Stimson Papers, box 482, Sterling Memorial Library, Yale University, New Haven, Conn.

41. Huntington Wilson's position was expressed in a memo, Feb. 26, 1912, in the Taft Papers, Presidential Series, no. 2, box 272 (China). See also Knox to H. Wilson, Aug. 3, 1912, H. Wilson Papers, box 5. For a scholarly view see Meribeth Cameron, "American Recognition Policy Toward the Republic of China, 1912– 1913," *Pacific Historical Review*, II (June 1933), 214–30.

The revolution and the rise of a republic under a "progressive" Yuan Shih-kai to replace the empire indicated to Americans that "China means to become a nation in the western sense of the word."[42] The goals of the Open Door would now be reached that much sooner with a government anxious to continue work to improve China's canals, modernize its industry and agriculture, and reorganize an antiquated administrative system.[43] The gospel of efficiency, so broadly accepted by 1911, was seen by Wisconsin sociologist E. A. Ross as the chief beneficiary of the revolution. An intelligent government, one that was just and efficient, would make enormous strides "in the introduction of western technique and organization," Ross reasoned for *La Follette's Magazine*. Seeing the revolution not in political terms but in terms of the commercial, financial, and reform goals of the Open Door, Ross was sure that it would mean machinery, railways, telegraphs, post offices, sanitation, education, conservation, and modern dress.[44]

While E. A. Ross went on to draw the "perilous" racial conclusions that the yellow man would now join the white in "controlling the globe" and eventually molding the "politics of the planet," others understood the revolution only in the language of efficiency and cooperation. "What a blessing it would be," long-time China hand General James Wilson wrote in late 1911, if there would be a "united and homogeneous people" to "start in the work of establishing a government and a scientific system of revenue."[45]

Yet American response to the revolution also revealed that the hopes of those who would have the United States compete for hegemony in the Far East were still alive. With the victory of cooperation in gaining the extension of membership in the consortium to six, the forces of competition started the struggle to rebalance the delicate American compromise between cooperation and competition almost as soon as the revolution began. Some pressured the State Department, as in the

42. *Outlook*, XCVII (Feb. 4, 1911), 249–50.

43. F. H. King, "The Wonderful Canals of China," *National Geographic Magazine*, XXIII (Oct. 1912), 931–58. *Outlook*, CII (Nov. 30, 1912), 700–01. *Journal of the American Asiatic Association*, XII (April 1912), 65, 76–77.

44. E. A. Ross, "The Overturn in China," *La Follette's Magazine*, III (Dec. 2, 1911), 7. Ross, "Race Mind of the Chinese," *Independent*, LXXI (Sept. 7, 1911), 526–28.

45. E. A. Ross, *The Changing Chinese* (New York: Century, 1911), p. 138. Gen. James Wilson to Millard, Nov. 15, 1911, J. Wilson Papers, box 16.

congressional Sulzer resolution, for unilateral and immediate recognition of the new republic. Others, convinced that "as the French Revolution was inspired by America's success, so China's revolution was brought about and won by America's education," sought to bolster such an accomplishment by increased efforts to train indemnity students, now the leaders of a new, republican China.[46]

On New Year's Day of 1912 three-time candidate for president William Jennings Bryan shipped an encyclopedia of Thomas Jefferson's views to Peking and greeted China's Yuan Shih-kai as the leader of a "United States of China." The image of China as a reincarnation, as a *tabula rasa* for American business and especially American reform, was never clearer than immediately after the revolution. "China is as large as the United States," Frederick McCormick suddenly remembered in December 1911. It also, he noted, "lies in the same latitude, has similar physical characteristics, and the same kind of climate." Sensing the same geographical analogy, agriculturalist F. H. King asked Americans to picture China's Grand Canal as similar to the stretch of land either from the Rio Grande to the Ohio or the Mississippi to Chesapeake Bay. In a most revealing "expansion of the frontier of the United States westward to the interior of China," as Roosevelt had described earlier, E. A. Ross found "the Far West of the Far East," the remote province of Szechuan, to be the most energetic and American part of China.[47]

Searching for similarities in ideas as well as geography which would justify and benefit an independent American role in China, the YMCA hit upon the idea of boys' camps popularized at home by Daniel Carter Beard and the Boy Scouts. Such groups, a YMCA spokesman felt, "can become as great, if not a greater influence for good in China than in America."[48] Bryan supporters in the Midwest also doubled

46. Consult a speech by Major Louis Livingston Seamen, president of the China Society of America, given to the Republican Club of New York, Nov. 18, 1912, found in the NYPL. *New York Herald*, Aug. 28, 1910. Also the *Journal of the American Asiatic Association*, XII (Dec. 1912), 329.

47. William Jennings Bryan to Yuan Shih-kai, Jan. 1, 1912, Bryan Papers, box 28, LC. Frederick McCormick, "Present Conditions in China," *National Geographic Magazine*, XXIII (Oct. 1912), 931–58. E. A. Ross, *The Changing Chinese*, ch. 9. See a general American view of the revolution in McCormick's *The Flowery Republic* (New York: D. Appleton, 1913).

48. See the note of J. C. Clark, Aug. 5, 1913, in the YMCA World Service Folder C, 1912–14.

their efforts after the revolution to achieve opium prohibition. Others
were concerned with another evil spirit or rather "prohibition" as the
term is more commonly used in the United States. Just at the time
China had thrown its doors wide open to the Christian West, one
Minnesota man wrote Bryan that the United States must curtail the
flow of alcoholic liquors to the Far East lest it substitute drunkards
for addicts.[49]

Summarizing such American interest in Chinese reform after 1911
and the revolution, The Outlook thought that "the new government
has the sympathy of Progressives everywhere." One such progressive,
Lillian Wald, took a late 1910 vacation from her Henry Street settlement on the teeming streets of Manhattan's Lower East Side to visit
what she found to be the far-more-depressing downtowns of the Far
East. Still, her lasting impression anticipated postrevolution enthusiasm. "We met people," Miss Wald commented, "interested in all
progressive movements in the diplomatic circles and the educational
centers."[50] Among all these, the "best man in China," according to
Miss Wald and other Americans like Horace Allen, was the successful
leader of the revolution, Yuan Shih-kai. Well known though frequently
in opposition under the Manchus and still not revealing his own later
imperial designs, Yuan seemed to Americans like Bryan to be a leader
able to take China along the road to free government like that of the
United States. Willard Straight, however, had real doubts if "the
people of China care greatly whether there be a republic or a constitutional monarchy as long as they are allowed to earn their livings
in peace."[51]

49. Vice Consul Charles F. Brissell to Knox, July 13, 1912, SDDF 893.114/43,
and H. A. Campbell to Bryan, June 13, 1913, SDDF File 893.114/102.

50. Outlook, CII (Oct. 5, 1912), 237. Lillian Wald to "Folks," May 8, 1910,
Lillian Wald Papers, cabinet 1, file drawer 1, NYPL, and Lillian Wald to Unie
Tsuda, July 23, 1910, Lillian Wald Papers.

51. Lillian Wald, 1910 Peking notes, Lillian Wald Papers; Horace Allen, "An
Acquaintance With Yuan Shih-kai," North American Review, CXCVI (July 1912),
109–17. Straight to Jacob Schiff, Jan. 22, 1912, StrP. On Yuan, see also Arthur
Brown, The Chinese Revolution (New York: Student Volunteer Movement, 1912),
ch. 7. An excellent study of China's political development and American solutions
to vexing problems can be found in Urban G. Whitaker, Jr.'s, "Americans and
Chinese Political Problems, 1912–23," (Ph.D. diss., University of Washington,
1954).

A political scientist with religious and academic ties to the work of Princeton in Peking had ideas much closer to Bryan's than to Straight's about the future of free government in China. "The awakening of the people of China to a consciousness of their possibilities under free government," Woodrow Wilson would later agree, "is the most significant if not the most momentous event of our generation." Operating under this assumption, once elected Wilson and his first secretary of state, none other than Bryan himself, could act upon the possibility of once again moving toward an independent American role in China to reverse the evolution of the Taft years toward a cooperative Open Door.[52]

The American Election of 1912

While infrequent specific reference to Far Eastern questions appeared in the 1912 presidential election campaign, that well-studied confrontation between the Republican president Taft, the Democrat Wilson, and the third-party Progressive Roosevelt did focus on the commonly accepted goals and pivotal tactical conflicts shaping American actions in China as well as at home. Defining the curious political spectrum in 1912, editor and diplomat Walter Hines Page wrote that "we now have Progressives, Halting-Progressives, Ultra-Progressives, Progressive-Conservatives, Conservative-Progressives and TR."[53] Page's clever play on a much-used label, actually revealed that the election of 1912 for all its heated debate had a wide range of agreement amongst the three leading candidates, permeated only by the brilliant Roosevelt personality. Neither the goals of American capitalism at home or abroad nor the pragmatic test of efficiency were debated by the three major candidates.

In search of a "Progressive Nationalism" which he defined as "honest and efficient political and industrial democracy," Roosevelt and his Bull Moose party agreed with Woodrow Wilson's belief that

---

52. The statement with which Wilson would have so much to do is the famous 1913 State Department repudiation of the six-power consortium; see *Papers Relating to the Foreign Relations of the United States*, pp. 170–171. On Wilson's background see Tien-yi Li, *Woodrow Wilson's China Policy* (Kansas City: University of Kansas City Press, 1952), p. 15.

53. Walter Hines Page to Ray Stannard Baker, Feb. 23, 1912, Ray Stannard Baker Papers, series 2, container 94, LC.

his New Freedom program would "depend upon efficiency."[54] Similarly, Wilson by his speeches and later presidential actions showed he understood and sympathized with the oft-repeated position of Roosevelt and Taft that trade and investment as well as political reform were necessary in China. Sounding like Brooks Adams or Philander Knox, Wilson proclaimed in accepting the Democratic nomination that "our industries have expanded to such a point that they will burst their jackets if they cannot find a free outlet to the markets of the world." While attacking the Wall Street "money trust" Wilson spoke out sternly against American banks doing too little rather than too much in support of international commerce.[55]

Where the candidates did differ was on the question of how to reach such goals both at home and abroad. Usually depicted as a purely domestic argument over the nature of business organization, the crucial issue in 1912 was the competitive-cooperative split which had shaped Open Door tactics since 1905. Roosevelt's New Nationalism advocated the practicality of the same kind of combination and cooperation which he had called for earlier in his advice to Taft to reach international agreements in order to protect the Open Door. This Roosevelt monopolization of the cooperationist position created as large an ideological dilemma for the Taft campaign as the breakaway of former Republican faithful behind Roosevelt produced a political headache. Certainly Taft had failed to show any leadership in his early presidential lack of decision and never regained the initiative he lost there. Even by a friendly assessment, his State Department "was guilty of so many egregious errors."[56] Yet for all this fumbling, real strides had been taken toward the substitution of cooperative for competitive financial assistance, the very kind of efficiency which Roosevelt supported and claimed only he could achieve.[57]

54. Theodore Roosevelt, "Progressive Nationalism," *Outlook,* XCVII (Jan. 14, 1911), 58. Woodrow Wilson's 1912 speeches have been collected in the very useful John W. Davidson, *A Crossroads of Freedom* (New Haven: Yale University Press, 1956). See Wilson's address at Denver, Oct. 7, 1912, p. 373.

55. Davidson, *Crossroads of Freedom,* Sea Girt, N. J., Aug. 7, 1912, p. 33; Bridgeport, Conn., Sept. 27, 1912, p. 299; Yorkville Casino, New York, Sept. 4, 1912, p. 114.

56. For a China hand's criticism of Taft in 1912 see James Bashford's unpublished diary in the Missionary Research Library, XXVII, 18–30. Also see Straight to Fletcher, March 26, 1911, StrP.

57. Silas Bent, "The China Consortium and the Open Door," *Nation,* CX

As Huntington Wilson understood, cooperation in foreign policy matters, facing less antitrust resistance, could evolve more completely than at home. Developing a broad philosophy for domestic as well as foreign policy, Taft men like Judge Gary and John Hays Hammond had to deal with the strong competitive tradition.[58] The 1909 compromise of limited cooperation to thwart a rival industry or nation had proved inefficient. The 1912 answer which Gary labeled "conservative progressiveness" called for a "policy of cooperation to conciliate our competitors." This idea of cooperation to conciliate not to thwart competition was reflected in the admission of Japan and Russia to the consortium and the simultaneous search at home for just such a "new competition" especially through the mechanism of the trade association.[59] Though still a compromise between cooperative and independent extremes, such a conciliation solution was certainly more oriented toward cooperation than were early compromises which combined against Japan or business rivals.

Woodrow Wilson was the only candidate to take onto himself the task of extolling the glories of the competitive way. Looking to the nineteenth century, the scholar-politician told a Philadelphia audience, "Domestic competition used to keep America quickened with life. Domestic competition used to beckon new men on all the time to the handsome adventures of American enterprise."[60] All this had been changed in Wilson's eyes by the rise of monopolies to curb such competition. Speaking about the great American trusts but using words

(March 20, 1920), 379–81, is an appreciative retrospective view of the Taft administration accomplishment.

58. See the speeches of Huntington Wilson as indicated in note 24. For Gary, consult an Oct. 19, 1911, speech before the American Iron and Steel Institute and also a May 17, 1912, address both found in Elbert H. Gary, "Addresses and Statements," vol. I, collected and bound by the Museum of the Peaceful Arts, found in NYPL. John Hays Hammond, "Why I Am for Taft," *North American Review*, CXCVI (Oct. 1912), 449–59.

59. It was in 1912 that Arthur Eddy wrote his *The New Competition*, as "an examination of the conditions underlying the radical change that is taking place in the commercial and industrial world—the change from a competitive to a cooperative basis" (Chicago: A. C. McClurg). Good information on the development of the trade association idea is scarce; see Harold U. Faulkner, *The Decline of Laissez-Faire, 1897–1917* (New York: Rinehart, 1951), 172–75.

60. Davidson, *Crossroads of Freedom*, Philadelphia address, Oct. 28, 1912, p. 488.

that could have been directed to Japan, the candidate threw down a gauntlet to "challenge those gentlemen to come into a fair field against the weakest and beat independent competitors. They cannot do it."[61]

Despite such statements, both as candidate and later as president, Wilson realized that to maintain "independent competitors" would mean not laissez faire but an active governmental participation or even intervention. Moreover it would probably require governmental regulation so as to prevent the rise of monopolies which had and could again grow out of just such a competitive situation as Wilson advocated.[62]

Roosevelt also envisaged the need for such a governmental function when he attacked Wilson's plan for "regulated competition" and sought to counter it with his own brand of "regulated monopoly." In reality neither Wilson nor Roosevelt adopted the extreme cutthroat competition or outright monopoly positions that each would have liked to pin on the other. The compromise solution of domestic regulation and international agreement was actually at least implied by all three major candidates. The difference was in emphasis, or to use a shorthand review: Roosevelt stressed cooperation, Wilson competition, and Taft compromise.

"New Freedom" and Renewed Competition

As the only even partial advocate of a competitive position in the race, Woodrow Wilson easily became the leader of those who sought an aggressive, independent American role in the Far East. To achieve Wilson's "fair field" was in fact the goal of these men who could now style themselves supporters of the New Freedom and agree with the philosophy of one Wilsonian, Louis D. Brandeis, whose guiding principle was defined later by Max Lerner as being "wherever monopoly has taken the place of former competitive units he wishes to restore and maintain competition."[63]

Wilson had spoken before the same 1911 peace convention that heard John Hays Hammond's plan to neutralize China. Yet as a poten-

61. Ibid., Denver speech, Oct. 7, 1912, p. 373. This speech is particularly interesting for Wilson does make reference to the lack of competition in China as explanation for the "acceptance of the inevitable" among Orientals.

62. Ibid.

63. Quoted in John Chamberlain, *Farewell to Reform* (New York: John Day, 1932), p. 233.

tial candidate the following year, he was making the kind of belligerent statements that could stir those seeking competition. Writing to
Bryan, Wilson proposed a "war for emancipation from the control of
the concentrated and organized power of money."[64] Men like Rea and
Crane would be sure to take such a statement as a declaration of at
least economic war with Japan.

Aware of such a possibility, Willard Straight warned following
Woodrow Wilson's victory over the divided forces of Roosevelt and
Taft that "the whole game may be stopped soon." Within a month of
Wilson's coming to office, Straight's warning had come true, though as
he later put it more accurately to a consortium friend, "We ourselves
are out of the game."[65] On March 18, 1913, the new American administration refused to extend its support to the international six-power
loan organization. Several weeks later, Washington reversed another
Knox action by independently recognizing the new republic of China.

Often depicted as a radical departure in the Open Door policy, these
early actions of the Wilson administration were rather a turning back
toward an independent, competitive posture to rebalance American
actions in China which had swung so far toward cooperation by 1912.
Both the bankers involved in the consortium and the new administration surely had personal reasons motivating the decision to suspend
operations on the international loan negotiations. The "American
group" was split by dissension and the delegation led by Henry Davison that went to Washington to discuss the matter in early March of
1913 was not anxious to continue in China unless specifically requested
by the new president. Given Wilson's political opposition to the "organized power of money" plus his latent southern sectional distrust of
"Wall Street," such a request was unlikely.[66] The withdrawal of support was not by any means, however, just a personal repudiation of
dollar diplomacy or a rejection of the goals of the Open Door. Both the
decision to pull out of the consortium and to independently recognize
China reflect an attempt to return to a more competitive position.

64. Woodrow Wilson to Bryan, March 15, 1912, Ray Stannard Baker Papers,
series I, container III.

65. Straight to Charles Wigham, March 13, 1913 and Straight to J. O. P. Bland,
Oct. 16, 1913, both in StrP.

66. Straight to Wigham, March 13, 1913, StrP. A good account is presented by
Griswold, *Far Eastern Policy*, pp. 172–73. See also Thomas W. Lamont's biography, *Henry P. Davison* (New York: Harper & Brothers, 1933.)

In the two-hour cabinet meeting of March 18 the independent reasoning behind the action is clear.[67] Desiring to enter through an open
door of friendship and mutual advantage, the president informed his
cabinet that further association with the six-power loan would lose
"the proud position which America secured when Secretary Hay stood
for the Open Door in China." Participation with others in a cooperative Open Door threatened China's political integrity, tied the United
States to a limited freedom of action and restricted to four banks the
number of Americans and American institutions which could become
involved in the vital questions of Chinese railway construction and
governmental reorganization.[68] "We ought to help China in some better
way," the new president observed. Such a way would include independent recognition of the republic, an alert to ships by Secretary of
the Navy Josephus Daniels about the potential danger of Japan, and
the discussion of suggestions made by George Bronson Rea to Bryan
that Americans alone could build ten thousand miles of railroads.[69]

Rather than a rejection of the Open Door goals, the American withdrawal from the consortium was an effort to speed up their attainment
by the United States alone. The influence of persistent pressure from
proponents of an independent role, like Rea, was shown in the State
Department's plans to improve upon cooperative international loans
by giving "American merchants, manufacturers, contractors and engineers the banking and other financial facilities which they now lack
and without which they are at a serious disadvantage as compared
with their industrial and commercial rivals."[70] Not surprisingly Rea,
then working with the American engineering firm of J. G. White and

67. David F. Houston, *Eight Years With Wilson's Cabinet* (Garden City, N.Y.:
Doubleday, Page, 1926), p. 45. E. David Cronon, ed., *The Cabinet Diaries of
Josephus Daniels* (Lincoln: University of Nebraska Press, 1963), p. 17.

68. Roy W. Curry, *Woodrow Wilson and Far Eastern Policy, 1913–21* (New
York: Bookman Associates, 1957), pp. 21, 313.

69. Arthur Link, *Wilson—The New Freedom* (Princeton: Princeton University
Press, 1956), pp. 283–88. Cronon, *Cabinet Diaries of Daniels*, pp. 18, 59–64.
Josephus Daniels, *The Wilson Era—Years of Peace, 1910–1917* (Chapel Hill:
University of North Carolina Press, 1944), I, 158–60.

70. See the State Department statement of March 18, 1913, SDDF 893.51/
1356a. An excellent collection of consortium material exists in the Breckinridge
Long Papers, box 179, LC. Long was involved in later American efforts to
reestablish a China loan group. Also Arthur Link, *Woodrow Wilson and the
Progressive Era* (New York: Harper & Row, 1954), p. 84.

Co. in conjunction with Sun Yat-sen and the Chinese National Railway Corporation, warmly endorsed such plans. Advocates of competition flooded the White House and State Department with praise for the anticonsortium decision. Henry George, Jr., speaking in the rhetoric of reform, saw the action as designed to "prevent the prostitution of our State Department by our princes of privilege." Others wired Bryan that such action would safeguard not a favored few but "all American men of business who care to treat with China."[71]

Of greatest importance after the 1909 showdown was the approval of Charles Crane. Crane was taking up a position in the Wilson administration as self-appointed advisor and banker behind the president's competitive stance. As an example he was in the process of purchasing *Harper's Weekly* as an administration news organ to be edited by his old friend Norman Hapgood, who had broken with *Collier's* in 1912 over that magazine's endorsement of Roosevelt. As late as January, Tom Millard had real doubts about "some visionary like Bryan as Secretary of State." By mid-March, however, Crane was applauding Woodrow Wilson, "Your China policy is wise, American and popular." Visiting his friends at the University of Wisconsin, Crane reported just a few days later that "all of the Progressives are enthusiastic about the way in which the new Administration is starting off."[72] The chief Wisconsin progressive, Robert La Follette agreed with the wisdom of repudiating the consortium. The Wisconsin link would in fact become all the more important as two members of the University's political science department, Paul S. Reinsch and Stanley K. Hornbeck, moved into the administration to develop the kind of independent tactics for which Crane had been dismissed in 1909.[73]

71. George Bronson Rea to Woodrow Wilson, March 26, 1913, SDDF 893.77/ 1263; Henry George, Jr., to Bryan, April 9, 1913, and Thurlow Weed Barnes to Bryan, March 14, 1913, both in the very rich SDDF 893.51/1356 reaction to the Wilson decision.

72. *Harper's Weekly*, LVII (March 29, 1913), 3. Millard to Crane, Jan. 21, 1913, Charles R. Crane Papers, held privately by John O. Crane, Institute for Current World Affairs, New York: also Crane to Woodrow Wilson, March 21, 24, 1913, both in the Crane Papers. Crane's congratulations can also be found in the Woodrow Wilson Papers, series 4, case file 227, LC.

73. See Link, *New Freedom*, p. 284. More will be said of the role of Hornbeck and Reinsch. See Hornbeck's *Contemporary Politics in the Far East* (New York: D. Appleton, 1916). See also his earlier "The Most Favored Nation Clause in Commercial Treaties," *Bulletin of the University of Wisconsin Economics and*

Basking in such praise, Secretary of State Bryan jubilantly reported his public opinion soundings to Wilson. "I have yet to find the first man who dissents from your position on the Chinese loan," he advised.[74] Clearly Bryan was not playing hide-and-seek too carefully in his own department. Huntington Wilson, who had intended to remain on the job for a transitional period, submitted his resignation almost immediately upon learning of the consortium rejection. His removal, heavily favored by Crane, would have been asked for had his resignation not been so quickly forthcoming. While a large residue of animosity obviously remained between Crane and Huntington Wilson from the 1909 feud, more than just personal issues were involved. "This is reactionary, ultra-conservative," Huntington Wilson admonished upon learning of the action against his cooperative system. "The diplomacy of the Taft administration," he observed, "was simply American diplomacy modernized."[75]

The former president agreed, going even further and blaming the New Freedom for the loss of American prestige in China and the stirring of Japan to fever heat. The only thing, in fact, upon which Huntington Wilson and Taft could find themselves in agreement with Woodrow Wilson and Crane about was that the renewed aggressive stand of the United States reflected the broad philosophy of the New Freedom at home as well. Huntington Wilson found solace that it seemed "more probable that President Wilson's repudiation of 'dollar diplomacy' may result in a great political issue, which will bring together again Roosevelt and Knox," in support of cooperation which he labeled "modern progressive diplomacy." Willard Straight concurred. Once "innocent enough to suppose that any consistent foreign policy was possible in Democracy," a sadder but wiser Straight wrote in late 1913 that such policy would "always be subordinated to the exigencies of domestic politics."[76]

Political Science Series, VI (1910), 327–448. On Hornbeck and Rea see the papers of the postwar inquiry, box 15, folder 9, Col. E. M. House Papers, Sterling Memorial Library, Yale University, New Haven, Conn. For Reinsch an excellent start is his own *An American Diplomat in China* (Garden City, N. Y.: Doubleday, Page, 1922).

74. For Bryan's conclusion see Daniels, *Wilson Era*, pp. 158–60.

75. Crane to Woodrow Wilson, March 21, 1913, Crane Papers; See also note in the Huntington Wilson Papers dated 1913.

76. Taft to Mabel Boardman, July 19, 1913, Mabel Boardman Papers, LC; Straight to J. O. P. Bland, March 25, 1913, StrP.

On the other side, the very same diplomatic-domestic tie was seen far more favorably. Defined by Arthur Link as an attempt to destroy monopoly and restore free competition, the New Freedom was to have its parallel in the New Diplomacy.[77] Each fought the same devils. The money trust whose bankers were eliminated from the consortium in March of 1913 was coming under the scrutiny of the congressional Pujo Committee for domestic malpractices at the same time.[78] Confident that the "sort of cooperation" personified by "young Huntington Wilson" had passed for good, a New Freedom supporter wrote his hero that "in giving a solar plexus blow to 'dollar diplomacy' you have complemented your work of reducing to a minimum 'dollar politics' . . . the two have been inseparable."[79]

Fallen from such a blow to the midsection, a hurt Willard Straight was fairly sure at first that he and his side had been counted out of the fight game for good. "Some day we may go back," he wrote in October 1913, "but I am inclined to doubt it." A more resilient Huntington Wilson believed without question that they could get off the canvas to fight and win again. No additional training would be necessary, he felt, merely "the passage of time." "We shall see," was the extent of his morning-after statement. Within a year, the defeated 1913 protagonists would not only be back but beginning to win their share against still strong opposition. Ironically it would be the groggy Straight and not the eager Wilson who would make the comeback. Having successfully revived a staggering competitive side, the New Freedom and the New Diplomacy would begin almost immediately, as Wilson had indeed known in the campaign of 1912, to make their own compromises with the forces of cooperation who were down but by no means out.[80]

77. Link, *Wilson and the Progressive Era*, p. 66. I am indebted to Robert E. Osgood, *Ideals and Self-Interest in America's Foreign Relations* (Chicago: University of Chicago Press, 1953), p. 104, for the relationship between a New Freedom and a New Diplomacy.

78. Harley Notter, *The Origins of the Foreign Policy of Woodrow Wilson* (Baltimore: Johns Hopkins Press, 1937), pp. 216–17. *The Washington Post*, Feb. 12, 1913, found in the Knox Papers, Scrapbooks, vol. 20.

79. Edward Ingle to Woodrow Wilson, March 24, 1913, Woodrow Wilson Papers, series 4, case file 227.

80. This interpretation fits with the view of Arthur Link, *Wilson and the Progressive Era*, p. 70, that domestically the New Freedom moved toward the New Nationalism. Actually Link underestimates the degree of New Nationalist or at least compromise-cooperation inherent in the 1912 Wilson New Freedom.

5

Return to Paradise
Woodrow Wilson's China Policy

THE maverick, muckraking impresario S. S. McClure, having lost control of his magazine to the West Virginia Pulp and Paper Company, retraced in 1917 the steps of others who had suffered similar disasters. Like Henry Adams after his personal tragedy, McClure set out for the Far East. To the Irish immigrant or the Boston Brahmin, the Orient was a perfect tonic. As his biographer reports, S. S. was "content in Japan" and "ecstatic in China." Wading, walking, or heaving on a handcar, the man who had revolutionized American journalism found adventure and danger galore. It was, he reported, "the best time I have had since I peddled. . . . I slept out doors, was naked a great deal, got an appetite perfectly incredible. I've gained about 10 pounds and learned a lot," McClure concluded. It was in China that McClure, like so many native or naturalized Americans, dreamed of the opportunities ahead. On a riverboat down the Yangtze to Shanghai, the displaced editor thought of a new magazine. To profit from his international travels, he would call it "Universal Weekly."[1] While McClure got no closer to such a publication than Adams did to China, his trip and his dream showed that in a year as filled with international dangers as 1917, China and the future were still American synonyms.

Despite changing casts of characters and ever-present domestic and

1. Peter Lyon, *Success Story: The Life and Times of S. S. McClure* (New York: Charles Scribner's Sons, 1963), pp. 383–84.

international tensions, America's vision of Princess Alice's wonderland remained intact for the bold and the blithe spirit alike. In 1915 such spirits had met at three separate locations. At San Francisco, the Panama Pacific International Exposition opened in July to celebrate the future of the Pacific basin and the new isthmian canal.[2] While the commercial, financial, and reform goals of the Open Door policy were expressed at this Pan-Pacific fair, meetings being held at two American universities revealed that the debate over how to reach those goals continued.

At Madison, Wisconsin, representatives of the university met to form their answer to Yale-in-China.[3] Imbued more with Robert La Follette's "Wisconsin Idea" of responsible government than with Yale's missionary spirit, the university was already involved in China through political scientist Paul Reinsch, American minister since 1913. In the continuing tactical debate, the Wisconsin idea favored an independent, competitive role for the United States. As developed in the "New Economics" of Richard Ely, or University President Charles R. Van Hise's book *Concentration and Control*, Wisconsin would discard laissez faire and the negative state but seek a compromise to preserve the competitive sphere in all but the "natural" or "social" monopolies like the public utilities.[4] Such ideas were fostered by Ely and Reinsch in their work to form both the American Economic and American Political Science Associations. Through Wisconsin-in-China they were to be pursued in the Far East by a "representative of the Wisconsin spirit."[5]

2. For a description of the fair see Frederick McCormick to Martin Egan, Jan. 12, 1916, Martin Egan Papers, held by Mrs. Cornelia Egan, New York. Also the William Jennings Bryan Letterbooks, box 43, Library of Congress (hereafter cited as LC), have much useful information.

3. An excellent review of the goals of Wisconsin-in-China appears in the Charles Crane Papers, appendix 2, dated Jan. 10, 1922, held privately by Crane's son, John O. Crane, Institute for Current World Affairs, New York.

4. James Bashford, "America and World Democracy," Missionary Research Library, China Pamphlets (New York: Union Theological Seminary, 1917). Merle Curti and Vernon Carstensen, *The University of Wisconsin, 1848–1925* (Madison: University of Wisconsin Press, 1949), II, 23, 338. Charles R. Van Hise to Ray Stannard Baker, Dec. 6, 1913, Ray Stannard Baker Papers, series 2, container 94, LC.

5. Sidney Fine, "Richard T. Ely, Forerunner of Progressivism, 1880–1901," *Mississippi Valley Historical Review*, XXXVII (March 1951), 599–624. Ely was the general editor of a series called Citizen's Library to which Reinsch contributed his 1900 *World Politics* (New York: Macmillan).

At Willard Straight's Cornell, advocates of cooperation met during a World Peace Foundation conference. Within the meeting's general theme of applying rational and scientific methods to the problems of war and peace, Professor Sidney Gulick saw America's Asiatic problem in "the light of Europe's tragedy." The answer Gulick proposed was a golden rule internationalism seeking the good Samaritan goals of the Open Door through the growth of Chinese science and political, economic, and industrial organization.[6] Fully converted to cooperation, Straight carried the Cornell message to the Southern Commercial Congress meetings in Muskogee, Oklahoma. "The progress of the world," he explained, "has been marked by the discovery and coordination of forces whose existence and mutual bearing have been previously unsuspected." Though he had once warned his countrymen against forsaking their individuality, Straight now emphasized that Americans were "not after all isolated from the rest of the world, or by no means independent of each other."[7]

The Right Man for Peking

Both the dream of China and the tension between competition and cooperative alternatives had been present before 1913. Still, the new Woodrow Wilson administration did manage to carve out, at least in its early actions, a unique Far Eastern personality. As telling as either the withdrawal from the banking consortium or the independent recognition of the Chinese republic was the selection of the proper man for the Peking ministerial post. Where Taft had suffered a setback in his efforts to fill the position, Wilson managed to find the right man to set the tone he desired. The task was still a difficult one, made no easier by returning minister William Calhoun's opinion that he had been a fool to subject himself to the smells, sand, and dust of Peking's physical climate let alone the heat of the political landscape.[8] With

6. *Proceedings of the Conference on International Relations* (Boston: World Peace Foundation, 1916), in particular Sidney Gulick, "America's Asiatic Problem."

7. Willard Straight address, "Foreign Relations and Overseas Trade," delivered at the Southern Commercial Congress, April 30, 1915, Willard Straight Papers (hereafter cited as StrP), Cornell University Library, Ithaca, New York.

8. See William Calhoun to Dr. Henry Baird Favill, Aug. 31, 1910. William Howard Taft Papers, series 2, case file 443, box 375, LC. The Calhoun description merits inclusion for the word-picture created: "men, women, children, donkeys,

Charles Crane serving as advisor not nominee, and with the help of Bishop James Bashford and YMCA-oriented industrialist Cleveland Dodge, Wilson sought one of the "new men," one of Christian service and university connections. An early candidate was William Jennings Bryan. When this man of pronounced "Christian character" was chosen secretary of state, others mentioned were the aging Harvard president Charles Eliot or John R. Mott, YMCA student volunteer leader.[9] Probably the very first man approached by Wilson, Eliot would not leave his Harvard post. Similarly Mott resisted personal pressure in order to continue a much-admired twenty-year career organizing students of the world for Christian service.[10]

Jeremiah Jenks fit the religious and educational requirements with his YMCA and Cornell ties but he was hardly a new man in China.[11] By April, Wilson, at Crane's urging, was studying the faculty of the University of Wisconsin. Sociologist and recent China visitor E. A.

---

camels, ponies, carriages, carts, wheelbarrows, jinrikishas, in a constant procession, interspersed by a huge, gaudy, barbaric funeral procession, which are of the most elaborate character, also marriage processions, very much the same in appearance as the funerals. It is impossible to walk there with either safety or comfort. And to walk on the sides of the streets is equally impracticable, because you have to watch every step you take to avoid holes, garbage and dogs. The next place to walk is on top of the great wall, but the top is so rough with broken brick and stone, with growth of weeds and thorny bushes, that there is neither pleasure nor comfort in walking there."

9. On the selection process see Tien-yi Li, *Woodrow Wilson's China Policy, 1913–17* (Kansas City: University of Kansas City Press, 1952), p. 83. Woodrow Wilson to William Jennings Bryan, Jan. 16, 1913, Ray Stannard Baker Papers, series I, container 3; Bishop Bashford note, Feb. 1913, Woodrow Wilson Papers, series 4, case file 226, LC. Also Robert L. Daniel, "The Friendship of Woodrow Wilson and Cleveland Dodge," *Mid-America*, XLIII (July 1961), 182–96.

10. See Charles Eliot to Wilson, Jan. 17, 1913, Wilson to Bryan, Feb. 5, 1913, and Wilson to Cleveland Dodge, March 30, 1913, all in Baker Papers, series I, container 3. On Mott see William Howard Taft to Philander Knox, June 2, 1912, State Dept. Decimal File (hereafter cited as SDDF) 393.116/21, National Archives (hereafter cited as NA), and John R. Mott to Fletcher Brockman, Feb. 5, 1912, World Service Folder C, 1912–14, Young Men's Christian Association National Headquarters Library, New York. Also Wilson to Dodge, March 10, 1913, and Wilson to Norman Hapgood, Feb. 27, 1914, W. Wilson Papers, series 4, case file 203.

11. Edward Jenkins to Wilson, March 14, 1913, W. Wilson Papers, series 4, case file 203, and undated Wilson to Dodge, Baker Papers, series I, container 5.

Ross was the first paraded before the president. After examination of his religious record by Mott, it was decided that though a student of Christianity in China, Ross failed the test of regular church membership.[12] Mott suggested educator Ernest Burton of the University of Chicago, but Crane had Wilson turned toward Wisconsin. After being suggested for a Latin American post, political scientist Paul Reinsch became, by process of elimination, the obvious choice. Other men considered appealed to Wilson's Princeton in Peking religious and educational predilections.[13] Reinsch, the scholar, attracted the attention of Wilson, the political scientist, thus revealing a significant third phase of the administration's orientation toward China. Having written for *La Follette's* in addition to his many publications, the most recent being a 1911 volume, *Intellectual Currents in the Far East,* Reinsch had strong scholarly credentials. That Professor Reinsch's observation that China "has become the focal point" should sound so much like John Hay's "storm center" statement made his nomination all the more attractive.[14]

More than anyone else Charles Crane knew the problem of a minister soon to depart. The once-almost-minister made certain that his friend Reinsch would receive a full week's Washington instructions plus the advice of men who knew China. Such instructions and advice would restate the tenets of the Wilson administration's original attitude toward China.[15] Talks with Wilson convinced Reinsch that now that America had withdrawn from a cooperative role it was "incum-

12. Charles Crane to Wilson, April 8, 1913, Crane Papers. See E. A. Ross, "Christianity in China," *The Century Magazine,* LXXXI (March 1911), 754–64, and Mott's report on Ross in the W. Wilson Papers, series 4, case file 203. Also Curti and Carstensen, *University of Wisconsin,* II, 338.

13. Crane to Wilson, March 21, 1913, Crane Papers; an excellent treatment of the roots of Wilson's attitudes in Roy Curry, *Woodrow Wilson and Far Eastern Policy, 1913–21* (New York: Bookman Associates, 1957), p. 15. Paul Reinsch, *Intellectual and Political Currents in the Far East* (Boston: Houghton Mifflin, 1911). Reinsch's most important scholarly work was *World Politics, at the End of the Nineteenth Century, as Influenced by the Oriental Situation* (New York: Macmillan, 1900). Among his other publications were: *Colonial Government* (New York: Macmillan, 1902) and *Colonial Administration* (New York: Macmillan, 1905).

14. Reinsch, *World Politics,* p. 85.

15. Crane to Wilson, Oct. 1, 1913, Crane Papers; Curry, *Wilson and Far Eastern Policy,* p. 39.

bent upon her to do her share independently and to give specific moral and financial assistance."[16]

With missionaries like Mott doing what Wilson felt was the "most important work in the world," the American spirit in international affairs would be the establishment of just this independent and distinctive role. Settling the dilemma of the Mexican revolution or serving as guide and teacher of East Asia, Americans were, in Wilson's words, to "offer the example" and to "stand for right and justice as towards individual nations."[17]

Much of the advice Reinsch received would be highly reminiscent of a decade before. Despite the desire for a distinctive role, the Open Door policy, as Wilson's second secretary of state, Robert Lansing, understood, was not to be "changed by the present administration."[18] The trade goal of American policy was reasserted in an "aggressive campaign to secure a share in the development of enormous resources in China." Working outside a tightly controlled Wall Street group, American financial leaders would find the door open wider than ever. Secretary of State Bryan, referring to the very important work of river conservation in China, declared as early as April 1913 "the desirability of the appropriation of funds for this work upon securing the loans sufficient for the purpose."[19] Of course reform remained a vital task for Reinsch and America. *The Outlook* summarized Open Door reform better than ever before. "The pigtails, the old pinched shoes, the para-

16. Paul Reinsch, *An American Diplomat in China* (Garden City, N. Y.: Double-day, Page, 1922), p. 63.

17. Crane to John O. Crane, Sept. 30, 1914, Crane Papers; E. David Cronon, ed., *The Cabinet Diaries of Josephus Daniels, 1913–21* (Lincoln: University of Nebraska Press, 1963), p. 34. Harley Notter, *The Origins of the Foreign Policy of Woodrow Wilson* (Baltimore: Johns Hopkins Press, 1937), p. 243. Wilson to Congress, Baker Papers, series I, container 1. The question of similar conceptions of Mexico and China needs and merits further study; see Sun Yat-sen to Wilson, Nov. 30, 1914, W. Wilson Papers, series 4, case file 227, and Wilson to Mott, Aug. 31, 1916, W. Wilson Papers, series 3, vol. 32, p. 172.

18. Robert Lansing to Congressman M. F. Farley (New York), Dec. 9, 1916, SDDF 693.011/149.

19. *Journal of the American Asiatic Association*, XV (Sept. 1915), 226. More will be said of the Hwai conservancy; see Mabel T. Boardman to John D. Rocke-feller, Jr., April 25, 1913, and C. D. Jameson to George W. Davis, March 21, 1913, both in the American National Red Cross File 898.5/2, Hwai River Conservancy, Finances and Accounts, American National Red Cross Library, Washington, D.C.

sols and banners must give way," the magazine demanded, "to parks, and sewers, and filtered water, and war on rats and mosquitoes." "The New China," the editors continued as if summarizing Lincoln Steffens's conclusions about America's cities, "must restrict child labor, elevate the status of women and provide for compulsory education. It must establish modern judicial codes, and above all, must stop graft."[20]

Other attitudes toward China, familiar a decade before, persisted as Reinsch prepared to depart. Anti-Japanese sentiment, growing after 1905, was a factor in all American actions by 1913. China was still the "storm center" and the extension of the great American western frontier, but Californians and labor unions were anxious to exclude its unskilled workers.[21] The relationship between domestic and international thinking remained as represented best in a man like Charles Crane who supported Wilson's antitrust revitalization of the domestic economy and his competitive rehabilitation of China.[22] Of greatest significance and similarity to a decade before, the New Freedom, despite its intentions to achieve such a competitive role, would be forced to seek some sort of compromise with financial and philosophical pressures for domestic and international cooperation. At first only Secretary of Commerce William C. Redfield spoke out within the administration for such compromise.[23] By the end of his first term Wilson would be

20. *Outlook,* CXI (Sept. 1, 1915), 16.

21. Robert E. Osgood, *Ideals and Self-Interest in America's Foreign Relations* (Chicago: University of Chicago Press, 1953), p. 212. On the extension of the American West see Frederick McCormick's observations in the *Journal of the American Asiatic Association,* XIII (Feb. 1913), 107; Jeremiah Jenks to Taft, Feb. 8, 1913, Taft Papers, series 2, case file 77, box 330, and Paul Glad, *The Trumpet Soundeth: William Jennings Bryan and His Democracy, 1896–1912* (Lincoln: University of Nebraska Press, 1960), p. 107. On the attitude of labor, consult Theodore Roosevelt to Baker, Nov. 10, 1911, Baker Papers, series 2, container 93, and Delbert L. McKee, "Samuel Gompers, the A. F. of L. and Imperialism," *Historian,* XXI (Feb. 1959), 187–99. For Californian attitudes see a speech by William Kent, July 15, 1920, before the Commonwealth Club of Boston, William Kent Papers, box 96, Yale University Library. Kent quoted his venerable Yale mentor William Graham Sumner as having said that "if he were a Californian, judging from the members of the race that he had met on campus, he probably would be as much opposed to Chinese as Californians were, with as little reason."

22. Crane to Joe Tumulty, June 26, 1914, Crane Papers; Crane to Wilson, Jan. 10, 1915, Crane Papers, and Crane to his daughter, Mrs. J. C. Bradley, Nov. 11, 1916, Crane Papers.

23. Cronon, *Cabinet Diaries of Daniels,* pp. 19–21, 40–42.

stressing regulation rather than competition and an independent American role in the Far East would be "more proclaimed than real." Having begun by rejecting Taft's policy in China, Woodrow Wilson was soon demonstrating that his purposes, aims, and problems were in fact very much like those of his predecessor.[24]

Reform Impulses Restrengthened

The China for which Paul Reinsch set sail was still a wonderland to American reformers. Lillian Wald summarized this feeling when she commented in 1917 that having done such a service to humanity in Mexico during the revolution, Americans "are now going to take up the Far Eastern question." For some time before, American influence and methods were indeed used to attack "China's most pressing and obvious problems."[25] Such attacks would be seen in the University of Nanking's Yale-inspired conservation work, the Rockefeller Foundation's efforts to cultivate untilled but arable land, and even the *Suffragist's* campaign to give women the vote in Shanghai and Peking. Americans in China sought to build up a primitive postal service, to introduce Marconi's wireless, and even to bar liquor from the legation in Peking.[26]

Much of this work to promote Chinese welfare, like the Social Gospel at home, was missionary-inspired. As the husband of evangelist Aimee Semple McPherson illustrated, "Every third baby that is born in the world is Chinese. Every third funeral is that of a Chinese; what

24. Several authors make this point: A. Whitney Griswold, *The Far Eastern Policy of the United States* (New Haven: Yale University Press, 1938), p. 173; Curry, *Wilson and Far Eastern Policy*, p. 320; Meribeth Cameron, "American Recognition Policy Toward the Republic of China, 1912–13," *Pacific Historical Review*, II (June 1933), 214–30; Mingchien Joshua Bau, *The Open Door Doctrine in Relation to China* (New York: Macmillan, 1923), p. 84.

25. Yamei Kin to Roger H. Williams, June 2, 1917, Crane Papers, and Thomas H. Simpson, "Restoring China's Forests, A New American Influence in the Empire," *Review of Reviews*, LIII (March 1916), 337–40.

26. Dwight H. Day to F. W. Williams, Feb. 25, 1919, Yale-in-China Papers, Forestry file, Yale University Library, New Haven, Conn.; *Outlook*, CXI (Oct. 6, 1915), 301; *Suffragist*, VIII (1920); *Review of Reviews*, XLIV (Dec. 1911), 724; "The Mails of the Mandarin," *World's Work*, XXXIII (April 1917), 637–44; on the wireless, Bryan to Paul Reinsch, June 26, 1914, SDDF 893.74/1; on prohibition *National Advocate*, LVI (June 1921), in SDDF 893.114/298, and Reinsch to S. I. Woodbridge, Feb. 16, 1917, SDDF 893.114/151.

a mighty task," Robert Semple concluded, "lies before Christianity."[27] Through the World Missionary Conference's continuation committee or the broader Asiatic Institute, Americans tried, in Bryan's words, to provide a "religious foundation" so as "to lift other nations out of darkness and put them on the high road to prosperity."[28] Like the peace movement, many of whose members were sponsors of missionary programs, the religious crusade of the early twentieth century was most practical and businesslike. Laymen's missionary meetings were not filled with fire and brimstone evangelists but rather, as Paul Varg has noted, with "men of large influence and big business responsibilities; manufacturers, merchants, lawyers, brokers, bankers, physicians, professors, editors and heads of corporations." Returning from a trip around the world, Bryan made this missionary-business link his personal gospel. "I believe that no Christian nation can justify doing business," Wilson's secretary of state had earlier told a missionary audience, unless its businessmen "interest themselves in the people among whom they go."[29]

As the original desire to send Eliot or Mott to Peking suggests, this interest would be directed to China's youth. "Young Chinese, with their fine physiques and Occidental speech and manners" could be trained in the classroom and in the less formal social welfare settlements of the cities to become "the most progressive element in the country."[30] To this end, educational advisors were dispatched, American university clubs established, and Christian colleges strengthened. As demonstrated in the work of Yale-in-China at Changsha, education

27. John W. Masland, "Missionary Influence Upon American Far Eastern Policy," *Pacific Historical Review*, X (Sept. 1941), 279–96; Paul Varg, *Missionaries, Chinese and Diplomats: The American Protestant Missionary Movement in China 1890–1952* (Princeton: Princeton University Press, 1958), pp. 91–93. Edwin D. Mead to Wilson, March 27, 1913, W. Wilson Papers, series 4, case file 227, and Aimee Semple McPherson, *In the Service of the King: The Story of My Life* (New York: Boni and Liveright, 1927), pp. 114–17.

28. Bryan to World Missionary Conference, 1910, in "Report of Commission III," pp. 433–34 and "Report of Commission VII," p. 168, Missionary Research Library. *Journal of the American Asiatic Association*, XIII (May 1913), 109. Harlan P. Beach, *The Findings of the Continuation Committee Conferences Held in Asia, 1912–13* (New York: Student Volunteer Movement for Foreign Missions, 1913).

29. Varg, *Missionaries, Chinese and Diplomats*, p. 65; Bryan to the World Missionary Conference, 1910, "Report of Commission VII," p. 168.

30. Simpson, "Restoring China's Forests," pp. 337–40.

was not an outlet for missionary fervor but a means to create a new civilization in the Far East, one that would be as Christian and professional as the American. "Modern education in China is only one side of a movement," the Peking University graduate study committee reported. The task "is not simply introducing new ideas into the country but modifying its industrial, social and political life and institutions."[31]

It was the YMCA that best represented the religious, educational, businesslike reform which interested Americans like Woodrow Wilson. Spiritual social workers not schoolteachers, John R. Mott, and the members of the Association in China's cities were to Wilson the "most active in establishing a new government and a new regime in China."[32] The YMCA had enjoyed the sympathy of President Taft who advised it to "get a Chinaman early," but it was in the Wilson years that it really strengthened its position in China.[33] In addition to the president's attachment to the YMCA's Princeton work in Peking, several of his Far Eastern advisors, such as political economist Jeremiah Jenks or industrialist Cleveland Dodge, were members of the Association's International Committee. That such men concerned with industrial and financial matters should be involved in the YMCA in China was in keeping with the practical missionary mood of the period and the relationship between the economic and philanthropic goals of the Open Door. Supporting Shanghai's settlement houses, American consul and Yale-in-China alumnus Amos Wilder could see that "viewed as a financial investment the support of these centers would appeal to businessmen who wish to see a leaven of progress injected into China."[34]

31. Reinsch to Lansing, July 11, 1917, SDDF 893.01A/39; Urban Whitaker, "Americans and Chinese Political Problems, 1912–23," (Ph.D. diss., University of Washington, 1954), ch. 4. See also a note to F. W. Williams, April 22, 1916, in the Yale-in-China Papers, F. W. Williams file.

32. Notter, *Origins of Foreign Policy*, p. 207, citing note from Wilson to Bryan, Feb. 1913. Crane to his daughter, Mrs. J. C. Bradley, May 31, 1916, Crane Papers.

33. Taft's address can be found in the Mabel Boardman Papers, Dec. 21, 1913, LC. See also D. Willard Lyon, *The First Quarter Century of the Young Men's Christian Association in China, 1895–1920* (Shanghai: Association Press, 1920).

34. Some of the titles Jenks published with the Association Press were *Life Questions of High School Boys* (1910) and *The Political and Social Significance of the Life and Teachings of Jesus* (1906). Also see Daniel, "Friendship of Woodrow Wilson." In the YMCA Papers see file x970.4, Lerrigo Correspondence, 1911, Robert Lewis to Mott, Feb. 29, 1908, World Service Folder a, and Amos Wilder's report, June 1914, World Service Folder c.

Although the Association never forgot that even in China the New Testament "is a book which we must all read," efforts were mostly directed toward sanitary improvement of China's prisons, parks, and places of business. The accent of such social uplift was always on the "new" or "young" China for "the children of today will become the rulers and leaders of tomorrow, and they must be nurtured and raised with the greatest care." As Yale sinologist S. Wells Williams had pointed out, work like that of the YMCA would breed sincerity and provide a corps of "physician-diplomats" who would rank with Commodore Perry in the development of an American role in the Far East.[35]

As an example of such work, Chinese "jinrikishamen" were to be turned into athletes fit for competition in future Olympic games. If qualified physical directors could be imported, the Association would "direct the policy and control the future of the athletic situation among four hundred millions of people." Using the familiar American image of China, J. H. Crocker looked ahead to China's future sports achievements. "The door," he noticed, "is wide open in all large cities." The "Great Commission" of the YMCA was indeed that of all American reformers in China; to wash, feed, clothe, educate, and employ an "awakened" country. D. Willard Lyon, an original Association China hand was confident America was uniquely fit to guide such a maturation process. "Having had experience in developing the resources of an expansive territory and having produced the machinery and methods necessary for carrying on large enterprises," Lyon observed, America "is in a peculiarly favorable position to supply what China needs."[36]

Another Chinese need after 1913 was not social welfare but contin-

35. Varg, *Missionaries, Chinese and Diplomats*, pp. 96–97; Lerrigo to F. M. Mohler, May 23, 1913, Lerrigo Correspondence, YMCA Papers. These YMCA papers are rich in field reports: for example, H. A. Wilbur and George A. Fitch, Foreign Work Reports, 1914–15; J. S. Burgess, "The Training of Social Workers in China," x951, 101, and "Peking as a Field for Social Service," World Service Folder c; see also "Ideals and Activities," a report by the Chinese Students' Christian Association of North America, May 1913, in the John R. Mott Papers, B690 at Yale Divinity School Library, New Haven, Conn.; Amos Wilder quotes S. Wells Williams in his report dated June 1914, YMCA, World Service Folder c; finally see the piece by a physician diplomat, W. W. Peter, in *World's Work*, XXXVIII (July 1919), 274–75.

36. J. S. Burgess, "China's Social Challenge," *Survey*, XXXIX (Oct. 13, 1917), 41–44. J. H. Crocker, Annual Report, Sept. 30, 1914, YMCA; D. Willard Lyon, Annual Report, Sept. 10, 1908, also YMCA Papers.

ued political advice on how to preserve an American-style republic. The YMCA felt it need do its best work in the wake of the 1911 revolution. American political scientists turned constitutional advisors were better qualified as teachers in this regard. While their interests were secular not spiritual, Reinsch, Frank Goodnow, and W. W. Willoughby believed just as firmly as did the YMCA that the "new republic" could best follow an American example.[37] All three had served on the first board of editors of the *American Political Science Review*. In the Orient they sought similarly to institutionalize and publicize their role through a Chinese social and political science association and a Far Eastern bar association. Since Wilson was also a political scientist by training, Reinsch could be his alter ego in China. The president kept an ear open to the "interesting suggestions" from Peking and refused to be persuaded that the minister should be promoted to a post in Washington.[38]

Wilson and Reinsch were in agreement on the need to preserve China's shaky republican government. All Americans felt a stable and orderly government essential. Goodnow and Willoughby thought this could be attained only through a strong executive, even if it meant catering to Yuan Shih-kai's increasingly obvious imperial pretensions.[39] Wilson hoped for the "permanency" of Yuan's government but warned that "the American people are watching with keen interest the development of representative government in China." Reinsch, a pragmatic political scientist who liked to talk of "specific relationships between definite individuals" and "social organization," also defended republicanism. Stressing the example of the United States, Wilson's minister

37. See Newton Hayes, Annual Report, World Service, 1911–12, YMCA Library; E. T. Williams to Bryan, May 6, 1913, Reinsch to Bryan, Jan. 24, 1913, J.V.A. MacMurray to Bryan, July 21, 1914 and Reinsch to Lansing, Nov. 16, 1918, in SDDF 893.01A/19, 22, 25, 41.

38. Whitaker, "Americans and Chinese Political Problems," ch. 4; Wilson to Reinsch, Nov. 9, 1914, Paul Reinsch Papers, State Historical Society of Wisconsin Library, Madison, Wisconsin. Wilson to Crane, Jan. 13, 1917, Crane Papers; Wilson to Reinsch, Dec. 27, 1916, W. Wilson Papers, series 3, vol. 37/298.

39. Bryan to Wilson, Oct. 6, 1913, W. Wilson Papers, series 4, case file 226; Whitaker, "Americans and Chinese Political Problems," Part III, an excellent approach to the "prerequisites" Americans held for successful government. See also MacMurray to Lansing, Sept. 9, 1918, Breckinridge Long Papers, box 179, LC, and Jenks to Taft, Aug. 30, 1915, Taft Papers, General Correspondence, box 319.

hoped a "peaceful, industrious . . . progressive" republican China would see America's free government not only as a model but an active source of "interest, sympathy and moral assistance."[40]

Excited Economic Aspirations

Such interest and sympathy were not all philanthropic. As the *Journal of the American Asiatic Association* reminded its readers in 1914, success of the Chinese experiment in popular government was in the "material interest of the United States."[41] The commercial goal of the United States's Open Door policy was as vital in Paul Reinsch's wonderland as it had been in Alice's. Reform in China was a lubricant making the hinges of the door swing open to trade, just as such trade made reform more necessary and possible. The one without the other was inconceivable to someone like Captain Robert Dollar. A China trader, Dollar was also president of the International Peace Committee of the Pacific Coast Churches. He openly assured the Chinese people that "we are thankful for our traditional friendship and for the commercial and international ties that bind us together."[42]

The reform-inspired belief that Americans should act alone in awakening China was reinforced by the view that the United States must compete for all, or at least the largest share possible, of China's commerce. With America no longer a party to a banking consortium, Wilson instructed Reinsch that it had become "incumbent upon her to do her share independently." Reinsch would never yield in his allegiance to that principle, even when it seemed to him that the president had altered his own views. From the first, the new minister would "claim for our nation every opportunity of engaging in . . . commerce, trade and industry." Anything done to support another's plan, Reinsch argued, would work only to America's disadvantage and slow the struggle "to rival and offset the influence exercised by other nations, often far from favorable to the further development of the Chinese people."[43]

40. Wilson to Yuan Shih-kai, Feb. 11, 1914, W. Wilson Papers, series 3, vol. X, p. 271; Paul Reinsch, *An American Diplomat*, pp. viii–42.

41. *Journal of the American Asiatic Association*, XIV (April 1914), 75.

42. For Dollar's proclamation of April 6, 1914, see the Paul Reinsch Papers.

43. Charles A. Beard, *The Idea of National Interest: An Analytical Study in American Foreign Policy* (New York: Macmillan, 1934), pp. 183–95. Reinsch comment of March 12, 1914, in Paul Reinsch Papers. Reinsch to Straight, Jan. 15, 1916, and Reinsch to State Department, March 16, 1914, Reinsch Papers.

Other long-time spokesmen of competition enjoyed their moments of victory in the early actions of the Wilson administration. George Bronson Rea informed all that the president had asked him to keep Washington posted on matters vital to American interests in China. Still shaken from the Taft switch from competition to cooperation, Rea warned that America must be armed with a redeclaration of the Open Door, lest "the end will soon come and the American position in the East will be irrevocably lost."[44] Most energetic and persuasive in the quest for an independent commercial role was Reinsch's protégé Stanley K. Hornbeck. A model of Wisconsin in China, Hornbeck was a 1911 Madison Ph.D. who followed Reinsch to China to become "sometime instructor in the Chekiang Provincial College and in the Fengtien [Mukden] Law College," before returning to Reinsch's old job at Wisconsin in 1914.[45] Hornbeck's chief concern as a political scientist was the theory and practice of international trade relations. In his publications and his own active career in the State Department especially as Chief of the Far Eastern Division during the 1930s, he showed himself one of the most systematic philosophers of commercial expansion. Having already dealt with the building block of trade relations in his 1910 theoretical study of the most-favored-nation clause, Hornbeck applied his knowledge to the storm center.[46] His speeches, reports, and major book *Contemporary Politics in the Far East* published in 1916 never stray from the underlying premise that "we have a right to a share in the commercial future of the Pacific."[47] American efforts to reform

44. George Bronson Rea to Reinsch, May 26, and June 30, 1914, Reinsch Papers.

45. More study is needed on the Reinsch-Hornbeck-Wisconsin relationship. See Curti and Carstensen, *University of Wisconsin*, II, 338. See also Stanley K. Hornbeck, *Contemporary Politics in the Far East* (New York: D. Appleton, 1916), especially the introduction which is an excerpt from Reinsch's 1900 *World Politics*.

46. Stanley K. Hornbeck, "The Most-Favored-Nation Clause in Commercial Treaties, Its Function in Theory and in Practice and Its Relation to Tariff Policies," *Bulletin of the University of Wisconsin Economics and Political Science Series*, VI (1910), 327–448. See also Earl H. Pritchard, "The Origin of the Most-Favored-Nation and the Open Door Policies in China," *Far Eastern Quarterly*, I (Feb. 1942), 161–72.

47. This discussion of Hornbeck's ideas is based on three documents he wrote during the years 1916–1918. See his *Contemporary Politics in the Far East*, passim; see also a report he prepared for the World War Inquiry panel of experts and for the Carnegie Endowment for International Peace in the files of the Inquiry, box

China's education were "philanthropically conceived" but Hornbeck made no effort to cloak the fact that they were "commercially carried out." He even admitted as few reformers would that the "awakened" Chinese had not lived up to the obligations and requirements of the Open Door and that "we forced ourselves upon Asia." There was at times in Hornbeck's writing the seldom-found notion that perhaps American policy had been operating without Chinese consent or even in outright opposition to China's wishes. "We compelled China and Japan to open their doors," Hornbeck told fellow Americans. "We made them accept relations with ourselves; and we have driven them to adopt, if only in self-defense, instruments and policies patterned on ours."

Such self-appraisal was not to serve as an argument for the abrogation of John Hay's notes, but rather as a reason for opening the door still further. Now, Hornbeck concluded, "the United States, for instance, has responsibilities in the Far East, we have an interest in the fate and fortunes of its peoples." Never questioning the dream of China's future, Hornbeck's conception of American responsibilities embodied in the Open Door, as in the Monroe Doctrine for the Western hemisphere, meant a restrengthened quest for industrial and commercial opportunity. Such a view also reinforced the idea of independent action by a country not only "uniquely qualified" but now "uniquely responsible." Linking the American frontier to China as so many had done before, Hornbeck noted that the search for markets and for resources was "as inevitable as has been the migration to our western prairies." Given such inevitability, a "young, virile, self-confident, wealthy, idealistic, missionary-inclined" American race had come of age and felt "confident of our fitness and ability to compete in the markets and to participate in the councils of the nations. . . . We are of pioneering stock."

America's chief pioneers after 1913 in "the biggest field for commercial enterprise that exists today" were the Bethlehem Steel and Standard Oil companies.[48] Not all American commercial efforts in China,

---

15, Yale University Library, New Haven, Conn.; see an address, "Trade, Concessions, Investments, Conflict and Policy in the Far East," given before the National Conference on Foreign Relations of the United States, Long Beach, N. Y., 1917, in George Kennan Papers, box 85, LC.

48. See a Reinsch interview dated Nov. 18, 1913, Reinsch Papers. The correspondence between Reinsch and the State Department concerning Standard Oil's interests in particular is voluminous.

however, were as ambitious as projects designed by these companies to build naval docks or drill oil fields. Through a National Association of Manufacturers's advisor, an American chamber of commerce for China, and attachés like Julean Arnold, all shapes and sizes of American business were encouraged for export. Though missionaries greatly disapproved some support even developed to transplant increasingly prohibited American breweries to China.[49]

Despite campaigns to export American business to China, Jeremiah Jenks and Willard Straight reported that many businessmen remained apprehensive about their relationship with the "anticonsortium" administration. Charles Crane of course knew better. When his faith in Wilson's desire to "clear the country for a great expansion of business" was matched by the joint-State and Commerce Department call for an "aggressive campaign to secure a share in the development" of China, the potential China market seemed nearer than ever.[50] The newly created National Foreign Trade Council summarized the commercial goal and the competitive strategy of the Open Door when it reminded Secretary of State Lansing in 1916, "the Government of the United States, acting through its Department of Commerce, has inspired the American people with visions of the possibilities of the Chinese market for the products of American workmen and American factories." With such advantage never fully realized, an aggressive, competitive American role was needed. Not only "the very vital interests of the members of the American Manufacturers Export Association," but also "the broader interests of the country are at stake," it was reported to the secretary of state.[51]

Japan's Special Position

These interests were most endangered, or so many feared, by the menace of Japanese hegemony in the Far East. An independent Ameri-

49. Reinsch to Bryan, May 28, 1915, SDDF 102.8/23; *Journal of the American Asiatic Association,* XVI (Feb. 1916), 8; MacMurray to State Department, July 6, 1915, SDDF 893.01A/31 and *Asia,* XIX (July 1919), 597–98.

50. Jenks to Reinsch, March 9, 1914 and Straight to Reinsch, Sept. 17, 1913, Reinsch Papers; Crane to Tumulty, June 26, 1914, Crane Papers; *Journal of the American Asiatic Association,* XV (Sept. 1915), 226, ibid. (Dec. 1915), 321; Frank Vanderlip to the American International Corporation and Straight to Henry P. Davison, both Nov. 1, 1915, StrP.

51. American Manufacturers Export Association and the National Foreign Trade Council to Lansing, Sept. 18, 1916, SDDF 793.94/532.

can role had first been defended after 1905 as a defense against the threat posed by Japan's easy victory over Russia. In the course of the next decade anti-Japanese sentiment had become so widely held that it could not alone explain the back-and-forth inconsistencies of American policy. Tension and compromise between competitive and cooperative keys to unlock the door, mirroring similar debates over domestic policy, had replaced a Japanese phobia as the chief determinant of Far Eastern actions. Fear of Japan was neither novel nor decisive after 1913. It was, however, a strong argument to convince those already so inclined that America must redouble its independent efforts to secure reform or trade in China.

The press was filled as it had been since 1905 with the fears of Rea or Frederick McCormick that China would be "Japanned" and that the door would be closed unless they could arrange to have "Uncle Sam's foot planted squarely in the opening."[52] Others in China were reporting to Wilson and Bryan that Japan was making inroads toward the control of commercial and railroad interests in Manchuria and the Chinese provinces of Shantung and Fukien. Such premonitions were crystalized in Japan's Twenty-One Demands by which China was asked to recognize its neighbor's informal spheres of influence and grant the former German claims in Shantung to Japan.[53]

Responding to this threat posed by Japan, some felt there must be another way than simply planting "Uncle Sam's foot." Still speaking in the rhetoric of laissez faire and antiimperialism, Oswald Garrison Villard could look back to the pre-1905 era and write that a friendly Japan might be allowed some sort of protectorate in China. Afraid more of Japanese in California than China, West Coast congressman William Kent advised that he "would rather that Japan took the lead" lest it start "looking in our direction for trouble." The strongest case for

52. Frederick McCormick, "America's Obligations in China," New York Times, May 9, 1915; New York Tribune, June 6, 1915, and March 19, 1916; Literary Digest, L (April 3, 1915), 737. Bishop Bashford to Bishop McDowell in Robert Lansing Papers, Feb. 9, 1917, vol. 24, LC.

53. George W. Guthrie to Bryan, 1914, Bryan Papers, box 30; Varg, Missionaries, Chinese and Diplomats, pp. 140–45; Consul Williamson (Antung) to Bryan, Aug. 26, 1913, SDDF 893.811/95; Reinsch interview with the Chinese Minister of Posts and Communication, Nov. 27, 1913, Reinsch Papers; Bryan to Wilson, Oct. 2, 1914, Bryan State Department Letterbooks, Bryan Papers, box 43; Griswold, Far Eastern Policy, pp. 185–98.

something other than a showdown came as expected from pro-Japan banker Jacob Schiff. Geographical proximity and administrative efficiency, Schiff reasoned, made it necessary and proper that Japan be China's "big brother."[54] America's task was to get alongside Japan, not to stand in its way. Even those unsure of Japan's good intentions felt an anti-Japanese stand could detract from the main task, "the great movement already under way toward developing China's resources." Japanese demands on China in 1915 were the catalyst forcing the continuing tension between competitive and cooperative alternatives in reaching the goals of the Open Door back into the open for the first time since Woodrow Wilson had withdrawn the United States from the consortium.

By 1915 the issue was as clearly drawn as it had been in 1912. China hand General James Wilson argued that cooperation would mean "not only Japan but all the world will find larger and larger profit in the commercial and economic development" of China. "This will tend," General Wilson added hopefully, "to the advantage of Japan as well as all other countries."[55] On the floor of the Congress, young Idaho senator William Borah, who had defended free competition at home in his speeches on the proposed Federal Trade Commission, took up the question of international competition. Often labeled an isolationist, as indeed he was in terms of European politics, Borah by his July 1916 address in support of a strong navy showed himself one of the period's most cogent and learned spokesmen for competitive, commercial expansion. "We must either go forward finding an outlet for our trade, a market for our goods and thereby a living wage for our workingmen, insuring efficiency and prosperity at home," Borah told his colleagues and his country, "or we must be content to be shut in and circumscribed, to see our markets glutted, labor underpaid and discontented,

54. *Nation*, C (May 13, 1916), 526; Oswald Garrison Villard, *Fighting Years: Memoirs of a Liberal Editor* (New York: Harcourt, Brace, 1939), pp. 141–42, 335–36. A good biography stressing Villard's late nineteenth-century orientation is Michael Wreszin, *Oswald Garrison Villard, Pacifist at War* (Bloomington: Indiana University Press, 1965). Also see Christopher Lasch, *The American Liberals and the Russian Revolution* (New York: Columbia University Press, 1962), p. 139. William Kent to Wilson, 1916, W. Wilson Papers, series 4, case file 226; Jacob Schiff to Frank Polk, Oct. 10, 1916, Frank Polk Papers, drawer 77, file no. 17, Yale University Library, New Haven, Conn.

55. See Gen. James Wilson's dialogue with Tom Millard, 1916, J. Wilson Papers, box 16, L.C.

internal dissension and dissatisfaction, and other things of which I do not care to prophesy." Besides drawing the relationship between internal and external events and repeating the philosophy of expansionists like Albert Beveridge, Borah sounded the warning should America fail to meet the Japanese challenge. "We have seen the Open Door, supposedly well guarded by our treaties and by our honor, closed in the Orient, and we now watch the process while the door which has been closed is being bolted."[56]

Within the State Department, Far East advisor E. T. Williams would move to unbolt the door with an American key. Encouraged by the work of Hornbeck and Tom Millard in holding Wisconsin seminars to stir anti-Japanese excitement, Williams sought to dismiss the cooperationist position of Jacob Schiff.[57] The real difficulty, Williams perceived, was that Japan was not about to be a brother to China, but rather a bully and a highwayman. With Americans in China calling for boycotts of Japanese products and the faster growth of American trade machinery financed by chambers of commerce or trade associations at home, Williams and Paul Reinsch pressured for strong diplomatic and naval responses to the Japanese claims.[58]

Faced already with crises in Mexico and on the Atlantic, Wilson and his secretaries of state, first Bryan then Lansing, sought, like the Roosevelt and Taft administrations, to compromise the Schiff and Williams alternatives.[59] Bryan, whose reluctance to accept a stern anti-

56. The William Borah Papers, LC, are as chaotic as they are crucial. Boxes 5–7 contain a well-ordered series of Borah's many congressional speeches, such as the FTC remarks, June 26–29, 1914, and the Navy address which is more readily found in U. S., Congress, 64th Cong., 1st sess., July 17, 1916, *Congressional Record*, LIII, Part 11, 11171.

57. *Outlook*, CXI (Sept. 29, 1915), 252, and ibid. (Oct. 13, 1915), 375–78. E. T. Williams to Polk, Oct. 11, 1916, Polk Papers, drawer 77, file no. 17.

58. For direct pressure see Reinsch to Bryan, Dec. 22, 1914; Williams to Bryan, Feb. 26, 1915; and Bryan to Wilson, Feb. 22, 1915, all in SDDF 793.94/216, 240. For a general survey of naval policy see Seward W. Livermore, "American Naval Base Policy in the Far East, 1850–1914," *Pacific Historical Review*, XIII (June 1944), 134.

59. The discussions can best be followed on the decision leading up to the American protest through the Bryan Letterbooks, Bryan Papers, box 43. See the following: Bryan to Japan, Feb. 18, 1915; Williams to Bryan, Feb. 26; Lansing to Bryan, March 1; Bryan to W. Wilson, March 22; Bryan to W. Wilson, March 25; Bryan to W. Wilson, April 15; W. Wilson to Bryan, April 27; W. Wilson to Bryan, May 10; and a Lansing interview, June 15. For a good review see Lansing memo, July 6, 1917, in SDDF 793.94/570.

German position on the Atlantic would lead to his departure from the cabinet, was equally hesitant to challenge Japan's special relations with China. While Wilson and Lansing denied the permanency of such relations and spoke through the spring and summer of 1915 in terms of the preservation of China's and America's independence, they too were anxious to reach a friendly or limited compromise with Japan. When Wilson did issue a protest reaffirming the Open Door policy, his supporters could assert that he had done a great deal in softening Japan's demands although surely the other powers and the Chinese had done as much to slow Japan. Actually the president himself was less than boastful. In seeking to do what he could "indirectly to work in the interest of China," Wilson was aware throughout the crisis that an overaggressive independent American response "would really do her more harm than good, inasmuch as it would very likely provoke the jealousy and excite the hostility of Japan which would first be manifested against China herself."[60]

Using historical hindsight, much has been made of Wilson's reaffirmation of the Open Door in 1915 in the face of Japanese pressure as a prelude to the Stimson nonrecognition policy of 1931–32 during the Manchurian crisis and to the outbreak of the Second World War in Asia.[61] Rather it should be noted that the 1915 protest merely reiterated the Root-Takahira agreement of 1908. The shaping of an American response to the Twenty-One Demands retraced familiar ground. Fear that a showdown with Japan was inevitable had been persistent for a decade. Faith in requisite cooperation to preserve peace had been asserted as early as 1908. By accepting compromise rather than outright competition in response to the Japanese menace, Wilson was paralleling the course that Roosevelt and Taft had taken. Tendencies toward compromise if not cooperation had been inherent if inhibited even in the Wilson campaign of 1912. As the original glow of the anticonsortium decision wore off, the New Freedom began

60. *Harper's Weekly*, LXII (Jan. 1, 1916), 1. Wilson to Reinsch, Feb. 8, 1915. W. Wilson Papers, series 3, vol. XX, p. 234.

61. See Arthur Link, *Woodrow Wilson and the Progressive Era, 1910–17* (New York: Harper & Row, 1954), p. 90, and Link, *Wilson—The Struggle for Neutrality* (Princeton: Princeton University Press, 1960), ch. 9. In general, Link makes too much of Wilson's defense of China. A better approach is Ernest R. May's, "American Policy and Japan's Entrance into World War I," *Mississippi Valley Historical Review*, XL (Sept. 1953), 279–90. See also Griswold, *Far Eastern Policy*, p. 197.

to accept elements of the New Nationalism as in the domestic Federal Trade Commission. Hardly a sudden or mystical transformation, the Wilson administration was compromising before the persistent pressures for cooperation.[62]

The Hwai River Investment in Cooperation

Among the strongest pressures was the interest of American bankers in search of the third goal of the Open Door, the investment of capital in China. Although the decision to work outside the tightly confined Wall Street consortium group had shaken all bankers for a while, most still found it quite natural and proper "to purchase the bonds that China might issue to secure funds to finance their operations." Investment like reform and commerce remained an almost universal Open Door goal. The three in fact were directly related for the "operations" financed would be in large part the very "electric light works, water works and other public utilities" American reformers and manufacturers concentrated on as well. All that was needed to overcome any banker reluctance, Willard Straight reported, was a sign that the American government would protect the investor as it did the missionary and merchant.[63]

In 1914 minister Paul Reinsch was assuring Straight that he recognized the "very great legitimate influence" of "immediate loans to China for constructive purposes." Secretary of State Bryan also declared the same theme when he delivered speeches written by Lansing or William Phillips before groups interested in the China market for goods and money. Finally by 1915 the president was verbalizing a principle he had always accepted. As long as more than just a handful of banks participated, Woodrow Wilson would "welcome action by American bankers" and "always seek to support citizens of the United States in all legitimate enterprises abroad."[64]

62. See Link, *Wilson and Progressive Era*, p. 70.

63. Straight to Reinsch, June 30, 1914, Reinsch Papers; *Journal of the American Asiatic Association*, XIV (Feb. 1914), 2, and Straight's speech, "Trade Relations with the Far East," delivered before the American Mercantile Marine, reprinted in the *Proceedings of the Academy of Political Science*, VI (Oct. 1915) and found in StrP.

64. Reinsch to Straight, March 21, 1914, Reinsch Papers; Straight to Fletcher, June 3, 1914, StrP, comments on Bryan's speeches. Reinsch to Wilson, W. Wilson Papers, series 4, case file 1953, and W. Wilson to B. Howell Griswold, Jr., 1915. W. Wilson Papers, series 4, case file 227.

It was a project of river conservation that provided what Straight described, mixing his metaphor, as "the bridge over which we can enter once again upon Chinese business."[65] The Hwai River restoration matched the hopes, beliefs, and abilities of America in China. The plan was to create outlets from the Hwai River basin to the sea, thus eliminating floods and creating new farmland. Paul Reinsch was ecstatic at this half-commercial, half-humanitarian plan which would be a happy example of how investment could be used for the active support of the Open Door. Best of all, Reinsch wrote, "No other enterprise could impress the Chinese mind so vividly with the true meaning of the word PROGRESS." Simultaneously he remembered the practical result of the development of China's resources "for while railways create means of communication, this enterprise will create the most fundamental of the constituent parts of wealth and welfare— agricultural lands of steady productiveness over an area nearly as large as the state of Maine."[66]

Recognizing, as Philander Knox had said, that "vast commercial and other interests, actual and perspective were involved," the Standard Oil Company had been active in financing similar work since 1903 with its loans secured by the granting of oil monopoly rights.[67] By 1914, the Wilson administration was in agreement that the Hwai project would be a singular evidence of serving a "great nation just awakening." With this support, Standard Oil's confidence and money were to be matched hopefully by that of American banks.[68] Characteristically, the spark needed to propose, plan, and prosecute the Hwai conservancy came not from a commercial or financial organization but rather from a group of American engineers under the supervision of

65. Straight to Reinsch, Feb. 25, 1914, StrP.
66. MacMurray to State Department, July 23, 1915, SDDF 893.811/196. Also Reinsch to Bryan, March 31, 1914, and to Lansing, Jan. 4, 1916, SDDF 893.811/ 122, 204–05. See Reinsch to Bryan, Dec. 2, 1913, Reinsch Papers; Reinsch to Bryan, Oct. 28, 1914, and to Mabel T. Boardman, Nov. 27, 1914, both in the extremely valuable American National Red Cross file 898.5/2, Hwai River Conservancy. Reinsch interview with Chinese minister for agriculture and commerce, Dec. 23, 1913, Reinsch Papers, and Reinsch to Gen. George Davis, Dec. 19, 1914, Red Cross 898.5/2.
67. Philander Knox to Fletcher, Nov. 2, 1909, Henry Fletcher Papers, LC. E. T. Williams press conference, Oct. 18, 1913, Reinsch Papers.
68. Wilson to Sen. George Chamberlain, April 7, 1914, W. Wilson Papers, series 4, case file 227. *Journal of the American Asiatic Association*, XIV (March 1914), 33–34, 39.

the American National Red Cross. A philanthropic piece of flood relief, the reclamation was also an effort at scientific conservation. Under President Mabel T. Boardman, not spiritual or secular social work, but conservation was "the principle of the Red Cross." River projects, Miss Boardman wrote, were "an honest and efficient piece of work" designed to achieve "economy and social advantage."[69]

The constant presence on the Hwai project of engineer C. D. Jameson reinforced the idea that engineering reforms rivaled or even surpassed education in the rank order of China's needs. Working for the J. G. White engineering firm, Jameson had learned his trade on the Panama Canal and had then taught it at Iowa State before coming to China.[70] As chief advisor on the Hwai project, Jameson harbored few illusions about educational or political reforms. His propensity to refer to a Chinese graduate of an American college as a "hopeless, half-baked, B.A. [Bally Ass]," probably lost him a job with the old consortium and certainly made it hard to gain his acceptance by the Chinese for work on the Hwai. Despite this both the Red Cross and the American State Department insisted he be accepted.[71]

This support of an obviously difficult personality resulted from the way in which Jameson, when not libeling the "new Chinese," put the spirit and purpose of the Hwai project, and of American goals in China, into words and actions. "Conservancy will do more towards opening up the country, alleviating suffering and conducing to quietness and productiveness among the people," the engineer boasted, "than any other proposition in existence." Jameson was summarizing the aims of the Open Door policy. There was a moral necessity to end the degeneration of millions "who are now becoming beggars and robbers." In addition these same millions would then be converted commercially from nonproducers to producers. Last but certainly not least, the project was "justifiable from a financial point of view" throw-

69. Mabel Boardman speech, 1910, before the National Conservation Congress, St. Paul, Minnesota, Mabel Boardman Papers. Also Boardman to John D. Rockefeller, Jr., April 25, 1913, Red Cross 898.5/2.

70. Much of this Jameson material comes from the Red Cross file 898.5/08, C. D. Jameson.

71. Jameson to Gen. Davis, Sept. 6, 1911, Red Cross 898.5/08; Willard Straight note, April 15, 1910, StrP; Jameson to Boardman, Aug. 20, 1912, SDDF 893.811/75; Reinsch to Bryan, Dec. 19, 1913, SDDF 893.811/98, and Reinsch interview, Dec. 23, 1913, Reinsch Papers, indicate Reinsch's and Williams's desire to have Jameson on the Hwai project.

ing open the doors to new financial groups to replace the tightly controlled Wall Street consortium quartet.[72]

Despite the presence on the Red Cross International Relief Board
of Senator Elihu Root, professor of international law John Bassett
Moore, or young Assistant Secretary of the Navy Franklin Delano
Roosevelt, it was Mabel Boardman herself who made "the necessary
arrangements with American financial and industrial interests."[73]
Charged by sections of the press with allowing the Red Cross to sacrifice philanthropy by "pulling Bryan's dollar diplomacy chestnuts out
of the fire," Miss Boardman did admit that "we are not a business
organization." It remained her "serious duty," however, to insure that
"American bankers and contractors may be willing to cooperate with
the American Red Cross in this work for China."[74] Several years
earlier Huntington Wilson had brought Mabel Boardman and the
House of Morgan's Henry Davison together for meetings on a similar
subject. In 1914, the head of an admittedly nonbusiness organization,
Miss Boardman described her role in the Hwai negotiations: "using
several other loan agreements approved and accepted by the Chinese
Government, I drafted one as a basis for decision. I then submitted
it," she continued, "to the Chinese minister . . . and to several promi-
nent bankers who are personal friends and with whom I have already
had brief conferences." The result was a proposed twenty-million-
dollar loan with revenues from the improvement, sale, and lease of
all reclaimed land as security, to be financed through the National
City Bank of New York, the International Banking Corporation and
the newly formed American International Corporation.[75]

72. Gen. Davis to Jameson, Sept. 12, 1912, Red Cross 898.5; Jameson to Gen.
Davis, March 21, 1913, also Red Cross 898.5/2 and Jameson's preliminary report,
1913, p. 43, Red Cross 898.5/08.

73. Boardman to Lansing, March 26, 1914, Lansing Papers, vol. II; Boardman
to Wilson, July 25, 1913, Red Cross 898.5/08; Magee to Jacob Schiff, Jan. 28,
1914, Red Cross 898.5, and the Chinese minister to Reinsch, June 11, 1914, Red
Cross 898.5/08.

74. *Boston Evening Transcript,* April 16, 1914, found in Red Cross 898.5/7
Publicity. Boardman to Robert W. deForest, Jan. 20, 1914, Red Cross 898.5, and
Boardman to Wilson, June 11, 1914, SDDF 893.811/152. Beard, *Idea of National
Interest,* pp. 183–95, based on Reinsch, *An American Diplomat,* passim, does
more than anyone else on dollar diplomacy of Hwai project.

75. Boardman to Gen. Davis, Sept. 16, 1912, Red Cross 898.5; also file 898.5/2
Loan Agreements, which contains the key document of Boardman to Reinsch,

In supporting the conservancy loan scheme, Harvard's Charles Eliot wrote to Charles Crane that the Wilson administration was doing "nothing inconsistent with its refusal to remain in the group." As engineered by the Red Cross, the Hwai project could "crown unselfish American enterprise in China for the betterment of human life and true progress." Paul Reinsch felt the whole enterprise was so representative of the spirit of American-Chinese relations that the United States could not fail to "reap the reward which always comes from taking the lead in great improvements of this kind." Merchants, missionaries, and industrialists would all benefit from efficient American engineering skill and financial assistance.[76]

Even die-hard independent George Bronson Rea, associated with the J. G. White firm at this time, was satisfied with the use of American contractors and money and the admittance of the Chinese to a small share in the conservation work, as he had proposed in 1910, in order to keep costs down. While such an American project served as a check on ulterior motives of other countries, Rea was not overconfident. With the danger of competitive Belgian financing or Dutch engineering on the Hwai, Rea warned that the door could be closed in China or even at the new Panama Canal should the United States lag.[77] Sharing the fashionable double image of faith and fear in the Chinese, Mabel Boardman was not without concern that the "wiles" of the "heathen Chinee" might upset the Hwai work. Again Paul Reinsch summarized this feeling when he called on America to act to "put other nations out of the field."[78]

There were only two things Reinsch need fear. They were of course the two things American competitors had feared since 1905: the rival demands of the Japanese and the cooperative tendencies of American

June 15, 1914, explaining her role. Also in 898.5/2 Loan Agreements, see John Bassett Moore to Boardman, Sept. 8, 1914. Important for the role of the newly formed AIC is SDDF 893.811/227, June 20, 1916.

76. Charles Eliot to Charles Crane, Feb. 7, 1914, Crane Papers; Reinsch to Wilson, Nov. 28, 1914, W. Wilson Papers, series 4, case file 1953; Reinsch to Gen. Davis, Dec. 19, 1914, Red Cross 898.5/2, and Reinsch to Bryan, SDDF 893.811/172.

77. George Bronson Rea to W. Wilson, March 26, 1913, SDDF 893.77/1263; William C. Redfield to Bryan, commenting on Rea, Bryan Papers, box 30; Reinsch to Bryan, Jan. 23, 1914, SDDF 893.811/109.

78. Mabel Boardman to Gen. George Davis, June 30, 1914, Red Cross 898.5/2, and W. H. Donald to Reinsch, March 12, 1914, Reinsch Papers.

bankers. By late 1915 Reinsch was livid at New York bankers who had to ask permission of competitors around the world before engaging in new business. These Wall Street interests, Reinsch observed, were the "most timid beings known to experience when it came to matters of foreign investment. In fact," the minister mocked in absolute disgust, America's competitors were so misguided they "still harbor the idea that Americans really desire to do business here."[79]

Of course as Reinsch defined it, the United States did not really desire to do business. However much the Hwai project might be applauded by the competitors at home, the involvement of banking interests brought pressure to cooperate or at least compromise with other parties, especially Japan. Predictably, Willard Straight now representing the American International Corporation, was at the forefront of the drive to reach an understanding with Japan. The classic example of a man who had moved from competition through compromise to cooperation, Straight would have America go the same route once again. Just three years after he had felt Woodrow Wilson was calling off the game forever, the former boy-diplomat was back listening to the claims of the Industrial Bank of Japan for a large share in the Hwai loan and proposing his own vision of a cooperative Far Eastern settlement.[80]

Persuasive Coordination

Paul Reinsch saw Japanese political interference in an "American industrial and humanitarian project" as most unsuitable. He surely felt that Straight had passed the bounds of sanity in his plans to join with Great Britain, France, Russia, and Japan to neutralize all of Asia, even if it meant giving up Manchuria to a Japanese sphere.[81] In proposing such a plan, Straight placed himself with Henry Adams and John Hays Hammond as a philosopher of cooperation. Another

79. Reinsch, *An American Diplomat*, p. 218; Reinsch to Lansing, Dec. 30, 1915, SDDF 893.811/202.

80. The evolution of Straight's cooperationist philosophy has been traced before. An interesting review can be found in: Roger Greene to Straight, May 12, 1908; Straight to Davison, Jan. 5, 1911; a May 2, 1913 speech "The Politics of Chinese Finance," and Straight to Herbert Croly, March 16, 1916, in which the international plan is discussed—all these documents are in the invaluable Straight Papers at Cornell.

81. Reinsch to Lansing, Dec. 29, 1916, SDDF 893.811/236.

convert to such thinking, William Howard Taft, concurred. Praising the "economy and efficiency of the Red Cross," the former president saw his friend Mabel Boardman's work as a hopeful sign of the end of "pettiness and suspicion" and the dawn of a scientific and international new era.[82]

This was to be a new era at home as well as in China. "The country neeeds more than anything else," Straight wrote to Theodore Roosevelt in 1914, "constructive-Nationalism-Americanism, hopeful, effective, and above all things, sane."[83] Linking America's problems to the taproot of industrial organization, Straight felt "the old vocabulary about monopolies, the wicked interests and corrupt big business, is pretty well out of date" and should be replaced by "constructive progressivism." Remembering the publicity lesson he learned during the Russo-Japanese War, Straight arranged and financed the rebirth of the dry *Journal of the American Asiatic Association* as the highly readable new magazine *Asia*.[84] He had also taken a similar step of greater proportions to interpret America as well as Asia by making possible his own *New Republic*, not the China of Yuan Shih-kai and Sun Yat-sen but the magazine of Herbert Croly, Walter Lippmann, and Walter Weyl. Much has been made of the intellectual marriage of these editors, their magazine, and their generation. More should be said in reporting the history of the *New Republic* of the role of Willard Straight, his "constructive progressivism," and his China-born concept of cooperation.[85] Straight gave Herbert Croly more than just an editorial or financial blank check. He contributed an outlook that

82. Taft's post-1912 position is best seen through the Mabel Boardman Papers. Working with Yale and the Red Cross in the period, Taft gave two important speeches both recorded in the Boardman collection, a 1915 San Francisco speech and an address of the same year at Clark University, "The Influence of the Red Cross for Peace."

83. Straight to Theodore Roosevelt, May 26, 1914, StrP.

84. For Asia see the *Journal of the American Asiatic Association*, XVII (March 1917) and *Asia*, XIX (Jan. 1919), 8–9. On the financing of these journals, especially the role of Straight's wife, Dorothy Whitney, who was an heiress to Standard Oil millions see Eric Goldman, *Rendezvous With Destiny* (New York: Alfred A. Knopf, 1952), p. 178, and Herbert Croly, *Willard Straight* (New York: Macmillan, 1925), pp. 354–65.

85. Studies of the *New Republic's* significance appear in Goldman, *Rendezvous With Destiny*, but most importantly in Charles Forcey's *The Crossroads of Liberalism: Croly, Weyl, Lippmann and the Progressive Era, 1900–25* (New York: Oxford University Press, 1961.)

matched in optimism and importance even that of Croly who had constructed his own version of America's promise. In rejecting the legacy of laissez faire that he found on the pages of *The Nation,* Straight reminded his editors that "without the ambition for proper and legitimate expansion not of our territory but of trade and activity, we will become atrophied and look upon the game with the eyes and the digestion and the imagination of an Oswald Garrison Villard."[86]

Straight need not have worried. Each of the *New Republic's* editors had already or would shortly concern himself with foreign as well as domestic problems, express a belief in China's importance and call for a cooperative open door. Such premises shaped Croly's *Promise of American Life.* In 1915 Walter Lippmann also defined China as the richest "stake" of diplomacy.[87] Competition in China, Lippmann noted, meant trouble for the whole world. The supreme task was internationalism or the organization of mankind. Walter Weyl, understanding American history as a progression from an atomistic, structureless society to a socialized and efficient "New Democracy," observed that "there can be no end of China." Much in the same way as Croly, Lippmann, or Straight, Weyl defined the task as "the integration of the world." China must be removed from the field of competition. Though the banking consortium had sought exorbitant profits, Weyl thought its inherent cooperation the only way to preserve peace and insure that the twentieth century's "gospel of steam" would reach the Far East.[88]

It is not surprising that the second issue of the *New Republic* led off with a story of Japan in China's future or that the third included a plan for a revolution in values to eliminate competing national expansionism.[89] Straight took an active part in the magazine through letters to his favorite, Croly. Often he would enclose an article, his or a friend's, for consideration. More frequently he corrected a mistake,

---

86. Straight to Croly, Dec. 29, 1914, StrP. Again Lasch's description of Villard. *American Liberals and Russian Revolution,* p. 139, is useful.

87. Walter Lippmann, *The Stakes of Diplomacy* (New York: Henry Holt, 1915), pp. 166–67, 224

88. Perhaps Forcey's greatest achievement was in reintroducing Walter Weyl. See Weyl's *The New Democracy* (New York: Macmillan, 1912); *American World Policies* (New York: Macmillan, 1917), pp. 76, 213–16; and *Tired Radicals and Other Papers* (New York: B. W. Huebsch, 1921), especially the essay "The Conquering Chinese."

89. *New Republic,* I (Nov. 14, 1914), 3, and ibid. (Nov. 21, 1914), 22.

scolded a misreading, or applauded a Croly piece from wherever in the world high finance took him. Once in a great while Straight really let them have it, or, as only he could say it, "Lord A'mighty, Phew!" Usually, however, he praised a "corker" and summarized the role the magazine played in his plans. "You've laid down a wonderful programme," he wrote about Croly's new book *Progressive Democracy*. "May the Republic serve to carry it out."[90]

By 1916, then, the Wilson administration was face to face with the financial and philosophical pressures that had forced Taft from compromise to open cooperation. Touring the Orient that year, United States Steel's Judge Gary repeated the argument he had been making since 1907. China, Gary observed, could go the way of harm or peace, toward war or internal development. With Japan as the model "in the progressive march," China could achieve education, health, morals, wealth, and strength only through individual, corporate, and national cooperation.[91] Faced with such pressures, the aggressively competitive position had always been compromised. "I recognize the values of competition," former minister William Calhoun announced proudly, "yet it has its limitations." Geographically robbed of its own "virgin market, a growing, expanding and absorbing market," Americans must cooperate to preserve similar frontiers around the world.[92]

Certainly there were those within the Wilson administration who understood the need for at least a limited cooperation. Secretary of Commerce William C. Redfield, the only member of the cabinet to support the consortium in 1913, had his own solution to the Wilson-Taft-Roosevelt debate. In *The New Industrial Day*, Redfield wrote that "our domestic business needs to feel the throbbing pulse of the larger world of foreign commerce." To reach this goal, he favored

90. Straight to Croly, Dec. 29, 1914, March 1, 5, 1915 (the latter from the Lusitania), StrP. For an interesting though unsuccessful indication of the way Straight's friends hoped to use the magazine, see Huntington Wilson and J. Reuben Clark to the *New Republic* trying to peddle a piece, Nov. 23, 1914, "The Effects of the War on Our Latin American Relations," Huntington Wilson Papers, Ursinus College Library, Collegeville, Pa.

91. Elbert H. Gary, "Addresses and Statements," collected and bound by the Museum of the Peaceful Arts, New York Public Library, vol. II, contains the record of Gary's 1916 visit to the Far East; see speeches in Honolulu (July), Manila (August), and Tokyo (September), and especially his review of the trip, a speech at St. Louis, Oct. 27, 1916.

92. For Calhoun's statement, *Journal of the American Asiatic Association*, XIV (Feb. 1914), 15–18.

applying industrial education and scientific management. Like Straight or Gary, Wilson's Secretary of Commerce would "base our hopes for the future on moderate progressiveness and on progressive moderation" or compromise in public as well as in business affairs.[93]

Much closer to the president, Col. E. M. House had developed his own view of the need for what Lipmann might call the "organization of mankind." In the romantic novel *Philip Dru, Administrator*, admittedly a "hastily and poorly expressed statement of my views in 1911," House secretly outlined a program for international cooperation remarkably reminiscent of Straight's later 1916 proposals.[94] When Philip's "life's work was done" and he set sail for paradise, which House interestingly perceived as somewhere west of the Golden Gate, the world would be guaranteed peace, efficiency, and commercial freedom through new supercentralized national governments. A vigorous republic of China would be at peace with Japan as both kept their zones open for the coaling stations and merchant marines of the world.

In his diary House noted that the anonymously published novel "expresses my thought and aspirations and at every opportunity I have tried to press rulers, public men and those influencing public opinion in that direction." Although after reading *Philip Dru*, Walter Lippmann thought the author's "imagination is that of a romantic boy of 14," the colonel's willingness to "press" made him a favorite correspondent of Straight, journalists Lincoln Colcord, Richard Washburn Child, and even Lippmann.[95] The advice for cooperation they passed on was in

93. Curry, *Wilson and Far Eastern Policy*, p. 21; Cronon, *Cabinet Diaries of Daniels*, pp. 40–42; William C. Redfield, *The New Industrial Day* (New York: Century, 1913), ch. 3, "What We Have to Do with Abroad."

94. Edward M. House, *Philip Dru, Administrator: A Story of Tomorrow, 1920–35* (New York: B. W. Huebsch, 1920), original copyright, 1912. The House Papers, a magnificent collection at the Yale University Library, contain some very interesting material on *Philip Dru*, especially campaigns in the 1930s and 1950s to persuade that House was a Jew, "E. Mandell House," and that his "Jewish conspiracy" was being realized in Roosevelt or later Truman. The *Liberty* and *Defender* magazines led the charge that House fit in with a curious conspiracy that began with banker Jacob Schiff, moved through Leon Trotsky, and culminated in Harry Truman. See House Papers, drawer 32, file no. 184.

95. See House's magnificent "Diary," March 17, 1917, vol. X; Lippmann's observation, Dec. 8, 1912, House Papers, drawer 32, file no. 184; Lippmann to House, Oct. 22, 1917, House Papers, drawer 12, file no. 29; and Richard Washburn Child to House, Sept. 8, 1917, House Papers, drawer 4, file no. 49, all in the Yale University Library.

keeping with *Philip Dru's* thought and aspirations for House was "eager to have Washington take a more sympathetic view of the Far Eastern situation . . . to bring seemingly chaotic conditions into a well ordered policy."[96]

The colonel's friends were concerned that Paul Reinsch had an absurd view of the capability of independent action, either American or Chinese, and an absolute anti-Japanese mania. Reinsch and his supporters, on the other hand, took heart from their information that House was not considered on Chinese affairs or very much else by the beginning of the second Wilson term.[97] Reinsch, Rea, Millard, and Crane might compromise enough to admit that Japan could be equally afraid of America and that "cooperation merits consideration when purely commercial." They would never yield in their belief that China was the "golden prize which is ours" to secure, just as their forefathers had not hesitated before the "great west." Similarly they could not accept a partnership with Japan or any "financial monopoly."[98]

Even during the honeymoon of the early Wilson years these competitors, however, were fighting a desperate holding action against the forces which Judge Gary found so valuable—namely, "concentrated wealth, integration of industry, large units, big and capable organizations." Such forces led naturally to "the maintenance of a constructive policy by our Government, one that is calculated to build up, to extend, to increase efficiency." In the shaping of foreign policy one

96. House, "Diary," Jan. 9, 1917, vol. X; Aug. 30, 1917, vol. XI; House to Wilson, Sept. 6, 1917, House Papers; J. Kingsley Ohl to House, May 16, 1917, House Papers, drawer 15, file no. 2. Christopher Lasch, *American Liberals and Russian Revolution*, pp. 78–82, is one of the few places where the role of House and a corps of journalists led by Colcord has been explored. Lasch has expanded the House-Colcord relationship into a chapter of his *The New Radicalism in America: The Intellectual as a Social Type, 1889–1963* (New York: Alfred A. Knopf, 1965).

97. Child to House, June 7, 1917, House Papers, drawer 4, file no. 49; Walter Rogers to Crane, June 25, 1917, Crane Papers; Breckinridge Long to House, Feb. 13, 1928, reviewing House's role, House Papers, drawer 12, file no. 36.

98. Reinsch to Lansing, Dec. 29, 1916, Jan. 24, 1917, SDDF 893.811/236,239. Reinsch interview, June 19, 1915, Reinsch Papers. Rea to Wilson, June 1, 1917, SDDF 893.00/2585, and Rea to Lansing, May 21, 1917, SDDF 893.811/257. Two articles by Jeremiah Jenks are most enlightening, "China, America's Silent Partner," and "Japan's Acts in China," in *World's Work*, XXXIII (Dec. 1916), 165–71 and ibid. (Jan. 1917), 312–28.

clear result of this constructive policy was the move culminating in the Webb Pomerene bill to authorize industries to combine, in violation of any antitrust laws, for purposes of foreign trade.[99] While this cooperation at home might, at times, be used to compete against more efficient, dangerous rivals, like Germany, it nevertheless had within it once again the basic logic of integrating the foreign marketplace for which all competed.

In fact, that spark needed to further transform cooperation designed to thwart America's rivals into one which might eliminate or reduce international competition was the United States's entrance into the world war. Since 1914, of course, Europe had been caught up in what many feared was the inevitable product of competition, war itself. The world war was "the biggest game" Willard Straight had "ever sat on the hoopskirts of."[100] It was also a lesson in the need for cooperation. American entrance into the military and political affairs of Europe did not create the need to cooperate but rather made it indispensable, and not just valuable that all combine against the one common enemy. While temporarily delaying projects like the Hwai conservancy, the war again did not create new aims for the Open Door policy. It did, however, place the well-known goals in a more "cooperative" perspective.[101]

"Every war has increased our Nationalism and conferred greater

99. A great deal of work is necessary on the "preparedness" of the Webb bill. See the recollections of Federal Trade Commissioner George Rublee, Columbia University Library, Oral History Research Project, vol. I, pp. 133–34. A speech by Willard Straight indicates the thinking behind such cooperation, Oct. 20, 1916, to the Annual Convention of the National Implement and Vehicle Manufacturers Association, StrP. Also a Gary speech, Gary, "Addresses and Statements," Jan. 5, 1918. For early thinking along these lines, Bryan to W. Wilson, Sept. 23, 1914, Bryan Letterbooks, Bryan Papers, box 43. Perhaps the fullest discussion thus far is in "Commercial Preparedness, 1914–21," a paper read by Lloyd Gardner at the 1966 American Historical Association meetings in New York.

100. The effects of the war shall be the subject of chapter 6. On the German competition in the Far East as a possible cause of war, see *Journal of the American Asiatic Association,* XVI (Feb. 1916), 2; *Asia,* XVII (Aug. 1917), 117; and Nelson T. Johnson's memoir in the Columbia Oral History Research Project, vol. II, pp. 441–44. For Straight's evaluation, see his note to Henry Fletcher, Dec. 22, 1914, Fletcher Papers, box 3.

101. See Gary, "Addresses and Statements," Jan. 5, 1918 speech. Gen. Davis to Bryan, Dec. 19, 1914, SDDF 893.811/167.

powers on the Federal Government than it possessed before," Robert Lansing noted.[102] In terms of China policy, the "centralization of power" which was "imperative in time of war" meant the victory of cooperation, a political rapprochement with the "allied" Japanese and the establishment of a second banking consortium.[103] All these had been possibilities before. The causes and nature of the war made them necessary and proper. The dreams and goals, the struggle and compromise that characterized America's Far Eastern policy would, however, survive emergency efforts at wartime cooperation as they had even the temporary triumph of Wilsonian competition.

In what form or balance they survived was the key question. Once again it was Lansing who perceived that the real decision for the future would come at the end of the emergency both at home and abroad.[104] Using the political terms *individualism* and *nationalism* where the organizational ones of *competition* and *cooperation* would have fit as well, Lansing pondered the "future effect upon our institutions."

"Will we be able after the immediate need is over to repeal, . . . to return to the same proportion of individualism and nationalism as existed in our political system prior to the war?" An educated guess would be that nationalism, centralization, and cooperation would continue to weigh more heavily after the war than they had before in the shaping of any necessary compromises. Discovering that answer and achieving those compromises both at home and in China would intrigue Willard Straight, anger Paul Reinsch, and in great part destroy Woodrow Wilson.

102. Lansing to Edward N. Smith, Dec. 20, 1917, Lansing Papers, vol. 33.

103. See the memo of E. T. Williams, Jan. 31, 1917, Breckinridge Long Papers, box 179; F. W. Williams, "China and Future Peace," *Nation*, CV (Nov. 22, 1917), 561–63.

104. Lansing to Smith, Dec. 20, 1917, Lansing Papers, vol. 33.

6

When Worlds Collide
The Far East and the Great War

SHORTLY after the United States entered the world war, at least one experienced China hand thought America was finally learning that the Open Door policy could no longer be carried out alone. Writing from Canton in November 1917, consul P. S. Heintzleman observed that the war was having a "sobering effect" on American policy. Trade, investment, and reform were still possible in the Far East but to reach these goals required international advice and support. Heintzleman understood, as Americans had for two decades, that "if China is to save herself, she must progress." After the war such progress would mean the cooperative assistance of the United States, Great Britain, and Japan.[1]

Two years later, a better-known American repudiated this sober forecast. In the *New Republic,* philosopher John Dewey asserted that American opportunity in China had survived the war. Indeed, Dewey predicted, the United States had "unparalleled opportunity." The war had conclusively shown that America "can act promptly, efficiently and on a large scale in foreign affairs."[2]

Neither the dominant attitudes of the period, nor the goals and tension shaping Far Eastern policy disappeared as a result of America's

1. P. S. Heintzleman to Robert Lansing, Nov. 15, 1917, State Dept. Decimal File (hereafter cited as SDDF) 793.94/610½, National Archives (hereafter cited as NA).

2. John Dewey, "The American Opportunity in China," *New Republic,* XXI (Dec. 3, 1919), 14–17.

participation in World War I. Yet, as Heintzleman perceived earlier, the war had a dramatic effect. At home and in China, the old dreams and debates were shaped anew by the challenges and opportunities raised by America's new role after 1917.

The need and ability to compromise the competitive and cooperative alternatives was the only traditional part of Far Eastern policy to suffer during the war. The crisis produced enforced cooperation at home as in the War Industries Board. Emergency executive authority and action temporarily overcame any reluctance to a politically and financially cooperative Open Door policy as well. In China, on the other hand, emergency conditions aided and created the kind of independent tactics disapproved by Washington and Wall Street. Cooperation and competition thus operated in two different theaters during the war. With a great distance between them, there was little chance to conflict. The usual need to compromise in order to produce a working policy was also absent. In applying the lessons of the war, however, to structure a new Far East, the two alternative strategies once again operated at cross purposes. The debate over the 1918 joint American-Japanese Siberian intervention was the first sign of the continuing postwar tactical clash. President Wilson's decision to concede the Chinese province of Shantung to Japan in order to preserve his League of Nations sparked a classic confrontation between the logic of cooperation and the challenge of Japan.

Familiar Concepts in a Different Theater

If possible, fascination with the Far East actually intensified during World War I. China, always the future Eldorado, took on added significance as perhaps the last prize to be left after the war's destruction —and if not the last, then surely the next. The immediate problem quickly became how to prevent the same temptations and impulses of the "world's dominating nations" from producing an even more fatal conflict around the "irresistible magnet" in the Pacific.[3] To some "the

3. See the articles of Samuel G. Blythe in the *Saturday Evening Post*, April 28 and May 12, 1917; also the report of J. E. Baker in the Breckinridge Long Papers, Nov. 1918, box 179. The Blythe articles are part of the excellent clipping files of the William E. Griffis Papers, Rutgers University Library, New Brunswick, N. J., boxes 26–29. The Long Papers, an indispensable source for the war years, are in the Library of Congress (hereafter cited as LC).

real cause of the present European war" had rested in "the exhaustless prizes of commerce which are offered in the western Pacific, . . . for back of all strivings of a thousand years has been the desire to reach the coveted riches which are concealed beyond these mysterious curtains." Even those not linking past and future so closely had little doubt that peace in Europe meant a renewed struggle in the Far East. China could be to the world, Walter Lippmann worried, what Turkey and the Balkans had been to Europe.[4]

If the European war had not been actually caused in the Pacific, its lessons could be applied there. Although German competition was easily identified by the Allies as the chief villain, differences developed over just what this proved.[5] To those favoring international cooperation, Europe's disaster demonstrated the evils of destructive competition. Advocates of an independent American posture felt the militant response to Germany should be extended to other rivals, especially the "Prussia-like" Japan.

Theodore Roosevelt urged going "whole-heartedly in with the allies" or there were "bad times ahead for civilization." The former president may have sought cooperation to produce a more efficient fighting machine; however, his logic was that of the prewar peace movement. Out of mixed emotions of irony, despair, and hope, remnants of that practical movement spoke out not so much against the war in progress as against the danger of more serious conflict in the Far East. Through the curiously named New Technique of Peace consisting of the old remedies of neutralization and financial cooperation, the Open Door was to be strengthened, China rehabilitated, and war prevented.[6]

4. Charles Harvey Fahs, *America's Stake in the Far East* (New York: Association Press, 1920) and the memoirs of Nelson T. Johnson in the Oral History Research Collection, Columbia University Special Collections, II, 441–44, are both excellent examples of views that the war had its origins in the Pacific. See also Frank B. Lenz, "China's Next Revolution—What Part Will America Play," *Overland Monthly*, LXX (Oct. 1917), 313–22, and Walter Lippmann, *The Stakes of Diplomacy* (New York: Henry Holt, 1915), p. 225.

5. On German competition see the *Journal of the American Asiatic Association*, XVI (Feb. 1916), 2, and the same journal renamed and restyled as *Asia*, XVII (Aug. 1917), 417.

6. Theodore Roosevelt to Willard Straight, May 16, 1918, Willard Straight Papers (hereafter cited as StrP), Cornell University Library, Ithaca, New York; Walter Hines Page to Lansing, Jan. 14, 1918, B. Long Papers, box 179; William C. Redfield to Frank L. Polk, March 8, 1919, SDDF 893.77/1735, and A. N.

This cooperation position grew, as those before it had, out of similar domestic pressures for concentration and consolidation. "Is there any reason," the *New Republic* asked, "why the process of forming trusts, mergers and cartels should stop short at frontiers?" Certainly not was the answer of industrial giants such as United States Steel or Du Pont who were negotiating with the Japanese Pacific International Iron and Steel Corporation or Nobel Explosive Limited of London for the rights to mineral deposits or the sale of commercial explosives in China.[7] "A half loaf is better than none," was the answer of Willard Straight speaking for banker Frank Vanderlip and the American International Corporation. Never in better humor than during the war, Straight knew that the United States could not be as aggressive as Germany or Japan and must cooperate. "I am not inclined to kick too hard against the bricks," he admitted, "unless I am sure I can wear hob-nailed boots instead of tennis shoes and if we can't kick we can certainly try to gain our purpose in some other way." By war's end, banker Thomas Lamont took a long look westward and informed merchants and manufacturers that they, like bankers, should insist "that international cooperation as contrasted with competition must be relied upon to establish permanent peace in the Far East."[8]

With such pressure on its side, international cooperation could be defined by 1917 as the official position of the State Department. The nations warring against Germany, Secretary of State Robert Lansing instructed his minister to China, Paul Reinsch, "must work in concert; the United States cannot act alone." It was not surprising to find Lansing or Col. E. M. House advocating cooperative measures to reduce

Holcombe, "Can the Nations Cooperate in the Rehabilitation of China," *Annals of the American Academy of Political and Social Science*, CLII (1930), 347–55. See the very important H. N. Brailsford, "A New Technique of Peace," *New Republic*, XXIX (Nov. 30, 1921), 12–15.

7. On the activities of U. S. Steel and DuPont, see Polk to Paul Reinsch, March 5, 1919, B. Long Papers, box 179, and in the same box, a Sept. 4, 1918, memo of Breckinridge Long.

8. Straight to Reinsch, Feb. 28, 1916, and June 21, 1916, both in the Paul Reinsch Papers, State Historical Society of Wisconsin, Madison, Wisconsin. Also a speech of Thomas Lamont, Oct. 20, 1920, given at the Cathedral of St. John the Divine in New York, StrP.

militarism in what House called "The China of Tomorrow."[9] The great effect of the war was to convert even President Wilson to a cooperative strategy just as at home it moved him further toward government regulation. Having come nearly full cycle from his 1912 campaign, Wilson was confident by 1919 that international coordination would leave the next few years free from the danger of accentuated foreign competition.[10]

Arguments for a competitive, anti-Japanese American position were not destroyed by war. In retreat at home much as they had been between 1909 and 1913, spokesmen for an independent rather than a cooperative posture redoubled their efforts if not their success. Minister Paul Reinsch never shifted his glance from the Far East as he reminded Americans that the "destinies of Serbia, Czechoslovakia and Greece are infinitesimal in their importance compared with those of China."[11] Although he agreed with the consensus opinion that "after the war China will loom larger in world affairs," Reinsch continued to support independent trade, shipping, and banking ventures. In particular Reinsch pleaded with companies such as National Cash Register, General Electric, and Singer Sewing Machine that now while the world looked towards Europe "is the most opportune time for American trade interests to lay a foundation for market extension."[12]

To veteran Japan-baiters like E. Carleton Baker, cooperation meant an American "minute-share" and the return to "spheres of influence." Cynical stories and anecdotes appeared in the press. Two favorites concerned the railway builder who pronounced, after seeing a European sphere-of-influence map, "and where the deuce is China," or the Chinese who, following a beating by Japanese toughs, gasped,

9. The department's view can be see in an E. T. Williams memo in the B. Long Papers, box 179. See Lansing to Reinsch, Jan. 14, 1918, Reinsch Papers; Col. E. M. House to Woodrow Wilson, Sept. 6, 1917, and J. Kingsley Ohl to House, May 16, 1917, both in the House Papers, Yale University Library, New Haven, Conn. Also a piece House later did for *McCall's* in 1926, "The China of Tomorrow," House Papers, drawer 32, file no. 15.

10. Woodrow Wilson speech, May 20, 1919, Woodrow Wilson Papers, file III-A, box 14, LC.

11. Reinsch to Lansing, Dec. 20, 1917, Reinsch Papers. See also Paul Reinsch, *An American Diplomat in China* (Garden City: Doubleday, Page, 1922), p. 366.

12. Frank Lenz, "China's Next Revolution;" Reinsch to Straight, Feb. 12, 1916, Reinsch Papers.

"I am it; China is dead, not dying but dead."[13] While Reinsch and George Bronson Rea kept up such attacks on Anglo-Japanese monopolization, they also turned their wartime guns on former hero Woodrow Wilson. The president might have withdrawn from the consortium in 1913 but he had not protested violently enough over the Twenty-One Demands. By 1917 Rea observed Wilson accepting new Wall Street maneuvers. When, after the war, the president proved willing to listen to Japanese claims to German holdings in the province of Shantung, the former Wilson faithful were horrified. "When I first came here," E. T. Williams wrote to Reinsch who sadly agreed, "Secretary Lansing told me that the President would stand right behind China. He did and pushed her over."[14] During the war Wilson came to see international cooperation as the only key to open the China door. His former competition-oriented supporters continued, however, to preach the same kind of YMCA "spiritual engineering" designed to produce an honest, patriotic, moral, and hygienic "Young China."[15]

Although both sides in the cooperation-competition debate sought to apply the lessons of the war, neither questioned what they felt they already understood. Some, like Wilson, moved closer to cooperation. Others simply redefined and reinforced previously held positions. Few if any pondered the basic attitudes or goals of policy in the Far East. The world war, in fact, strengthened the belief that America's destiny was to expand westward. Writing in the period before another war, Henry L. Stimson made the historical link between the war and the West. In the war, Americans, Stimson observed, were symbolized by the cry "let's go" as they "trespassed casually over the boundaries of No Man's Land with the same cheerful abandon with which their

13. For a sample of these stories, see Samuel Blythe's articles in the *Saturday Evening Post* in the Griffis Papers and E. Carleton Baker to the State Department, April 8, 1918, Reinsch Papers.

14. Growing anti-Wilson sentiment can be traced through Reinsch to Frank Polk, Nov. 9, 1915, Frank Polk Papers, drawer 89, file no. 13, Yale University Library, New Haven, Conn.; Bishop James Bashford to Bishop McDowell, Feb. 9, 1917, Robert Lansing Papers, vol. 24; George Bronson Rea to Lansing, May 21, 1917, SDDF 893.811/257; Rea to Wilson, June 1, 1917, SDDF 893.00/2585; Wharton Barker to Lansing, Nov. 7, 1917, SDDF 793.94/592; Reinsch to the State Department, July 11, 1919, SDDF 893.51/2130; and a summary in E. T. Williams to Reinsch, May 1919, Reinsch Papers.

15. George Lerrigo to Charles Lerrigo, Aug. 15, 1918, YMCA National Headquarters Library, New York, Lerrigo General Correspondence, x970.4.

forefathers had trespassed over the hunting ground of the Iroquois." These were the same breed of men who had "carried their race across the successive frontiers of this continent until they found themselves penned up against the boundaries of the Pacific Ocean." Such a race, Stimson understood, "will not be satisfied with a walled-in territory, however ample." Defining American goals before and after the war, he was confident that "in default of more wilderness to conquer," America "will vent its commercial instincts in trading with and building up other peoples of the earth."[16]

Necessary Partnerships with Japan

In virtually the first act of his administration, Woodrow Wilson had broken William Howard Taft's working agreements with American bankers and the Japanese by withdrawing support from a banking consortium. Among the earliest actions of Wilson's government once America was at war were the reestablishment of these ties through the Lansing-Ishii agreement and the creation of a second banking consortium.

Early in June, 1917, Secretary of State Lansing informed Colonel House that a Japanese commission "important as any which has visited us" would soon arrive. The appearance of these guests, led by Viscount Kikujiro Ishii, gave Oswald Garrison Villard another chance to call for friendly relations with Japan, England's and now America's ally in the fight against Germany.[17] It also put Lansing face to face with the same problem Wilson and Bryan had wrestled with in 1915— Japanese claims to former German territories in China. Two years before, Lansing criticized Bryan's implication and Jacob Schiff's declaration that Japan had a semipermanent "special interest" in China based on geographical proximity and administrative efficiency. In the summer of 1917, pressure from Japan and those who had long

16. Stimson's speech, "America Must Trade Abroad," was delivered before the Foreign Policy Association and World Peace Foundation (both World War I–experienced organizations), 1934; it can be found in the Henry L. Stimson Papers, box 482, Yale University Library, New Haven, Conn.

17. Lansing to House, June 8, 1917, Lansing Papers, vol. 28; Oswald Garrison Villard, *Fighting Years: Memoirs of a Liberal Editor* (New York: Harcourt, Brace, 1939), pp. 335–36; and F. W. Williams, "China and Future Peace," *The Nation*, CV (Nov. 22, 1917), 561–63.

supported cooperation convinced the president and the secretary of state to allow some guarded mention of Japan's special position in exchange for a defense of the status quo in the postwar Far East.[18] With China, in the person of American educated minister V. K. Wellington Koo, literally seated in the diplomatic waiting room, Lansing and Ishii rejected the term *special relation* but agreed that Japan had a *special interest*.[19]

In the face of immediate protest from Reinsch and Tom Millard that China's political independence and the Open Door had been handed to Japan as an exclusive right, Lansing assured them that the United States saw nothing paramount or permanent about Japan's interest. The secretary had opposed the suggestion of a special Japanese anything in 1915. With the war requiring cooperation, Lansing still argued the agreement concerned only what he now defined as Bryan's sole criterion in 1915, "territorial contiguity."[20] Needless to say the Japanese interpreted the document without Lansing's limiting definition. Similarly they rejected President Wilson's emphasis that the United States had said nothing about political influence in China and merely extended the hands-off concept of the Monroe Doctrine to the Far East.[21]

Writing almost twenty years later, Robert Lansing admitted the words *special interest* had been misconstrued.[22] In part this was intended. The Lansing-Ishii agreement did not represent sloppy diplo-

---

18. For a review and a preview of a vital relationship see William A. Williams, "China and Japan: A Challenge and a Choice of the 1920's," *Pacific Historical Review*, XXVI (Aug. 1957), 259–79.

19. The actual negotiations are reported in SDDF 793.94/583½–589 and the B. Long Papers, Sept. 26, 1917, box 179.

20. Tom Millard to Charles Crane, March 12, 1918, Charles Crane Papers, held privately by John O. Crane, Institute for Current World Affairs, New York. Reinsch to Lansing, Jan. 30, 1917, SDDF 893.77/1588. For a review see Wilson to William Jennings Bryan, May 10, 1915, Bryan Letterbooks, box 43, Bryan Papers, LC. There is an interesting interview with Lansing, July 6, 1917, in SDDF 793.94/570. Finally see Payson J. Treat, *The Far East* (New York: Harper & Brothers, 1928), p. 444.

21. Lansing to Sen. William King, Aug. 19, 1919, Lansing Papers, vol. 45, and Wilson to Lansing, July 3, 1917, SDDF 793.94/570½.

22. There is some interesting information in J. Chal Vinson, "The Annulment of the Lansing-Ishii Agreement," *Pacific Historical Review*, XXVII (Feb. 1958), 57–69; Lansing's own (later) review is in Robert Lansing, *War Memoirs of Robert Lansing* (Indianapolis: Bobbs-Merrill, 1935), ch. 10, "The Far East and the War," pp. 283–306.

matic vocabulary any more than it did a rekindled love affair between the two countries. Rather it was the carefully guarded admission, as Lansing had noted earlier, that wartime emergencies required unusual cooperation. Certainly such an admission could not escape the criticism of Paul Reinsch who would at most only support special interests in exchange for a reciprocal agreement on similar American rights in Manchuria.[23] Two years before and two years after Lansing himself would reject any special Japanese position, yet in 1917 he would put his own name to it. Like the earlier Taft-Katsura and Root-Takahira notes, this agreement was surely intended to keep the door open against a mounting Japanese challenge. The earlier agreements, especially the 1908 Root notes, were part of a developing movement for cooperation. In the emergency of war, Lansing had to admit hesitantly, much as Henry Fletcher had concluded a decade before, that for all Paul Reinsch might huff and puff he would not be able to blow Japan's house down in the Far East.

Secretary Lansing went even further in describing the philosophy behind the agreement to the British ambassador. Lansing observed that the war had produced a new day of international dealing "when international exchange and coordination have assumed an unprecedented importance."[24] Matching the political importance of the Lansing-Ishii agreement was the financial significance of a second banking consortium. The interest of the American International Corporation had been stimulated before the war through the Hwai River reclamation work. With Willard Straight and the National City Bank's Frank Vanderlip controlling that project, it took little spark to recrystallize the plans and the organization of the old consortium. Again, the worldwide cooperation made possible and necessary by the war proved to be this spark.[25]

23. Reinsch to Lansing, Jan. 30, 1917, SDDF 893.77/1588. A. Whitney Griswold, *The Far Eastern Policy of the United States* (New Haven: Yale University Press, 1938), p. 215, sees the agreement as an "expedient." A better approach showing the agreement consistent with Lansing's desire for cooperation is Burton F. Beers, *Vain Endeavor: Robert Lansing's Attempts to End the American-Japanese Rivalry* (Durham: Duke University Press, 1962), ch. 9.

24. Lansing to the British Ambassador, Sept. 20, 1917, in *Papers Relating to the Foreign Policy of the United States, 1917* (Washington: Government Printing Office, 1926), p. 198.

25. Paul H. Clyde, "Railway Politics and the Open Door in China, 1916–17," *American Journal of International Law*, XXV (1931), 642–57; Frank Vanderlip to Reinsch, Jan. 12, 1916, Reinsch Papers; also 'Financing Other Nations," *Nation*, CVIII (May 24, 1919), p. 843.

From its first rumored reappearance in 1916, the new banking venture spelled out goals and tactics similar to those of the previous consortium. Three international loans were to be negotiated with the Chinese. Two were the familiar currency reform and Canton-Hankow railway loans and the third provided for an emergency war fund of fifty million dollars. As others had hoped before, these new investments were needed "not so much because of what China means at the present but for the potency she has for the future as regards our relations with the Far East."[26]

There were to be major differences in membership from the first consortium. At home greater diversity would be achieved, it was hoped, through thirty-seven banks rather than four taking part. The leadership still rested, however, with the old Wall Street quartet plus Lee, Higginson and Company of Boston and John Jay Abbott's Chicago Continental and Commercial Trust. Internationally, all German interest would naturally be eliminated and reassigned. The greatest differences, however, would result from the immediate recognition of the need for cooperation. Far removed from his 1913 position, Wilson allowed complete governmental support not only for American participation but for actual American creation of the new international organization.[27] In addition, Japan was to be accepted, albeit reluctantly, by the consortium.

All the steps in Taft's gradual shift from compromise in 1909 to cooperation in 1912 were rapidly repeated between 1916 and 1918. Strong anti-Japanese pressure came as it had before from Reinsch and Rea.[28] Early overtures towards partnership were justified, on the

26. The second consortium needs further study matching Vevier's research on the first's negotiations. At present the best information must be gathered from several useful manuscript collections—in particular the Breckinridge Long Papers, box 179, especially a note from E. T. Williams dated Jan. 31, 1917, and a letter from the American International Corporation to John J. Abbott, July 30, 1917. The best single review, also in the Long papers, is B. Long to W. Wilson, Feb. 11, 1918. See also some early notes in the Reinsch Papers, dated Aug. 21 and Nov. 1, 1916; Lansing to Polk, July 3, 1916 in the Polk Papers, drawer 77, file no. 19, and a Thomas Lamont press conference, May 1, 1919, House Papers, drawer 30, file no. 110. Finally consult Lamont's Across World Frontiers (New York: Harcourt, Brace, 1951), p. 228.

27. B. Long to W. Wilson, June 20, 1918, House Papers, drawer 12, file no. 35, and Polk to Reinsch, March 19, 1919, SDDF 893.77/1734a.

28. George Bronson Rea to Polk, Jan. 31, 1920, Polk Papers, drawer 77, file no. 46, and a Reinsch memo, Aug. 1918, Reinsch Papers.

other hand, as administration efforts to thwart or to "prevent independent action by Japan."[29] By early 1918, defense of cooperation to
conciliate and not to thwart began to appear. "It was more simple and
more expeditious," Lansing told Secretary of Commerce William C.
Redfield, who had long agreed, "to join Japan in financial undertakings
in China." Finally the Japanese, as they had in 1912, underwent a
remarkably well-timed transformation in American eyes. With a new
and hopefully friendly government established in Tokyo it was obvious,
or so Paul Reinsch was informed from Washington, that the Japanese
"evidenced a willingness to cooperate."[30]

Willard Straight had personally undergone this conversion experience almost a decade before. Happy to see the consortium reestab-
lished, Straight suggested still stronger steps. International neutralization of China's eighteen provinces so as to produce a "balance not of
conflicting but of cooperative powers" and a commercial Open Door
was his 1917 proposal.[31] Straight's fatal last bout with pneumonia while
in France in 1918 robbed him of the chance to work for this plan as
he hoped to do with Colonel House. He might have easily seen in the
months before his death, at age thirty-eight, that pressures for cooperation, as demonstrated in the Lansing-Ishii agreement and the new
banking consortium, were more pervasive than at any time since 1912.
But the proper touch of cynicism he cultivated after Woodrow Wilson's
action withdrawing from the consortium in 1913 probably would have
allowed Straight to see, as well, that neither the cooperative victory
nor the friendliness of the Japanese would go unchallenged very long.

Convenient Opportunities for America

The likelihood of a competitive, anti-Japanese challenge was increased by wartime events in China. Despite cooperation's victory at

29. Lansing to Polk, July 3, 1916, Polk Papers, drawer 77, file no. 19; Reinsch to
the State Department, Sept. 16, 1917, Reinsch Papers. Some studies of Wilson's
policy go no further than the anti-Japanese early position; see Roy W. Curry,
Woodrow Wilson and Far Eastern Policy, 1913–21 (New York: Bookman Associates, 1957), p. 318. Contrast his interpretation with Burton Beers, *Vain Endeavor,*
passim; or William L. Neumann, *America Encounters Japan: From Perry to
MacArthur* (Baltimore: Johns Hopkins Press, 1963), ch. 8, "Reluctant Allies."

30. Lansing to William C. Redfield, Jan 11, 1918, B. Long Papers, box 179;
Polk to Reinsch, May 31, 1919, Reinsch Papers.

31. Straight to Polk, March 26, 1917, Polk Papers, drawer 77, file no. 21.

home, an independent American role in the Far East was strengthened by China's entrance into the war. Before 1917 a mixture of propaganda and fear produced mild pro-German sentiment in China. Of more immediate concern was an internal struggle between the northern military oligarchy faithful to the party of the recently deceased Yuan Shih-kai and an opposition southern National Assembly behind Sun Yat-sen.[32] Out of this 1917 chaos, Paul Reinsch saw the possibility of creating an anti-German, anti-Japanese, "conservatively progressive" China. Reinsch's greatest fear was China's entering the war under the aegis of Japan. To prevent that he urged the United States to guarantee Chinese sovereignty over Shantung province, to supply an immediate ten-million-dollar loan and to suspend indemnity payments in order to convince the Chinese to enter the war under Allied and not just Japanese supervision. To Reinsch "the vital interests of China including the maintenance of national unity and the ability to be of use in this war" were at stake. At the same time of course, American national security, as Reinsch defined it, demanded China as an ally, especially once the United States entered the war itself. Such partnership could "strengthen American influence" and allow the "immediate completing" of the Hankow-Canton Railway.[33]

At first, Secretary Lansing was dubious of Reinsch's plan to bring China into the war. He was certainly anxious, however, to achieve the political reform of "one central united and alone responsible government."[34] Redfield and War Railway Administrator William Gibbs McAdoo stressed the commercial advantage that could be derived from free access to China's "allied" ports. Thus commercially as well as politically China's entrance could be accepted as a rededication to the goals of the Open Door. On August 14, with American support, the military government of Tuan Chi-jui declared war on Germany. Tuan sought a seat at any postwar conference to check Japan and to preserve his own rule against mounting parliamentary and southern opposition. Within days of China's declaration, however, Redfield and

32. The best published accounts of China's entrance are Kenneth S. Latourette, "China, the United States and the War," *League of Nations, World Peace Foundation*, II (1919), 168–91, and Thomas E. LaFargue "The Entrance of China into the World War," *Pacific Historical Review*, V (1936), 222–33.

33. Reinsch to Lansing, Feb. 6, 7, 8, 12, 1917, all in B. Long Papers, box 179; Reinsch to Lansing, Aug. 9, 1917, SDDF 893.77/1619.

34. Lansing, *War Memoirs*, pp. 287–90; E. David Cronon, ed., *The Cabinet Diaries of Josephus Daniels, 1913–21* (Lincoln: University of Nebraska Press, 1963), pp. 133–35.

others were more concerned with the effect on the Open Door of "big developments" in shipping and the financial and industrial changes sure to take place in a wartime China.[35]

The war effort produced a ready-made opportunity to develop China's manpower and material resources, presumably to supply the Allies. Given the vast amounts of money and machinery needed to modernize China, any war advances would be aimed as well towards future progress. The hundreds of thousands of dollars in Liberty Bonds sold in Shanghai were not as crucial as the work of War Trade Board representative Charles Denby to "hold and increase good feeling toward us."[36] Even the success of Denby, an advocate of a competitive American role, was surpassed by the continued wartime work of the YMCA. There was some talk in Washington and Peking about sending Chinese divisions to France. A fighting role, as earlier envisaged by Homer Lea, would provide the Chinese an equal voice with Japan at the conference table. A more realistic proposal, as carried out, entailed the shipping of more than a hundred thousand Chinese laborers to work at the front.[37] In France these "new Chinese" would naturally come under the educational and religious guidance of the Association's United War Work Campaign. The war therefore provided the "greatest school for Chinese" ever seen by those involved in bringing American civilization to the Far East. Its graduates returned with the lessons of this civilization or its wartime facsimile. Some even took up rural and industrial YMCA work in China.[38]

Even this educational opportunity to reach Chinese youths paled in comparison with the American chance to achieve "direct communication" during the war. Ever since 1905 journalists had been excited by the possibilities of a permanent publicity program in China. Despite the plans of Straight and George Marvin, it took another war to achieve this "American voice" through a Committee on Public Information, better known as the Creel Committee. Under the leadership

35. Redfield to Lansing, Aug. 17, 1917, SDDF 102.8/196, and William G. McAdoo to Polk, Oct. 1, 1917, Polk Papers, drawer 89, file no. 87.

36. *Asia*, XVIII (Dec. 1918), 803. Papers of the War Trade Board, Record of the Executive Office, Record Group 182, NA, contain the information on Denby; see entry 11, box 5.

37. B. Long to Wilson, Oct. 20, 1917, a nine-page memo in B. Long Papers, box 179.

38. D. Willard Lyon, *The First Quarter Century of the Young Men's Christian Association in China, 1895–1920* (Shanghai: Association Press, 1920). Also at the YMCA Library, World Service Folder e, 1918–19, contains reports of the war work.

of young journalist George Creel, the committee sought to take advantage of a modern communication revolution by establishing a global news network with a Chinese outlet at Shanghai and another important base at Vladivostok in Siberia. If "America's influence in China may not be felt to the extent that America deserves," Creel assured, it will not be "because her voice will not be heard."[39] Prior to the war, all American news in the Far East had been provided by the English agency, Reuters, and its Tokyo ally, Kokusai. More often than not, these reports belabored the crime and corruption of the United States. "It will interest you to hear," a colleague learned from Creel, "that I have been told by a well educated Chinese friend that he has not seen any news in the local press of the arrival of American troops in France." Making matters worse in Creel's fiercely competitive eyes, the only rival to Reuters before 1917 had been a German agency which was "spreading reports that the Americans have no heart in fighting against them."[40]

This American image was to be changed by daily war reports. Paul Reinsch happily supplied the wireless services of the Peking legation and attempts were even begun to supply translations for Chinese papers to reprint. Even this might reach only the educated elite. Four hundred volunteers were recruited, therefore, from American missions and businesses. Their function was to plaster wall-posters all over the offices of the Standard Oil, the Singer Sewing Machine, and the British-American Tobacco companies, as well as assorted chapels, reading rooms, and mission schools.

Beyond daily news accounts, the committee developed a publishing house and a mailing list to print and distribute translations of President Wilson's speeches, trade magazines, textbooks, crop reports, and even American college catalogues.[41] On a less frequent basis the Creel

39. There are only two good places to look into the Creel Committee, first the published George Creel, *How We Advertised America: The First Telling of the Amazing Story of the COPI that Carried the Gospel of Americanism to Every Corner of the Globe* (New York: Harper & Brothers, 1920), "The Work in the Orient," pp. 358–64, and the papers of the committee, especially "America's Voice in the Orient," Record Group 63, Committee on Public Information (hereafter cited as CPI) 17-C7, NA.

40. Ibid.

41. See also the memoirs of Nelson T. Johnson in the Oral History Research Collection, III, 510–17, and Eugene E. Barnett of the YMCA to Crane, Jan. 22, 1919, in the Crane Papers.

Committee work in China included drumming up the sale of Liberty Bonds and an occasional foray into diplomacy as in rebutting the favorable publicity received by the French and Italians upon the visit to Peking of a Papal representative or the conversion of Wellington Koo to Catholicism.[42] The most creative effort of the Committee on Public Information's work in China was the importing of American motion pictures to show the "social, industrial and agricultural progress" realized at home and possible in China.[43] Wartime communication had a negative side as well. Certain news, especially damaging casualty reports, was bad publicity. "You know how well our cable censorship works," Creel wrote to banker Martin Egan, a former Russo-Japanese War journalist, "and we guarantee that this news will not get out of the country."[44]

On-the-scene leadership in China came from the experienced corps of American reporters. All close friends of Charles Crane, the Creel Committee team consisted of the "aggressively American" Tom Millard, the "efficiency minded" John B. Powell and the "communications expert" Walter Rogers.[45] Its captain and coordinator was Carl Crow. Arriving in China before the war as a merchandising agent, Crow evolved into the Far East's first public relations man specializing in guidebooks designed to sell "pills for the ills" of China's four hundred million customers. Before the war he had pressured for improved cable, postal, and news services as well. His wife, Mildred, lobbied for women's rights and sold typewriters. In one of the clearest expressions of American business and reform in China, Mrs. Crow defined her job:

42. Carl Crow to Walter Rogers, Oct. 19, 1918, R. G. 63, CPI 17/A2, and Charles F. Merriam to Ray Stannard Baker, Jan. 30, 1919, Ray Stannard Baker Papers, series 2, container 97, LC.

43. George Creel to Martin Egan, March 30, 1918, in the Martin Egan Papers, held in New York by Egan's widow. Julean Arnold to Robert Lansing, Dec. 24, 1918, SDDF 102.8/511.

44. In the Egan Papers, see Creel to Egan, March 30, 1918, and Polk to Egan, Sept. 28, 1916.

45. John B. Powell, "Newspaper Efficiency in the Small Town," *University of Missouri Bulletin*, XVI (April 1915), and by the same author, *My Twenty Five Years in China, 1917–42* (New York: Macmillan, 1945). Also Walter Rogers to Crane, June 25, 1917, Crane Papers, Crane's "Memoirs," unpublished, p. 73, held by his son in New York; and Reinsch to Creel, Sept. 14, 1918, R. G. 63, CPI 17/A2. The only good treatment of American journalists as a group in China appears in Urban Whitaker, Jr., "Americans and Chinese Political Problems, 1912–23" (Ph.D. diss., University of Washington, 1954), ch. 5.

"The typewriter is one of the great emblems of civilization and progress and there will be no more talk of poor, backward China when
the typewriter is as common there as in America."[46]

The lessons of the Creel Committee to people like the Crows were
obvious. War was just the beginning of a broad news organization and
a spectacular advertising campaign. On billboards and in newspapers
unexploited fields could be reached by American goods and ideas so
that "peoples are not bound down through ignorance in a way so as
to be a potential menace to a world of enlightened democracy."[47] By
March 1919, advocates of an aggressive American position in the Far
East were suggesting to the State Department that "it would be well
to continue our propaganda activities, both as regards dissemination
of literary matter and the use of suitable films."[48] In this line, of special
future concern would be the struggle of the Federal Telegraph Company with Japan for radio concessions in China and the former German
rights to a vital Yap Island communication link.[49]

A Postwar Open Door, I: Siberian Experience

At the same time that the Creel Committee planned future communication with China it was involved in the immediate repercussions
of the 1917 Russian revolution.[50] The nature of this revolution and the
way it affected American attitudes toward the war and the Far East

46. See *Outlook,* CXI (Oct. 13, 1915), 375–78. Some of Crow's titles include
The Travelers' Handbook for China (1913, 1921); *Four Hundred Million Cus-
tomers* (1937); *I Speak for the Chinese* (1937); *Foreign Devils in the Flowery
Kingdom* (1940); and *China Takes Her Place* (1944). See also Rogers to Crow,
Sept. 17, 1918, and Crow to Creel, Dec. 10, 1918, both in R. G. 63, CPI 17/A2.
On Mildred's activities see *The World Outlook,* Aug. 1916, found in the William
E. Griffis Papers.

47. *Review of Reviews,* LIX (March 1919), 312. Julean Arnold to B. S. Cutler
of the Department of Commerce, July 17, 1918, R. G. 63, CPI 17/A2.

48. Alvey Adee to Harvey O'Higgins, March 7, 1919, R. G. 63, CPI 17/A2.

49. See SDDF 893.74/88, 92–100, 106a. Also Rogers to R. S. Baker, August
25, 1919, R. S. Baker Papers, series 2, container 97. On Yap Island see the Lansing
Papers, vol. 56.

50. Creel to Egan, March 30, 1918, Egan Papers. An excellent article is Claude
E. Fike, "The Influence of the Creel Committee and the American Red Cross on
Russian-American Relations, 1917–19," *Journal of Modern History,* XXI (June
1959), 95–109. Also Reinsch to Lansing, June 27, 1918, R. G. 63, CPI 17/A2,
and Creel to Polk, Feb. 6, 1918, SDDF 861.77/276.

has been much studied. In particular, as one observer has recently
noted, "a great deal of scholarly energies have recently been turned
on the subject of the Siberian intervention."[51] This project was, in
theory, a joint American-Japanese expedition organized in 1918 to
assist allied Czechoslovakian troops fighting their way to the Pacific.
In practice and in historical debate, the intervention has become the
subject of varied interpretations.

In terms of the shaping of American policy in the Far East, the
Siberian episode was the first incident, after the United States entered
the war, to call forth the traditional Open Door tension between
cooperative and competitive strategies. At home the world war produced a temporary victory for cooperation even with Japan. In China,
the emergency created and refined new competitive tactics. First
during the Siberian expedition and more seriously in the debate over
the Versailles peace of 1919 these alternatives to reach the widely
shared goals of the Open Door would once again be the subject of
conflict and compromise.

Descriptions of the Siberian intervention have suffered from the
difficulty of defining its demonology. Was it designed or carried out
to overthrow the Bolsheviks in Russia, to check the Japanese in the
Far East, or to defeat the Germans in the war? In part, of course, the
answer is all three. A better beginning is to view it as a positive effort
to further open the door. Part of the expedition was to be defensive.
Some seven thousand American troops were deployed in Siberia to
protect white girls who "in their extremity are selling themselves for
a consideration" and to free Russian-held Chinese "forced labor."[52]
More essential in studying the intervention, however, is to see these
troops as but the advance arm of an American "commission of mer-

---

51. This is the comment of William Neumann, *America Encounters Japan*,
p. 329. One recent work, Christopher Lasch, "American Intervention in Siberia:
A Reinterpretation," *Political Science Quarterly*, LXXVII (June 1962), 205–23,
makes an important prefatory distinction between the Siberian intervention and
another Allied strike into North Russia. I repeat it here: "That [North Russia]
was an entirely separate affair and was undertaken for quite different reasons. It
has never been as controversial as the Siberian expedition. . . ." For that reason
and because the focus of this study is the Far East, I, like Lasch, shall restrict
this discussion to Siberia.

52. Lansing to the American consul in Shanghai, Aug. 31, 1918, B. Long
Papers, box 179; the memoirs of DeWitt C. Poole in the Oral History Research
Project at Columbia University, III, 368.

chants, agricultural experts, labor advisors, Red Cross representatives, and agents of the Young Men's Christian Association" whom Wilson would send to relieve the immediate necessities of the people and educate them for the future.[53]

As early faith in Russia's revolutionary desires to be free turned into pessimism and disgust for bolshevism and "revolution as a mode of progressing," the expedition could keep the door open for American trade, investment, and reform not only in Siberia but in Russia itself. "There is an old tradition," Charles Crane advised Woodrow Wilson in August 1918, "that Russian will some day be saved by Siberia and I hope to have some word with Reinsch about it." Intervention, the minister agreed, could "save" Russia for the Allies.[54] To achieve this, another expedition of those interested in the future of American business and reform, such as Crane and John R. Mott, traveled to Russia under the leadership of Elihu Root in 1917. The aim as in the Siberian intervention was anti-Bolshevik—not pre-1905 or post-1945 fears of Russian expansion, but post-1917 hopes that America could reconstruct "a genuine Russia." Of those suggested for the Root Commission, many were businessmen; some, like Joseph Davies and George Rublee, had experience with the Federal Trade Commission. Apparently, as George Creel believed, "a genuine Russia" could be reconstructed only by those who understood trade organizations and had a "knowledge of the great basic industries."[55]

53. Wilson's cable to Secretary of War Newton D. Baker, July 23, 1918, R. S. Baker Papers, box 1, series 1.

54. American opinion toward the Russian Revolution has been studied by Christopher Lasch, The American Liberals and the Russian Revolution (New York: Columbia University Press, 1962). See the Diary of Colonel House, March 17, 1917, vol. 10, House Papers; Lansing to George Kennan, May 20, 1917, George Kennan Papers, box 4, LC; Crane to his daughter, Dec. 17, 1917, Crane Papers; and Reinsch to Lansing, May 9, 1918, B. Long Papers, box 179, for some changing opinions on the revolution.

55. Anti-Bolshevik roots of the intervention have been traced by William A. Williams. See his American-Russian Relations, 1781–1947 (New York: Rinehart, 1952) and the more recent articles, "American Intervention in Russia," which he wrote for Studies on the Left, vol. III (Fall 1963) and vol. IV (Winter 1964). Williams's conclusion is that the "action was anti-Bolshevik in origin and intent." Also tracing this problem is George F. Kennan, Soviet-American Relations, 1917–20 (Princeton: Princeton University Press, 1956, 1958); two volumes, Russia Leaves the War and The Decision to Intervene, are most important. In manuscripts for anti-Bolshevist roots see Crane to Wilson, March 21, June 21, 1917, Crane Papers; Eliot to Crane, Aug. 26, 1918, Crane Papers; Creel to Wilson, July 23, 1918, George Creel Papers, LC.

The anti-Bolshevik aims of the Siberian intervention were an expression of the goals of the Open Door policy and almost as widely shared. Anti-Japanese motivation, as might be expected, was the product of an aggressive and highly competitive campaign to reach those goals. What good would defeat of the Bolshevik revolution be if it left the Japanese a free hand, or so E. T. Williams and Tom Millard reasoned.[56] At first President Wilson remained reluctant to become involved in another military expedition. By midsummer of 1918 he became convinced that Japan acting alone might easily seize the Chinese Eastern railway in Siberia, convert its gauge to that of the South Manchurian line, and "swallow the whole Manchurian transportation system." To match the rumored seventy thousand Japanese troops, Americans were sent into Siberia. Of particular importance was a corps of top engineers under John Stevens who were ordered to guard supplies at Vladivostok and Archangel and to protect the Chinese Eastern from the Bolsheviks, the Japanese, and even the Germans.[57]

Anti-German origins of the Siberian expedition have received all too little attention. German aid to Russian revolutionaries and the separate peace of Brest-Litovsk were convincing arguments that Bolshevik success, if only by removing a threat on the eastern front, had been part of a German plot. "Bolshevism in Eastern Asia," the new magazine *Asia* reported, was a German threat. By the revolution in Russia the kaiser had opened his way to India. In the most striking example of how the Open Door had become the American frontier, John Foord wrote, "The Teuton in Asia, is the Teuton at our doors."[58] Fears of German benefit in Asia as a result of the Russian revolution

56. See E. T. Williams to Lansing, Feb. 25, 1918, B. Long Papers, box 179; Tom Millard to Crane, March 12, 1918, Crane Papers. The weight of publication has come down heavily on the side of an anti-Japanese motivation: consult two monographs—Betty Miller Unterberger, *America's Siberian Expedition, 1918–20* (Durham: Duke University Press, 1956) and John Albert White, *The Siberian Intervention* (Princeton: Princeton University Press, 1950).

57. American consul Caldwell in Vladivostok to Lansing, Aug. 26, 1918, SDDF 861.77/453. Also a conversation between P. P. Batolin and Breckinridge Long with Prof. Samuel Harper interpreting, in House Papers, Sept. 7, 1918, drawer 34, file no. 118; Newton D. Baker to W. Wilson, Nov. 27, 1918, R. S. Baker Papers, series 1, container 1. John Stevens to Lansing, March 28, 1918, B. Long Papers, box 179.

58. Anti-German roots have been picked up by Christopher Lasch, "American Intervention in Siberia: A Reinterpretation." For a contemporary fear of Germany read the pages of *Asia*, vol. XVIII, any month, especially April-July 1918.

were based on misconceptions and wartime hysteria difficult to comprehend. They allowed the Siberian intervention, however, to be seen by Robert Lansing and others in Washington as still another way to build a difficult but necessary international cooperation with Japan.[59] Less lucid or influential than a few years before, Theodore Roosevelt could still argue for cooperation more effectively than most. Fearing that Germany might organize Russia and through Austria and Turkey keep control of western Asia and southeastern Europe, Roosevelt anxiously advised the administration to aid Japan in taking temporary possession of eastern Siberia.[60]

Describing the Siberian intervention as well as the attitude of historians studying it, Robert Lansing later observed that the United States "did the best we could in an impossible situation." The best, as in virtually all conflict between competitive and cooperative strategies, was a compromise. Major troop concentrations might have been directed to check the Germans in the West and the Japanese in the East. The decision was made, however, to limit the force and use it to "rescue" Czech forces.[61] In the light of American entanglement in western Europe such a plan was realistic. It was also ambiguous enough to allow contemporaries and historians to take their choice as to the various villains of the piece. As was so often the case in a carefully structured compromise, it failed to defeat any of them, Russian, Japanese, or German.

This impossible situation provoked some of the first questioning of the nature of American policy. "If I had my own way about Russia," Secretary of War and former Cleveland mayor Newton D. Baker mused, "I would like to take everybody out of Russia except the Russians, including diplomatic representatives, military representatives, political agents, propagandists, and casual visitors and let the Russians

---

59. Beers, *Vain Endeavor*, ch. 10; Basil Miles to Lansing, Feb. 12, 1918, SDDF 861.77/290, and a note from David Francis, minister to Russia, Feb. 24, 1918, in SDDF 861.77/311.

60. Roosevelt to Straight, May 16, 1918, StrP.

61. Lansing to Kennan, Feb. 2, 1920, Kennan Papers, box 4; see the excellent memo of Breckinridge Long in his papers, box 187. Also the aide memoirs, "The American Policy in Siberia," July 17, 1918, in *Papers Relating to the Foreign Policy of the United States, Russia, 1918* (Washington: Government Printing Office), II, 287–90.

settle down and settle their own affairs." By his own admission "this of course, is impossible."[62] To Baker, America's financial supremacy and the need to maintain it against Japan in the Far East overcame qualms that America should withdraw from Russia. Although he certainly did not apply it to China, Baker's untenable "own way" was among the period's most serious critical appraisals of the philosophy behind the Open Door policy.

Rather than Baker's wishful withdrawal, young diplomat William C. Bullitt questioned America's reluctance to go further in the Siberian intervention. Not sharing the growing disgust with the bloodthirsty Bolsheviks, Bullitt would not compromise anti-Japanese and anti-German attitudes but compete against both. Bullitt gazed into his crystal ball and announced, "We shall have to throw Japan out of Siberia some day." Going further he predicted that Japan and Prussia might form a militarist alliance. Still fighting one world war, Bullitt foresaw another when "the fight would be the cleanest thing in the world. The democracies of America, Russia, England, and France would be arrayed against the imperialistic autocracies of Germany and Japan. That fight," he mimicked Woodrow Wilson, "would indeed be for a new world order."[63]

After wartime years of separate preparation and training, the delicate balance of cooperation, competition, and compromise in shaping Far Eastern policy reappeared together in the decision to intervene in Siberia. In the process of making that decision two men questioned the traditional prewar pattern. One, Newton Baker, wondered why America need be involved at all. Another, William Bullitt, could not understand why the United States clung to a delicate, carefully balanced, and pacific foreign policy. Despite these criticisms, the prewar ingrained goals and tactics of the Open Door policy would be very much in evidence in attempting to solve the problem recognized as crucial since 1917, how to best structure a postwar Far East.

62. Newton D. Baker to W. Wilson, June 19, 1918, Newton D. Baker Papers, LC, box 8. Also in his papers see a speech he gave in Jersey City, Oct. 1916, on the Mexican revolution, box 244. Finally a letter to W. Wilson, Nov. 27, 1918, Newton D. Baker Papers, box 8.

63. William C. Bullitt to Frank Polk, March 2, 1918, Polk Papers, drawer 85, file no. 38.

A Postwar Open Door, II: Shantung Decision

To prepare for the problems of peace, a panel of government-sponsored experts known as The Inquiry studied the world situation and America's role in it. The general future of colonial administration and tariffs or the "Open Door around the world" was the domain of historians George Louis Beer and F. W. Taussig. The Far East became the particular sphere of journalists Walter Lippmann and Samuel Blythe, Clark University historian George Blakeslee, economist A. P. Winston, Reinsch protégé Stanley Hornbeck, and the virtually unknown Wolcott Pitkin.[64] In detailed studies of China's economic or transportation systems or general observations about international trade these scholars accomplished little save a restatement of the goals and logic of the Open Door. They supported this policy for it provided markets for material and money without imposing spheres of influence or empire on China. Indeed far from destroying Chinese integrity, Blythe praised the reforms and modernization the Open Door policy had achieved in China's political, financial, educational, and even postal systems. F. W. Taussig and The Inquiry staff were certain as had been the prewar "practical" peace adherents that the Open Door "is a plain and simple policy of a liberal sort. It may be described," observed the noted student of trade and tariffs, "as a sort of colonial disarmament."[65]

By stressing what businessmen, diplomats, and reformers had long understood as the goals of American policy before the war, The Inquiry revealed the relevance of these goals for Americans in any postwar settlement. In addition the reports suggested that debate between cooperation and competition would also continue to play a

64. Lawrence E. Gelfand, *The Inquiry: American Preparation for Peace, 1917–19* (New Haven: Yale University Press, 1963) pp. 63–65. Walter Lippmann to Newton D. Baker, March 20, 1918, Newton D. Baker Papers, box 6. The Inquiry papers are in the Yale University Library, New Haven, Conn. See a report of F. W. Taussig, "Colonial Tariffs and the Open Door," Inquiry Papers, box 28, folder 8. Taussig was a leading student of commercial relationships; see his *Principles of Economics* (1911) and his much cited *The Tariff History of the United States* (first published 1888). G. L. Beer was a distinguished student of English colonial policy; see his *British Colonial Policy, 1754–63* (1907) and *The Old Colonial System, 1660–1754* (1912).

65. Hornbeck's reports were originally prepared for the Carnegie Endowment for International Peace, Inquiry Papers, box 15, folder 9; Samuel Blythe's reports dated March 6, 1918, Inquiry Papers, box 15, folder 11.

major role after the war. Colonel House thought the experts might create a Philip Dru-like progressive program which would "leave the Open Door, rehabilitate China and satisfy Japan."[66] Young Wolcott Pitkin paid homage to the House-Lippmann creed of cooperative international action to prevent the further use of force. He could not hide his belief, however, that "this country acting alone" would be best "from the viewpoint of the Far East." Pitkin refused the House or Jacob Schiff idea of a "satisfied" or "big brother" Japan. Looking toward the Versailles conference, Pitkin warned as many, like Tom Millard, had since 1905 that "Japan is clearly the most dangerous element in the Far Eastern situation."[67]

The most serious confrontation over this Far Eastern situation since 1913, perhaps since 1899, came in the debate and defeat of Woodrow Wilson's Versailles peace treaty in the summer and fall of 1919. To realize postwar cooperation in a League of Nations, the president was willing to sacrifice his opposition to the harsh peace with Germany desired by England and France. More serious from the viewpoint of many Americans, he would also accept the inevitable Japanese claims to former German possessions in the province of Shantung.

The debate did not touch on the need for American commerce, investment, or reform in China but whether full cooperation was the way to achieve those. Early in 1917 the European allies decided that it was. Through secret treaties, much-debated at the war's end, Japan, in return for entering the fight, was promised its special interests in China including a share in the Chinese Eastern railway and the German sphere in Shantung. First published when the Bolsheviks tore open the Russian archives, these treaties were the subject of widespread rumor in the American press.[68] Wilson and Lansing both later asserted that their first knowledge of the existence of such documents came at Versailles in the spring of 1919. Both Walter Lippmann and Oswald Garrison Villard insisted, probably correctly, that the State Department and Colonel House knew enough about the treaties

66. House to Wilson, Sept. 18, 1917, cited by Gelfand, *The Inquiry*, p. 261, W. Wilson Papers, LC.

67. The unknown lawyer Pitkin was a curious choice; see his reports, Inquiry Papers, box 18, folder 5, and box 24, folder 12. Also Gelfand, *The Inquiry*, pp. 258–67.

68. E. T. Williams to Lansing, March 5, 1918, reports the Russo-Japanese treaty of July 3, 1916, Polk Papers, drawer 85, file no. 39.

in 1918 to have maps outlining their proposed territorial settlements. Before he went to Versailles, Lansing, if not Wilson, had been informed by E. T. Williams and Hornbeck that "agreements have been concluded (or under discussion) since the beginning of the war."[69] With Wilson's express opposition to such secret agreements a part of his wartime creed, the Fourteen Points, controversy over American knowledge of these treaties is an interesting but specious historical debate. Even if unknown, agreements with Japan were fully consonant with the State Department's cooperative stance during the war. "To give capital seeking joint investment, greater assurance of stability," these treaties would further enhance the financial cooperation of the second banking consortium.[70]

Paul Reinsch, however, had promised Shantung to China if it entered the war in 1917. As late as January 1919, in fact, American policy was to stand firm in denying Japanese territorial claims to the coastal province of Shantung which "in its strategic location south of Peking, would, with the Japanese control in Manchuria, leave Peking, Tientsin and the whole of the great gulf of Pechili, completely helpless."[71] At Versailles Wilson had to struggle to save the greater good of the League's cooperation. Having come full circle from his 1912 defense of regulated competition, the president saw his structure threatened by an Italian withdrawal after failure to satisfy its irredentist territorial claims. A premature death for the League of Nations was a possibility if Japan followed Italy, as indeed it seemed likely when a pledge for racial equality was blocked by the English. In the most classic confrontation between the logic of cooperation and the challenge of Japan, all concerned agreed that the crucial "decision lay with the President." On the advice of House and the English that the Japanese might walk out, Wilson made the decision on April 28 to allow Japanese claims in Shantung and Kiaochow. "It is all bad," the

69. Villard, *Fighting Years,* pp. 470–72; Walter Lippmann to Ray Stannard Baker, Jan. 2, 1922, R. S. Baker Papers, series 2, container 98. Lansing's Aug. 11, 1919, testimony to the Senate Foreign Relations Committee is revealing; Lansing Papers, vol. 45. B. Long to House, Feb, 1928, reviews the question, House Papers, drawer 12, file no. 36. Finally the reports of Williams and Hornbeck, Jan. 12, 1919, Lansing Papers, vols. 41–42.

70. Minister Guthrie to Lansing, Jan. 15, 1917, SDDF 793.94/593.

71. Wilson to Lansing, Feb. 3, 7, 1919, Lansing Papers, vols. 41–42; Lansing to Reinsch, June 17, 1918, B. Long Papers, box 179; a statement of American policy in House Papers, Jan. 30, 1919, drawer 30, file no. 108.

cooperation-minded House told Wilson. Yet, he added, "it is no worse than the things we are doing in many of the settlements in which the Western Powers are interested."[72]

Colonel House perceived the dilemma correctly. It was one other Americans had failed to solve. "We had best clean up a lot of old rubbish with the least friction," was his advice, "and let the League of Nations and the new era do the rest." Wilson agreed this could be done only by sacrificing anti-Japanese attitudes to secure cooperation. As he understood it, "the only hope was to keep the world together, get the League of Nations with Japan in it and try to secure justice for the Chinese not only as regarding Japan but England, France, Russia, all of whom had concessions in China." The president anxiously advised that his decision be seen as a cooperative defense of China and not an acquiescence to Japan's closing the door. He constantly reiterated that Viscount Uchida promised to hand back full sovereignty in Shantung to China once a special police force had been established and former German economic privileges in the settlement of Tsingtao secured. Despite this pledge, Ray Stannard Baker reported that of all the Versailles decisions the Shantung settlement worried Wilson most.[73]

A Postwar Open Door, III: Shantung Debate

The president's fears were well founded. Immediate opposition came from the Chinese delegation, especially the American-educated Wellington Koo. Denied official American advisors, the Chinese were being tutored by the Creel Committee's most aggressive anti-Japanese voice, Tom Millard. Millard's view, shared by Williams and Hornbeck, was that Wilson should "let the Japanese go home" rather than compromise

72. For the decision see Charles Seymour, *The Intimate Papers of Colonel House* (Boston: Houghton Mifflin, 1926), IV, 449–55, 469–70. These papers include vital letters from House to Wilson and from Wilson to Baker both dated April 29, 1919.

73. Ibid. Also in the W. Wilson Papers, file III-A, box 15; Robert Lansing, *The Peace Negotiations: A Personal Narrative* (Boston: Houghton Mifflin, 1921), ch. 18, "The Shantung Settlement," pp. 243–67. A good review appears in Herbert Hoover's *The Ordeal of Woodrow Wilson* (New York: McGraw-Hill, 1958), pp. 207–11.

America's freedom of action.[74] From Peking the leading spokesman of this competition-oriented group, minister Paul Reinsch "hesitated to believe" America could perpetuate "Prussianism" by handing over Shantung to Japan. In Reinsch's eyes, all his and America's work to bring China into the war, to create a peaceful industrial state, and even to guarantee "the future of our country" were to be sabotaged by Wilson's procooperation decision on the "cardinal question."[75]

Most worrisome, however, was the opposition of Wilson's own advisors. To Millard and Reinsch, Wilson had become another Taft, rejecting competition. To Lansing and Baker, he had become another Roosevelt, rejecting limited compromise. Ray Stannard Baker thought such compromise might involve joint American-Japanese agreement to settle for the postbellum reward of the elimination of a German menace from Far Eastern markets. Going further, Secretary of State Lansing broke with the president's decision to save the League but abandon China. The American commissioners, including Lansing, Gen. Tasker Bliss, and experienced diplomat Henry White were unwilling to openly rebel by resigning or refusing to sign. Privately they asked for stronger guarantees that the Japanese would return railways, mines, and ports in the province lest the Shantung decision be an "iniquitous agreement" for the future of the Open Door.[76]

The principals in the renewed consortium negotiations were among the few to accept Wilson's decision as a necessary evil in the pursuit of "standardization and unification," the higher goals of cooperation.[77] The New Republic, Willard Straight's magazine, wished many more

74. Polk to Lansing, Dec. 16, 1918, B. Long Papers, box 179; Tom Millard, "China's Case at the Peace Conference," Century Magazine, XCVII (April 1919), 797–802. Hornbeck to House, May 5, 1919, House Papers, drawer 30, file no. 11. An interesting anecdote appears in William Allen White, The Autobiography of William Allen White (New York: Macmillan, 1946), p. 556. See also Russell H. Fifield, Woodrow Wilson and the Far East: The Diplomacy of the Shantung Question, 1915–22 (New York: Thomas Y. Crowell, 1952), p. 299.

75. See a stream of Reinsch to Lansing letters, Jan. 14, 1918, B. Long Papers, box 179; Feb. 24, 1919, May 6, 16, 1919, SDDF 793.94/767, 816, 819. Also Reinsch to Polk, April 11, 1919, Polk Papers, drawer 74, file no. 59.

76. For Baker see his papers, series 2, container 97; Lansing, Peace Negotiations, reports Bliss's comments as well as the author's own attitude, pp. 256, 259, 264.

77. H. D. Marshall to B. Long, May 29, B. Long Papers, box 180 (the whole file is worthwhile for the second consortium details). Also therein find George Whitney to H. D. Marshall, June 2, 1919. Lamont's Across World Frontiers, pp. 114–15.

thought that way. If only as much energy went into building a strong and capable League of Nations, the editors conjectured, as was presently spent denouncing Japan, the Shantung arrangement could be justified.[78]

No one worked harder than Woodrow Wilson to convert his own personal energy into the light he hoped would emanate from a League of Nations. At first the president did not mention the Shantung provision in asking the Senate, as he must, for its advice and consent on the Versailles treaty. Even in his early speeches on an extensive and exhausting western tour, made to elicit support for the treaty, Wilson alluded only briefly to Shantung. When he did, it was again in defense of the League and cooperation. "I do not like it any better than you do," he told a Des Moines audience in early September, but what was the alternative? Surely the answer was not to refuse the treaty, the League, and thereby a say in China's future.[79]

As the tour progressed, the president came more and more to stress not the league itself but the very future of China, the Open Door, and cooperation. In the treaty and on the tour, Wilson saw only John Chinaman's good side. In the fullest stereotype of the day, Chinese were "thoughtful, ancient, interesting, imaginative, industrious, accomplished, honest, learned, patient and diligent." They were also helpless and easily exploited by those too concerned with just the "Open Door to goods," be they American or foreign. Never dismissing the need for "our goods to be sold in those markets," Wilson stressed his long-held belief that America must sell reform as well. Through a League of Nations, reform would be genuine and lasting, for it would be internationally guaranteed. Just three days before he was stricken at Pueblo, Colorado, as a result of the strain of Versailles and after, the president symbolically vowed that to defend China, "I for one am ready to do anything, or," he added significantly, "to cooperate in anything in my power to be a friend."[80]

With equal determination Wilson's opponents in the Senate ratifica-

78. *New Republic*, XIX (May 17, 1919), 66; *Review of Reviews*, LIX (June 1919), 575, and LX (Oct. 1919), 349.

79. Wilson's speeches appear in his papers, file III-A, July 10, 1919, to the Senate, box 14, tour speeches, box 15, especially St. Louis—Sept. 5, Des Moines—Sept. 6, Helena—Sept. 11.

80. Ibid. Los Angeles—Sept. 20, Reno—Sept. 22, Salt Lake City—Sept. 23, Cheyenne—Sept. 24, and Denver—Sept. 25.

tion debate felt "it can't be right to do wrong even to make peace."[81]
Much has been written about the political and psychological foundations of the debate and Wilson's defeat at the hands of a coalition
of "irreconcilable" and milder "reservationist" critics of America's
role in a League of Nations.[82] In this literature some, focusing on the
Far East, go so far as to see Shantung more important "than any
other single issue." Others bend back the other way to view it as a
subordinate question. Given Wilson's growing attention to Shantung
on the tour, it may be said that the decision to sacrifice China was,
as Russell Fifield notes, "a significant factor in the rejection of the
Treaty of Versailles in the Senate of the United States."[83]

It was also a symbolic factor. The *New Republic* thought Shantung
gave anti-Wilson Republican forces a moral issue symbolizing "the
whole failure at Paris."[84] Beyond personal or party hostility, the debate
mirrored the persistent tension between cooperation and competition.
The League of Nations was the clear victory of the forces of international cooperation. Japanese demands for Shantung became then the
inevitable example of a requisite and unacceptable concession to keep
that cooperation alive. The ranks of the irreconcilables, those who
would accept nothing short of full competition at home and abroad,
were, as they had been since 1909, vocal but small. Those who would
compromise, the reservationists in the syntax of the ratification debate,
were in the majority. Woodrow Wilson had surely been with them at
Versailles. Having gotten so close to the cooperative goal, the tragedy
and uniqueness of the man was his inability of compromise further
in the final crucial moments.

81. Tasker Bliss, April 29, 1919, R. S. Baker Papers, series 1, container 1.

82. The classic, recently released, but more-dated study is the William C. Bullitt
–Sigmund Freud treatment of Wilson. *Thomas Woodrow Wilson: Twenty-Eighth
President of the United States, A Psychological Study* (Boston: Houghton Mifflin,
1932 and 1967.)

83. Powell, *Twenty-Five Years in China*, p. 71, and Wen-hwan Ma, *American
Policy Toward China as Revealed in the Debates of Congress* (Shanghai: Kelly
and Walsh, 1934), both feel Shantung was decisive. Robert Hosack, "The Shan-
tung Question and the Senate," *South Atlantic Quarterly*, XLIII (April 1944),
181–94 takes the view that it was unimportant. The role of public opinion and
Shantung is highlighted in John Morton Blum's *Joe Tumulty and the Wilson Era*
(Boston: Houghton Mifflin, 1951), p. 181. Finally see Fifield, *Wilson and the Far
East*, p. x.

84. *New Republic*, XIX (July 30, 1919), 404–09.

With student riots throughout China, advocates of an independent American role, such as Reinsch, Hornbeck, Millard, and even members of the YMCA in China, pleaded with the Senate to reject the Shantung provision and the entrenchment of a Japanese "Prussia" in China.[85] Their protests registered sharply with those irreconcilables or competitors in the Senate such as Borah, La Follette, George Norris of Nebraska, and Hiram Johnson of California. These men opposed the League in principle. They would certainly brook no compromise let alone cooperation with the mistrusted Japanese when a territory they liked to describe as being "as big as Illinois" was at stake.[86]

Norris, Borah, and their allies dominated the headlines by parading opponents of the League and the Shantung cession, including even Secretary of State Robert Lansing, before summertime hearings of the Senate Foreign Relations Committee.[87] Throughout these sessions and the October floor debate, however, the groundwork for compromise was being readied. The forty-five amendments proposed by Henry Cabot Lodge as chairman of the Foreign Relations Committee, especially the six on Shantung, bore the definite stamp of a man schooled in compromise, the former secretary of state and now senator, Philander Knox.[88] To compromise, the committee would simply substitute China for Japan in the Shantung section thus denying the Japanese an official sovereignty which even the Germans never possessed. Knox and Lansing agreed that Wilson exaggerated Japan's reluctance to sign without an outright cession of Shantung. The solution allowed the League to survive, America to save its soul and Japan to maintain its unstated but implied special interest in China.

85. Reinsch to Lansing, June 9, 1919, SDDF 793.94/928. Reinsch to Lansing, Oct. 10, 1919, Lansing Papers, vol. 47. Hornbeck to Lansing, July 12, 1919, also Lansing Papers, vol. 47. See the papers of Yale-in-China, Dec. 1919, for reports of student unrest in China, Yale-in-China Papers, Yale University Library, New Haven, Conn.

86. Tom Millard to Sen. Hiram Johnson, Lansing Papers, vol. 44; Sen. Secretary George A. Sanderson to Wilson, Aug. 18, 1919, SDDF 793.94/962. Wen-hwan Ma, *American Policy Toward China*, p. 247. *New York Tribune*, July 20, 1919, and George Norris, *Fighting Liberal* (New York: Macmillan, 1945), pp. 208–10.

87. On the Senate Foreign Relations Committee, Lansing Papers, vol. 45; W. Wilson Papers, file III-A, box 15; Fifield, *Wilson and the Far East*, pp. 341–45; Hosack, "The Shantung Question and the Senate."

88. Philander Knox to Huntington Wilson, Nov. 6, 1919, H. Wilson Papers, Ursinus College Library, Collegeville, Pa.

Jeremiah Jenks, who for almost two decades had been struggling with this problem of cooperation and competition, expressed the proposed give-and-take. "If the Senate amendment should be adopted," he wrote Lansing, "it would deprive the Japanese, so far as the United States influence goes, of any legal title. . . . Even with that large deduction," Jenks continued, "the Japanese of course would possess far more property that could be used for business purposes than the citizens of any other nation except China."[89]

Even this compromise, which would have provided de facto if not de jure cooperation, was unacceptable to Wilson, who ironically had begun his own administration by striking down the cooperative structure his predecessor had built. With the president marshaling enough Democratic votes in the Senate, the committee amendments were defeated as were further efforts to strike references to Shantung. By his own irreconcilable position on these amendments or later reservations, Wilson stymied a possible compromise over the League, drove the reservationists into outright opposition and caused the defeat of his treaty in the Senate.[90] By doing so, this time by his opposition and not by his support, the president gave competition its greatest triumph since his own decision to withdraw from the consortium in 1913.

Woodrow Wilson proved at the cost of his own health that he could temporarily block compromise over the League. This was not a permanent setback by any means. Indeed Wilson's failure meant the continued importance of compromise between the two alternative strategies in structuring Open Door policy. Lacking a new world order or a new leader, Americans sailing in search of China's "unparalleled opportunity" had to draw on the experience of the war and pre-war years. This was true of those like John Dewey who ventured west for the first time after the war, or of old hands such as Charles Crane returning to the scene of their earlier hopes and failures.

Based on past experience a continued tension and compromise could be predicted between a cooperative strategy, successfully tested by wartime organization and a competitive tradition, clearly not one of

89. Jeremiah Jenks to Lansing, Sept. 20, 1919, SDDF 793.94/1016.

90. The Senate debate is one of the most interesting and important found in the *Congressional Record*. Debate on Secs. 156–58 of the treaty or Senate Resolution 122 took place between July 15 and Oct. 16. U. S., Congress, 66th Cong., 1st Sess., *Congressional Record*, vol. 58, pp. 2579–7013.

war's victims. Most certainly it would include the constant challenge of Japan in China. Finally, as should never be forgotten, such tension and compromise concerned, even during the heated Shantung debate, only the means to an end. The dream of the Open Door survived even the trauma of war.[91] The dangers of the struggle indeed intensified belief that not just China's but America's future was at stake in the Far East. "If America can't sell her goods," Assistant Secretary of State Breckinridge Long worried in November 1919, "stagnation will result here, factories will close, wages will drop, prices will rise, cold and hunger will prevail, and the prevailing unrest will grow to open disorder."[92] A man, who, like others, would take the lessons of the war into the next few decades, had written the epitaph of one period and the preface to the next.

91. The memoirs of Nelson T. Johnson, Oral History Research Project, Columbia University, III, 554–56.

92. Breckinridge Long to Rear Admiral Cary T. Grayson, Nov. 29, 1919, House Papers, drawer 12, file no. 35.

7

Since Yesterday
From Versailles to the American Century

WOODROW WILSON's decision to allow the Japanese temporary possession of Shantung drove Paul Reinsch into a self-imposed exile as legal advisor to the Chinese. It also gave Charles Crane his long-denied chance to be minister to China. In Peking, as Philander Knox and Huntington Wilson had feared, Crane was his usual garrulous self. His statements, however, were hardly as controversial as they were perceptive. The man who was president of the Municipal Voters League and advisor on China policy told the tale on progressivism and the Open Door.

"The most important things going on, religious, educational, scientific, political," he informed Harvard's Charles Eliot, "were exactly the sort of things we had been doing all our lives in Chicago." In addition to recognizing the great similarity in goals and methods at home and abroad since John Hay and Theodore Roosevelt, Crane felt that new blood and new ideas were needed. The visit of Mr. and Mrs. John Dewey, the minister thought, was "fine testimony of the changes going on in China," since the educator and his wife were "the most influential foreigners here." Crane certainly would not dismiss, however, the lessons he and his generation had learned in the Far East. In a move revealing the continuity as well as the change in China, the minister suggested Paul Reinsch's protégé Stanley Hornbeck for a

Harvard post. This young political scientist, according to Crane, had a "lot of material to pass on the to the next generation."[1]

In the years following the world war and the defeat of Wilson's League of Nations in the United States, traditional American policy and problems in the Far East were restated if not reexamined. As Charles Crane understood, this postwar period, sometimes styled a return to normalcy at home, would witness a perpetuation of the link between domestic and diplomatic attitudes and actions. Some, like Dewey, would go to the Far East for the first time, deeply imbued with a faith in America's future. Others, more experienced in those environs, though still young and optimistic, would remain concerned with the continuing tactical debate between cooperation and competition. Perhaps most important, Crane, Dewey, Hornbeck, and so many others shared a faith in America's goals and role, a belief in their ability to compromise and a knack for dismissing fears that, for all their effort, they might fail.

Our Man in Peking, Finally

Charles Crane's 1920 appointment met with little of the fanfare and controversy that greeted his 1909 selection. It was, the *Nation* reported, a "most helpful move," perhaps "saving" Asia from the vacuum following the League's defeat. The new minister was the same outspoken man who had almost gone in 1909. World war had only restrengthened his resolve to carve a unique American role in the Far East. Interpreting recent history for President Wilson, Crane had observed in 1917 that "we went into a war to free Cuba and came out of it with heavy responsibility in the Philippines. The present war is vastly greater and we may come out of it with vastly greater responsibilities."[2] Just how the responsibility might be greater was an interesting, indeed provocative, question in the postwar period. Nevertheless

1. Once again the Charles Crane Papers, held privately in New York by Crane's son, are invaluable. See Crane to Dr. Charles Eliot, June 21, 1921; Crane to his daughter (JCB), June 21, 1921; and Crane to Archibald Cary Coolidge, Dec. 28, 1920, all in the Crane Papers.

2. *Nation*, CX (April 3, 1920), 413; Crane to Woodrow Wilson, June 21, 1917, Crane Papers. E. David Cronon, ed., *The Cabinet Diaries of Josephus Daniels, 1913–21* (Lincoln: University of Nebraska Press, 1963), p. 515.

the intention shared by Crane and America remained the export of business and reform. In the pursuit of "progress and efficiency" Crane emphasized the part American science, engineering, medicine, education, and religion could take in China. In fact, on his arrival in 1920, Crane planned a momentous show to pit the "evil" Japan against "progressive" America.

"We have a great role to play here," the minister instructed. "It is all perfectly clear; it is a role we can play, and a role that is entirely American and cannot be counterfeited by any other nation."[3] Forty million starving Chinese provided the tragic setting around which Crane hoped to reunite the now well-known stars of the Hwai River conservancy such as engineers, bankers, and the Red Cross in a new project of famine relief.

At first the American National Red Cross had been buying and transporting some fifteen thousand tons of grain to feed the starving masses. Crane's inspiration was to convert this relief into payment for Chinese labor on a reawakened river-reclamation plan.[4] This cheap and efficient labor could be housed in "cheap movable shacks" and employed building roads, railways, and dams. Through large-scale public works programs, Crane hoped his show might transform the Chinese character. Soon the workers would have "the ability to organize" and "the pride in achievement" necessary to create "a self-reliant, progressive power." The relief projects even might "form the nucleus of a movement for unifying China politically."[5]

As expected in any Crane plan, Americans would be the chief actors and beneficiaries. Red Cross and YMCA volunteers would be present along with American engineers such as Brown-in-China repre-

3. See Crane to David F. Houston, July 19, 1920, and Crane to Dr. Eliot, April 28, 1920, both in the Crane Papers. Also Crane's "Memoirs," p. 247, an unpublished manuscript also in the Crane Papers.

4. Ralph A. Graves, "Fearful Famines of the Past," *National Geographic Magazine*, XXXII (July 1917), 89; see the "Report of the China Famine Relief," dated Oct. 1920 to Sept. 1921, in the American National Red Cross Library, Washington, D. C. Also J. E. Baker to the Red Cross, Director of Foreign Operations, Nov. 30, 1920, Red Cross File 898.5.

5. The International Reform Bureau to Woodrow Wilson, Feb. 4, 1921, State Dept. Decimal File (hereafter cited as SDDF) 893.48g/107. "Report of the China Famine Relief," p. 8; Crane to Dr. Eliot, Feb. 5, 1921, Crane Papers. On the idea of works-projects and their domestic application see Paul Reinsch to Robert Lansing, Oct. 26, 1917, SDDF 893.48/75.

sentative John Freeman whose job was to divert the Yellow River for irrigation.[6] Star-billing in the show remained the property of American bankers who, in Crane's theater lexicon, could use the famine relief as "the full dress rehearsal of the consortium principles." In particular Thomas Lamont, John Jay Abbott, Frank Vanderlip, James Stillman, and Mortimer Schiff were featured players. Once listed in the beginning as the American China Development Company, these second consortium bankers appeared on Crane's program as the Red Cross American Committee for China Famine Relief.[7]

The famine relief idea seemed to satisfy many diverse interests. Commercial and shipping concerns saw the chance to supply needed materials. For comic relief even the Wrigley Chewing Gum Company thought it might save starving Chinese with forty-nine cases of its finest product.[8] Railway and banking groups had visions of famine relief as a "moral investment" finishing old projects and starting new ones.[9] Agricultural reform groups thought the time had finally arrived for the wholesale extension of reforestation, irrigation, and seed selection programs in China.[10] On China's perenially magic stage, the famine relief idea was to be the epitome of the kind of adventures America could produce.

It would be in the "interest of America" and the "welfare of China,"

6. See a report on the Foochow cholera epidemic in the Red Cross File 898.5. A general Wilson notice on the famine relief, 1920, Woodrow Wilson Papers, file III-A, box 15, Library of Congress (hereafter cited as LC). On John Freeman see his folder in the Yale-in-China Papers, Dec. 17, 1920, Yale University Library, New Haven, Conn.; Crane to the State Department, Oct. 4, 1920, SDDF 893.48g/3, and Bainbridge Colby to John Stevens, Oct. 4, 1920, SDDF 893.48g/10a.

7. Reinsch to Lansing, Feb. 23, 1918, SDDF 893.48/83; the American Committee for China Famine Fund to Norman Davis, Jan. 15, 1921, SDDF 893.48g/101, and Crane to Eliot, June 21, 1921, Crane Papers. Crane's exact words were: "I planned not only to take care of the famine but to give a kind of full-dress rehearsal of the consortium principles."

8. Frank Polk to Reinsch, July 26, 1918, Breckinridge Long Papers, box 179, LC; *Asia*, XVIII (Nov. 1918), 859–64. The Wrigley plan is discussed in the Red Cross, "Report of the China Famine Relief," p. 233.

9. Crane to Sec. of State Charles Evans Hughes, May 26, 1921, SDDF 861.77/2088, discusses future plans for the Chinese Eastern Railway. Roger Williams to Crane, Jan. 25, 1921, Crane Papers.

10. See *Review of Reviews*, LX (Nov. 1919), 515–18 and *Asia*, XIX (Nov. 1919). Also see the papers of the Red Cross, North China Famine, 1920–21, Finance and Accounts, file 898.5/2.

Crane thought, if a whole series of such projects could establish a national system, technical organization, and progressive government in China. The metaphor of Crane's show was later reworked at home in depression public works projects. It reveals the leitmotif linking progressivism and the Open Door. Through welfare and educational reforms, Americans sought "the advancement of modern business adminstrative methods, . . . general progress, . . . and the matchless opportunity for the development of manufacturing enterprises."[11] Consul General Thomas Sammons best summarized these goals when he advised that American reforms in China must have a rank-order of priorities. "While it is most important to carry out a systematic educational program," Sammons began, "it is of the most urgent importance for the progressive Chinese to master the details of modern administrative procedures." Then, he concluded, the goal would be reached as "the foreign commercial possibilities of the country may receive the most desirable and constructive attention."[12]

For all the support it received, the famine relief never got beyond Crane's dress rehearsal. It conflicted with a remarkably similar project of Herbert Hoover, the feeding of thirty million war-starved European children.[13] More devastating than the publicity battle with Hoover's work was a feud among the chief participants of the China famine relief project. Crane felt the moral of the whole show should be the impossibility of working together with the English and the Japanese. In a revealing aside in the midst of the proceedings, Crane ordered that American funds be placed with several banks on a week-to-week basis so that competition might breed the best interest rates.[14] To the minis-

11. Merle Curti's *American Philanthropy Abroad: A History* (New Brunswick: Rutgers University Press, 1963), pp. 348–53, fails to understand the economic motivation behind the desire to spread reform but is still one of the few broad studies of America's parental role in China. See Crane to President J. Leighton Stuart of Peking University, June 11, 1921, Crane Papers. A report by D. M. Brodie, Autumn 1921, in the Crane Papers, and *New Republic*, XIX (May 10, 1919), 45–47.

12. Thomas Sammons's statement, Oct. 10, 1919, SDDF 693.001/151.

13. Crane to Wilson, Sept. 22, 1920, Crane Papers; Roger Williams to Crane, Jan. 25, 1921, Crane Papers; and William Howard Taft to Mabel T. Boardman, Nov. 28, 1920, Mabel Boardman Papers, LC. It appears that the famine relief, unlike the Hwai project, was Crane's and not Miss Boardman's show.

14. Crane, "Memoirs," p. 156; Crane to Norman Hapgood, Dec. 10, 1920, Crane Papers; Eliot to Crane, March 10, 1921, Crane Papers. Crane to Sec. of State Bainbridge Colby, March 23, 1921, SDDF 793.94/1170; Tom Millard to Crane, March 4, 1918, SDDF 893.48/87; and the very important two-bank plan of Crane in a letter of his to Colby, Jan. 11, 1921, SDDF 893.48g/88.

ter and his long-time associate Tom Millard, the famine relief was an allegory designed to show the advantages of competition and the uniqueness of aggressive, independent American action.[15] To the bankers involved, the object was the opposite: increased cooperation with all consortium partners, including Japan.[16] A parable of America's policy dilemma since 1905, the famine relief project appealed to all interested in commerce, investment, and reform in China. Some of those excited by the proposal favored competition, others cooperation. Rather than the potentially powerful project intended, the famine relief idea suffered from confusion and chaos over the means to be employed in staging Crane's show.

An Innocent Abroad

While Crane's plans floundered, philosopher and educator John Dewey was observing what he later described as his own "characters and events" in China.[17] Traveling and teaching in the Far East, Dewey symbolized a large group of Americans, mostly reformers, who had joined together during the war to form the League of Free Nations Association. Supporters of Wilson's effort to construct a liberal world, this group remodeled itself into the Foreign Policy Association after the war.[18] Like Dewey, historian Charles Beard, Herbert Croly, and Lillian Wald they had been involved in domestic and international reform movements for at least two decades. They lacked, however, specific knowledge of the Far East possessed by China hands such as Crane or Jeremiah Jenks. Conscious of new roads, both macadam and

15. Crane to Archibald Cary Coolidge, Dec. 28, 1920, and Crane to Eliot, June 21, 1921, both in the Crane Papers. Also the International Reform Bureau to Wilson, Feb. 4, 1921, SDDF 893.48g/107.

16. Hughes to Crane, March 29, 1921, SDDF 893.74/106a. Martin Egan to Frederick W. Stevens, Aug. 16, 1920, Martin Egan Papers, held privately by Egan's wife in New York. Charles A. Stone to Colby, Feb. 14, 1921, SDDF 893.811/386, and J. P. Morgan to Colby, Oct. 23, 1920, SDDF 893.48g/20.

17. John Dewey later wrote some essays in social and political philosophy, collected and titled *Characters and Events* (New York: Henry Holt, 1929). There are two volumes; vol. I, book II, chs. 4–17, pp. 170–323 deals with China.

18. There is much good information on the League of Free Nations Association in the Lillian Wald Papers, file case no. 3, drawer no. 2, New York Public Library; see a later publication of the Foreign Policy Association simply titled *Ten Years of the Foreign Policy Association*. Subsequent revisions were made following this original volume which covers the decade 1918–1928. The F.P.A., right down to the present, is badly in need of historical study.

cultural, leading from "Washington to Europe, to Latin America and China," the FPA was established to raise the level of knowledge about China.

Into the 1920s, Americans often learned little about China beyond the clever luncheon banter that America had given China light, heat, and power in the Standard Oil Company, the American Tobacco Company, and missionaries while China reciprocated with cleanliness, heat, and power through laundries, chop suey, and students.[19] Many, such as Lillian Wald or Mabel Boardman, had traveled to China before. Postwar visitors such as Jane Addams and Dewey were to be more students than sightseers, more teachers than tourists.[20] After the turmoil of war, the opportunity was present for a philosopher of Dewey's perceptivity to question and perhaps restructure American attitudes about China. Yet Dewey's experience in the Far East produced few new insights. Rather it resulted in a restatement of the problems and answers of the past.

John Dewey's thinking about China underwent a change between 1919 and 1921. It was, however, the same change others had undergone at least fifteen years earlier. Through a steady stream of articles and letters, those at home could follow the familiar metamorphosis. Dewey arrived in Japan in the summer of 1919 planning a three-month stay there and a brief visit to China. He stayed almost two years in the Far East, nearly all of it in China, at Peking University. His first and most lasting impression prompted the schedule change. China, as it had been to earlier American visitors, was a wonderland. "Simply as an intellectual spectacle, a scene for study and surmise," Dewey wrote for *Asia*, "nothing in the world today, not even Europe in the throes of reconstruction, equals China."[21] Just like those faced in 1905 with boycotts and financial fiascos, Dewey could not help but be struck by the gap between the potential and the realized opportunity. The "rotten, crumbling remnant" he visited and studied was charac-

19. This analysis was made by Dr. PingWen Kuo of the World Federation of Educational Associations and is reported in "Conflict of Policies in China," a publication of the Foreign Policy Association dated 1925 and found in the Library of Congress.

20. Urban Whitaker, Jr., "Americans and Chinese Political Problems, 1912–23" (Ph.D diss., University of Washington, 1954), ch. 6, "Tourists."

21. An excellent beginning to a study of Dewey in the Far East is Thomas Berry, "Dewey's Influence in China," in John Blewett, ed., *John Dewey: His Thought and Influence* (New York: Fordham University Press, 1960), pp. 199–231.

terized by "educational backwardness . . . physical degeneration . . .
political corruption and lack of public spirit."[22]

The old, sleeping, drugged, Confucian China sparked in Dewey, as
it had in others, hope and not despair. Reform could produce a new,
awakened, scientific, pragmatic China. The great hope, the tool to
mold industrial and political progress was China's youth. Dewey opposed "the classicists in education" who "have a noble example here
in China of what their style of education can do if only kept up long
enough." He rejoiced at China's "unused resource," the mature, eager
students of Peking University. Even an American schooled in an age
of zealous urban reform could not believe the optimism of this "Young
China." Dewey conveyed his amazement to his own children. "To think
of kids in our country from fourteen on, taking the lead in starting
a big cleanup-reform-politics movement and shaming merchants and
professional men into joining them. This is sure some country."[23]

Such reform could be extended to industrial and social reorganization if only the American example was followed. As Willard Straight,
E. A. Ross, Paul Reinsch, and a score of others had known before him,
Dewey came to believe that the "United States as a nation is the
living embodiment of what the young Chinese hope China some day
will be."[24] Even his opposition to organized religion was overcome
in this reform effort. In China, Dewey confessed, missionaries led
by the YMCA had become social workers and Christianity truly a
social religion.[25]

As might be expected from one reliving the evolution of America's
policy after 1905, Dewey came to recognize the menace of Japan.
"I didn't ever expect to be a jingo," he apologized shortly after arriving, but the United States should "wash its hands entirely of the Eastern question" or be as positive and aggressive in calling Japan to
account.[26] Followed by Japan's secret service even though an honored

22. Fortunately Dewey's letters have also been published. See John and Alice
Dewey, *Letters From China and Japan* (New York: E. P. Dutton, 1920); in particular see two dated May 12 and June 2 for early impressions.

23. *New Republic*, XXI (Dec. 24, 1919), 117. Many of Dewey's pieces appeared
in the *New Republic* or *Asia*. See also Harold Isaacs, *Scratches on Our Minds:
American Images of China and India* (New York: John Day, 1958), pp. 51–52.

24. J. L. Childs to E. A. Ross, Aug. 7, 1921, YMCA National Headquarters
Library, New York, cites Dewey's work.

25. John and Alice Dewey, *Letters*, July 24, 1919.

26. Ibid., May 13, 1919.

guest, the American philosopher-king clearly chose the latter. Fifteen years after others had begun to recognize the same thing, Dewey agreed Japan had assumed the old Russian role in continuing China's nightmare. Convinced America and Japan were in a contest for "prestige and moral authority," Dewey violently opposed Wilson's Shantung decision.[27] In an American imagery that would have done William Jennings Bryan proud, Dewey likened Japanese control of the disputed province to their capture of Wilmington, Delaware, and the mainline of the Pennsylvania Railroad. The report that the Chinese at Versailles had actually refused to sign the treaty seemed "too good to be true," to the American visitor.[28]

Following the progression of American policy in an almost mystical way, by 1921 Dewey had retraced America's steps to the watershed of 1909. To that point he had rebuilt the foundation for a competitive, anti-Japanese position. Yet he also recognized that the crucial transition from an old to a young China would be possible only with a reform in China's finances. Suddenly it dawned on him that a cooperative mechanism, "some kind of international foreign control of finance," was not only a financial necessity, "but a political, industrial and moral necessity."[29] Dewey thus proved he could define the tension as well as the goals of American policy. How could the dilemma of Japan's ambitions and the logic of international financial cooperation be reconciled? Perhaps, he reasoned, the Japanese could not match American abilities to organize and handle financial matters on a large scale. Failing that, he hoped, Japan could be satisfied elsewhere.[30] Even for a

27. Reinsch to Lansing, June 5, 1919, SDDF 793.94/931, talks of Dewey and Japan. See Dewey's "The American Opportunity in China," *New Republic*, XXI (Dec. 3. 1919), 14–17, and also *New Republic*, XXIII (June 30, 1920), 145–47.

28. John Dewey, *China, Japan and the U.S.A.: Present-Day Conditions in the Far East and Their Bearing on the Washington Conference,* New Republic Pamphlet no. 1 (New York: Republic, 1921). John and Alice Dewey, *Letters,* July 2, 1919. An interesting treatment stressing Dewey's role in the Far East is Warren I. Cohen, "America and the May Fourth Movement: The Response to Chinese Nationalism, 1917–1921," *Pacific Historical Review,* XXXV (Feb. 1966), 83–100.

29. Dewey did a piece for *Asia* titled "Young China and Old," May 1921. It may be found in his *Characters and Events,* I, 261.

30. As early as "The American Opportunity in China," *New Republic,* XXI (Dec. 3, 1919), 14–17, Dewey had been mulling over the subject of possible compromise with Japan.

logician of Dewey's talent there was still no anwer save warlike competition, unthinkable cooperation, or hopeful compromise.

In a work aptly titled *China, Japan and the U.S.A.*, John Dewey fell back upon the goals he understood to solve the dilemma he did not. The answer, as Americans had been telling themselves for two decades, must be found in the Open Door. This would be a commercial Open Door to be sure. "But the need is greater," Dewey concluded, in articles also appearing in the *New Republic*, "that the door be opened to light, to knowledge and understanding." Rather than brooding over failures and conflicts, Dewey optimistically urged Americans to apply the lessons learned in the schools, the cities, and even the battlefields of the early twentieth century. In search of a "new mind" and real communication, Americans could "work for the opened door of open diplomacy, of continuous and intelligent inquiry, of discussion free from propaganda."[31]

Charles Crane's show and John Dewey's metamorphosis symbolized two groups of Americans and their interest in China after 1919. The members of Crane's group were Chinahands, more experienced and concerned wtih continuing and compromising the tactical debate between competitive and cooperative strategies. The other group, Dewey, the Foreign Policy Association, and the new administration of Warren Harding, were more excited, at least at first, with the China dream than with the tension over tactics. Each group accepted the need for America's role in the Far East. Each served to structure America's China policy in the next few decades.

Competition, Cooperation, and Compromise

Some of the China hands were just beginning long careers in the State Department. Among these were Hornbeck, William Phillips, J. V. A. MacMurray, Warren Austin (an American International Corporation attorney and later ambassador to the United Nations), and John Leighton Stuart (a YMCA volunteer and future China ambassador). Not the least of these was Lansing's nephew John Foster Dulles, who at nineteen had been a secretary to the Chinese dele-

31. In conclusion again see Berry, "Dewey's Influence in China," p. 223. Also John Dewey, "Transforming the Mind of China," *Asia*, XIX (Nov. 1919), 1103–08 and Dewey, *China, Japan and the U.S.A.*, especially articles written in May and Oct. 1921.

gation at the 1907 Hague Peace Conference and later served as a young second consortium lawyer.[32] Others with more than a passing interest in the Orient, engineer Herbert Hoover and Franklin D. Roosevelt of the China-trade family of Delano, would become presidents.[33] Still others, including Colonel House, Frank Polk, Newton D. Baker, Philip Jessup (Elihu Root's law partner), and Henry Luce (a Yale-in-China offspring who became editor of *Time, Life,* and *Fortune*) would serve in advisory capacities on organizations such as the Institute of Pacific Relations. All looked back upon the beginning of the century as their years of growth, "an age almost of innocence— of youthful thrilling adventure."[34]

More often though they remembered that in their youth they first learned of conflict and disappointment as well as adventure. They recalled, and if not they were quickly reminded by Huntington Wilson or Tom Lamont, that "cooperation would certainly have a great deal of influence in steadying present international relations." Yet they also listened to George Bronson Rea's continued protest against international consortiums in the face of Japan's grip on East Asia. The task before these experienced China hands was twofold. They had to teach Rea that "American cooperation with Japan in China seems to have the unqualified support of the biggest interests of the United States." At the same time Lamont could not be allowed to forget that unrelenting Japanese pressure might force America to "revert to the old form of national and individual action in spite of all its disadvantages of competition and conflict."[35]

Finding the middle ground, the classic balance, the acceptable compromise was the legacy of the first two decades of the twentieth

32. John Leighton Stuart, *Fifty Years in China* (New York: Random House, 1946). John Foster Dulles to Lansing, Nov. 3, 1921, Lansing Papers, vol. 58, LC.

33. Isaacs, *Scratches on Our Minds,* pp. 168–71.

34. See the Colonel House Papers, drawer 32, file no. 184, and the Frank Polk Papers, drawer 86, file no. 37, both in Yale University Library, New Haven, Conn. Also J. V. A. MacMurray to Huntington Wilson, July 24, 1942, Huntington Wilson Papers, Ursinus College Library, Collegeville, Pa.

35. H. Wilson to William Phillips, and Phillips to H. Wilson, June 2, 1933, H. Wilson Papers. See also Huntington Wilson's review of F. V. Field's *American Participation in the China Consortiums* (Chicago: University of Chicago Press, published for the Institute of Pacific Relations, 1931), found in his papers at Ursinus College. See George Bronson Rea to Polk, Jan. 31, 1920, Polk Papers, drawer 77, file no. 46, and Rea to Lansing, Sept. 9, 1919, SDDF 793.94/1072.

century at home and in China.[36] Stanley Hornbeck became one of the best at it. Trained in an anti-Japanese, independent approach by Paul Reinsch, Hornbeck tempered his master's words. If not a League of Nations, at least, a "league of forces, economic and political" was necessary. Hornbeck proved unwilling, at least through the 1920s, to accept Reinsch's axiom that Japan must be driven out of China. To do that, Hornbeck decided, would be "playing Japan's game" and blocking any effective "clearing up" in the Far East. As chief of the Far Eastern Division in the 1930s, he worked to achieve order and peace through another consortium's efforts at railway and public utility building. He could never forget, however, the other side of the balance. "Sooner or later," Hornbeck wrote in 1919, "the Japanese will have to be made to understand that the United States is indeed earnest."[37]

The cooperative logic and the competitive tradition had been expressed as possible alternatives to open the door in China as early as 1907 by United States Steel's Judge Gary and Crane's friend Tom Millard. Some three decades later Stanley Hornbeck was still attempting to find a compromise satisfactory to both. In this effort he had a great deal of help. Two of the most active and experienced supporters of John Hay's Open Door policy, Jeremiah Jenks and John Hays Hammond, had made the broadest attempt to understand the cooperation-competition dilemma as it affected what they called the great American issues.[38] Like others involved in bringing business and reform to China, Jenks and Hammond were members and officers of both the American Asiatic Association and the National Civic Federation. Under the leadership of Mark Hanna and Samuel Gompers, this federation had been founded in 1900 to apply voluntary concilia-

36. One of the best studies of this "classic balance" is Sidney Fine, "Richard T. Ely, Forerunner of Progressivism, 1880–1901," *Mississippi Valley Historical Review*, XXXVII (March 1951), 599–624.

37. Hornbeck's ideas can be traced through *Trade Concessions, Investments, Conflict and Policy in the Far East,* an address delivered to the National Conference on Foreign Relations of the United States, Long Beach, New York, June 1917, found in the George Kennan Papers, box 85, LC; also Hornbeck to Reinsch, Sept. 5, 1921, Paul Reinsch Papers, State Historical Society of Wisconsin, Madison, Wisconsin; in 1934 Hornbeck's consortium plans appeared in SDDF 893.51, June 11; my thanks to Howard Jablon for sharing his research on this later period with me; finally, a note, July 12, 1919, in the Lansing Papers, vol. 44.

38. John Hays Hammond and Jeremiah Jenks, *Great American Issues: Political, Social, Economic* (New York: Charles Scribner's Sons, 1921).

tion to problems involving labor, management, and the public.[39] Jenks and Hammond followed this tripartite division, which they labeled social, economic, and political, in their postwar book. They brought with them more than just the organizational structure of the Civic Federation. Their book *Great American Issues* represented the fullest statement of the social, economic, and political foundations of progressivism at home and the Open Door in China. Like experienced China hands, the authors did not need to belabor the goals they had known so well and so long. In fact the watchword of their work was the need for practical not philosophical programs.

Each brought forth a pet "practical" project. Jenks stressed the idea of currency reform and Hammond the possibility of neutralization of China's railways. More important they defined the tension and the proposed solution of America's policy at home and in China. In a section headed "Competition and Monopoly," Jenks and Hammond urged a compromise guaranteeing efficiency, order, stability, and organization. These were to be voluntary, and not state-enforced. They were to be produced by more trade associations, business commissions, and foreign trade incorporation acts, such as the Webb-Pomerene bill.

In fact, a China trade act, to provide an incorporation law for exporters in the China market, had already been introduced in the Congress when Jenks and Hammond wrote.[40] To protect American business, to stretch the possibilities of cooperation without destroying antitrust safeguards, and to do it through a law breeding uniformity and stability were the continuing aims of Jenks, Hammond, Hornbeck, and other Americans who had grown up with China since 1900. The China Trade Act, passed in 1922, was a rare successful compromise. Yet it left many questions unanswered. Was it the beginning of an attempt to bypass a competitive tradition and achieve international cooperation? Or was it, as Robert La Follette under-

---

39. Recent research on the period has resurrected the National Civic Federation as an important and characteristic organization. For an older view of its origins see Oscar Straus, *Under Four Administrations: From Cleveland to Taft* (Boston: Houghton Mifflin, 1922), pp. 194–95.

40. Precedents for the China Trade Act can be found a decade earlier in State Department Numerical Files 14716 (1909) and 20930 (1910), where individual corporations sought government protection. The 1922 debate can be followed in Wen-hwan Ma, *American Policy Toward China as Revealed in the Debates of Congress* (Shanghai: Kelly and Walsh, 1934), pp. 219–27.

stood, a way to strengthen small business and improve America's competitive position against the English and the Japanese?[41] Alternative and ambiguous interpretations of the Open Door's proper tactical approach remained possible despite the perceptive and revealing words of Jenks and Hammond or the action of the Congress to organize and incorporate America's future in China.

The future would, of course, be greatly affected by Asian developments, such as the continued revolutionary disruption of China or the immense role of Japan which cannot be even roughly outlined in the scope of this study. Yet it need be noted that the tension and compromise over competition and cooperation which had developed between 1905 and 1921 must be understood to examine and generalize about continuities in American policy toward China in subsequent decades. John Hay's original Open Door note spoke only of commercial equality and opportunity. His second, following the Boxer rebellion, moved into questions of territorial sovereignty and integrity. Despite protests to the contrary and efforts to remain aloof from the teetering balance of power in Europe, America's commercial career had given it political responsibilities. The history of the period, 1905–1941, may be written, in part, as an effort to prevent this from meaning a military commitment as well. As early as 1913, Willard Straight realized that competition with Japan, an independent American position in the Far East, "would necessitate active military support."[42] Straight and the pre–World War I "practical" peace movement came to apply the logic of cooperation to conciliate Japan in order to prevent war. Down to 1941, American-Japanese relations were the catalyst for the continuing tactical debate between the alternative strategies of cooperation and competition. In other terms, however, those who would cooperate at home and abroad accepted an American share in the commercial and political future of the Far East. Those who would compete in the United States and China were more belligerent, willing to run the risk of a requisite military role

41. John B. Powell, *My Twenty-Five Years in China: 1917–42* (New York: Macmillan, 1945), pp. 67–69, has an interesting discussion of La Follette's anti-English orientation and his desire for America not to be outdone by the English through Hong Kong.

42. Paul Reinsch was one who protested that America had not adopted a political role; see his early note to Bryan, Dec. 2, 1913, Reinsch Papers. Willard Straight thought otherwise; see his Feb. 13, 1913, talk to a missionary group in the Goucher Papers, no. 521, Missionary Research Library, Union Theological Seminary, New York.

in support of an aggressive American position. The majority still sought a delicate compromise between extreme cooperation and competition, between America and Japan, and between the political and the military role. On December 7, 1941, it was demonstrated that compromise had failed.

Even after 1945, in the collective security basis of the United Nations and regional security pacts such as SEATO, and essentially unilateral involvements and interventions in Asia and elsewhere, the tactical schism of the Open Door was still much in evidence. Still alive also in post-World War II America was the debate at home between the pressure for consolidation, merger, and conglomeration and a viable competitive, antitrust tradition. It would be a speculative, though perhaps not hasty, generalization to surmise that the struggle between individual leaders, private organizations, and governmental departments for direction of more complex and powerful midcentury diplomacy continued to mirror the well-developed pattern of cooperative, competitive, and compromise approaches to American domestic and foreign policy.

Rhetoric and Stereotype in Wonderland

The most celebrated event of the early 1920s concerning the future of America and China was the Washington Naval Conference of 1921–22. Experts on China like Hornbeck were on hand. This meeting, however, belonged in spirit to new American leaders who were still novices in the Far East. Hornbeck and the China hands in the State Department attempted to steer Far Eastern policy down a different passage rather than veer towards either of two conflicting courses. The new administration of Warren Harding and Secretary of State Charles Evans Hughes was not skilled in the intricacies of navigation but could reassert its faith in the general direction America was heading.

Harding had an aunt who was a missionary and, as he told journalist John B. Powell, he "had always been curious about China." In fact, as China hand Powell liked to report, the president's aunt had been in India, never China.[43] In his all-too-common confusion, Harding was representative of other Americans, untutored about the distant and mysterious Orient. The president also spoke for these untutored Ameri-

43. Powell, *My Twenty-Five Years in China*, p. 63.

cans when he applauded the United States and China for what he felt was an unceasing and reciprocal friendship, confidence, and good will. Harding was as ignorant of the problems facing the Open Door policy as he was about his aunt's geography. Yet the president's belief in the friendship between the two countries combined with Secretary Hughes's idea of the need for "expansion into the potentially rich markets of China" to reinforce the Open Door policy as part of an America returned to "normalcy."[44]

The United States went to war in 1917 firmly believing in the Open Door policy. It came out of war with that belief unshaken but at least slightly sobered. Even this tempering effect was gone in 1921. Present at the Washington Conference, Robert Lansing, like Millard at Versailles, represented China and not America.[45] The conference saw Harding and Hughes trying to build their own Far Eastern policy in the image of John Hay. If Hay was first to state the Open Door policy as American dogma in the Far East, Hughes gave it a first real treaty definition.[46]

The arms limitations agreements produced at Washington were in keeping with the ideas of those working to compromise the tactical debate over the Open Door. They provided unity, coordination, organization, and an air of wary friendship between the United States and Japan.[47] In Hughes's terms, however, they were more important as a vitalization and legalization of Open Door goals than as carefully conceived compromise. The secretary trusted wholeheartedly in the commercial, financial, and reform aims of American policy.[48] Like John

44. Warren Harding's China ideas can be read in a statement prepared for the American Committee for China Famine Fund, March 29, 1921, Red Cross Papers, file 898.5/02. Charles Evans Hughes to J. P. Morgan, March 23, 1921, SDDF 893.51/3329.

45. Lansing to Alfred Sze and V. K. Wellington Koo, Feb. 18, 1922, Lansing Papers, vol. 59.

46. This is the position of J. Chal Vinson, "The Annulment of the Lansing-Ishii Agreement," *Pacific Historical Review*, XXVII (Feb. 1958), 57–69, and Paul H. Clyde, *United States Policy Toward China: Diplomatic and Public Documents, 1839–1939* (Durham: Duke University Press, 1940), pp. 281–90.

47. Such a position which he defines as the "syndication" of the Open Door is discussed by H. N. Brailsford, "A New Technique of Peace," *New Republic*, XXIX (Nov. 30, 1921), 12–15.

48. American Chamber of Commerce of China to Hughes, Sept. 14, 1921, SDDF 693.001/162, and a Hughes statement, 1921, SDDF 893.74/115.

Dewey he would rely on them and their constant invocation to overcome a dilemma he did not yet fully understand.

The idea that progress towards these goals at home and in China could solve all problems was best expressed on the eve of the conference by Sun Yat-sen.[49] Sun's career had many ironies. Schooled in American-style reform, especially that of single-tax spokesman Henry George, Sun was anxious to preserve Western civilization. Yet his anti-Manchu political revolution was fast becoming a social rebellion frightening to America's search for stability.[50] Despite alienation from much American support, Sun continued to understand the rhetoric and the logic of United States policy. Hughes traced his position back to John Hay. Sun could go all the way to Confucius, linking China in the Chow dynasty with America in the twentieth century. "When the great principle prevails the world will be a common possession of all men," he wrote to President Harding, "and there shall be no stratagems and intrigues; and there shall be an end to robbers and thieves; rebels and traitors; and the outer door of every house shall go unbarred."

The policy of Harding and Hughes was rooted in rhetoric and stereotype. This was equally true of most of the attitudes shaping the general direction of American policy in the Far East before, during, and after the Washington Conference. "We stand for the Open Door," read the *New Republic*'s creed on Asia. Such statements, without definition, were based on images such as that of the industrious, shrewd, peaceloving and friendly John Chinaman.[51] In this stereotyped thinking, China was an ancient civilization and would again be the center of the world. All that was needed was the regeneration of China's soul. This it was believed without question was America's role, duty, responsibility, and opportunity all rolled into one.[52] China and the future were synonyms in the American thesaurus. They were

49. See an address by Dr. Alfred Sze, 1922, Lansing Papers, vol. 59 and the most interesting letter Sun Yat-sen to Harding, Sept. 20, 1921, SDDF 793.94/ 1137–38.

50. Whitaker, "Americans and Chinese Political Problems," p. 40; Leonard Shih-lien Hsu, *Sun Yat-sen: His Political and Social Ideals* (Los Angeles: University of Southern California Press, 1933).

51. *New Republic*, XXVII (July 6, 1921), 154; for a typical image see Thomas Lamont, *Henry P. Davison* (New York: Harper & Brothers, 1933), pp. 170–71.

52. George D. Herron to Crane, Nov. 2, 1920, Crane Papers; Lebbeus Wilfley to Egan, Dec. 19, 1921, Egan Papers.

rarely used except with the most glowing and exaggerated adjectives. They were always linked to the role America could and should take.

Repeated disappointment in realizing this potential did little save to stir more spirited studies of how to succeed. China's art was displayed in American galleries, its capital remodeled in the image of the Chicago World's Fair's White City, and its civilization joined with the American in an "associated enterprise" designed to meet the industrial revolution.[53]

Not the least of this relationship was America's right to export its potential surplus of farm and factory. Of all the images of China, that of the great market for American goods was the strongest. The idea that the future of both countries would be secure only when tires made in Akron could roll on highways built by Americans in Asia survived even the Great Depression of the 1930s.[54] This image was an outgrowth of the belief in the need for an American frontier. As such it was more a necessity than an opportunity that brought America to China. "The trend of business in our country was, and yet is, westward," announced a 1932 National Foreign Trade Convention spokesman.[55] With the idea ever stronger after 1893 that the free land of the country was used up, a westward leap across the Pacific was natural.

Commercial expansion to China might satisfy Brooks Adams's geographical law of civilization, yet it could not by itself satiate the energy and zeal that had gone into domestic territorial expansion. Other all-encompassing images and frontiers were necessary at home. Perhaps the most viable was the belief in organization and rationalization, or as Warren Susman has put it, the gospel of "business efficiency

53. The State Department Decimal Files, like so many government documents, contain much collateral information. See April 11, 1921, 893.48g/172, for a discussion of an art exhibition and Feb. 9, 1912, 893.00/1154, for Sun's plan to bring Chicago architect Daniel Burnham to Nanking to remodel it in an American image. Charles Beard edited a collection of essays in 1928 titled *Whither Mankind* (New York: Longmans, Green, 1928). Among the contributors were Bertrand Russell, Julius Klein, the Webbs, Havelock Ellis, Lewis Mumford, John Dewey, Stuart Chase, and Carl Van Doren. The very first essay was by Chinese philosopher and American-educated Hu Shih who called for the "associated enterprise."

54. The most perceptive study of the persistence of the American stereotypes about China is William L. Neumann's "Determinism, Destiny and Myth in the American Image of China," in George L. Anderson, *Issues and Conflicts—Studies in Twentieth Century American Diplomacy* (Lawrence: University of Kansas Press, 1959), pp. 1–22.

55. Ibid., pp. 10–13.

as the new frontier."[56] To export not just goods and money but reforms, built around this efficiency, allowed Americans to conceive of a new manifest destiny. The old frontier was the West. The new one was efficiency. In China, America could have both. American engineers and philosophers of technology such as Thorstein Veblen focused their attention on the making of a new China. By applying the tool of technical education to the practical fields of forestry, horticulture, animal husbandry, metallurgy, paper manufacturing, and railway administration, to name a few, Americans in China could realize the future and both their frontiers.[57]

To some born in China like novelist Pearl Buck, "Asia was the real, the actual world and my own country became the dream-world,"[58] This was the exception. Usually the two countries were visualized in similar images, with China the *tabula rasa* making possible the westward expansion of America's civilization. Another American born in China, who founded *Life, Time,* and *Fortune* in the United States, best expressed the spirit of opportunity and responsibility learned in the Far East. Henry Luce grew up in his father's mission in China between 1898 and 1912. In the United States he managed the magazines and wrote the words that Willard Straight might have, had the boy-diplomat lived past 1918.[59] Straight and Luce agreed that the twentieth century was the American Century. "It is ours," Luce wrote in February 1941, "not only in the sense that we happen to live in it but ours also because it is America's first century as a dominant power

56. Warren Susman, "The Useless Past: American Intellectuals and the Frontier Thesis, 1910–1930," *Bucknell Review,* XI (March 1963), 1–20. Mention of the work of Louis Galambos should be made again; see ch. 2.

57. There is a great bulk of information on the engineering ethos. Joseph Dorfman, *Thorstein Veblen and His America* (New York: Viking Press, 1934, 1961), pp. 360–61, cites Veblen's 1917 concern with China, the war, and the future peace. See SDDF 693.001/167; Thomas Sammons to the State Department, 1916, SDDF 493.11/604; the John R. Mott Papers, B699.1, Yale Divinity School Library, New Haven, Conn.; "American Help in Chinese Technical Education," *Journal of the Association of Chinese and American Engineers,* II (July 1921), 2–4, and a 1924 YMCA pamphlet "Makers of New China in College in America," YMCA Library.

58. Pearl Buck, *My Several Worlds: A Personal Record* (New York: John Day, 1954), pp. 89–90.

59. Herbert Croly, *Willard Straight* (New York: Macmillan, 1924), p. 469, suggests that Straight would have returned to edit a newspaper or magazine.

in the world."[60] Henry Luce lectured Americans on the need for all-out participation in the Second World War. Yet, Luce's essay, "The American Century," was far more than an interventionist tract. It was an appeal to get in and get out of war with Germany in order to face the opportunity ahead. Luce dismissed the belief in a tradition of American isolationism. In doing so, he defined "America's Vision of Our World" in terms so common in the China of his boyhood. "First," he began, was "the economic." America must defend free enterprise and demand dynamic world trade. His entire conception of this American Century grew from the image of the China market.[61] Americans think of Asia, Luce argued, "as being worth only a few hundred millions a year to us." In fact, Asia was a virtual index of America's manhood. In this century "it will be worth to us exactly zero or else it will be worth to us four, five, ten billions of dollars a year. And the latter are the terms we must think in, or else confess a pitiful impotence."

Such trade was not just economic but "has within it the possibilities of such enormous human progress as to stagger the imagination." Americans, like Luce and his father, wished to "create the world of the Twentieth Century." Sounding like Woodrow Wilson or George Creel, Luce would send "engineers, scientists, doctors, movie men, makers of entertainment, developers of airlines, builders of roads, teachers, educators" throughout the world. "We must undertake now," he concluded, "to be the Good Samaritan of the entire world." The world leadership Luce sought for America had its roots in the effort to import business and reform into China between 1900 and 1920. If successful, the American Century would see the Open Door around the world.

The shady side of John Chinaman's image was present though subdued in what Harold Isaacs describes as the early American Century's Age of Benevolence towards China. The standard stereotype of a gambling, graft-ridden, and inefficient China remained for all to see. George Creel, a precursor of the public relations or image-building agent, drew the best vernacular word-picture of the stereotyped

60. "The American Century" first appeared in *Life* for February 1941. It was subsequently printed with other comments by Luce's contemporaries (New York: Farrar and Rinehart, 1941).

61. Luce's essay ran some forty pages; the key comes, however, in the final eight pages, from which this discussion is taken.

"chink" as "a sort of walkin' banana that anybody could skin an' did. A simple childlike soul, bringin' his wife's family to live with him, regularly handin' over his pay envelope to his great-grandmother, or the oldest survivin' ancestor, an' eatin' nothing stronger than chop suey."[62]

To many, this image was a constant reminder of the need for America to awaken a "young China" and to direct an industrial, social, and political renaissance. To a very few others, however, John Chinaman's negative side was a sign that some of America's "undue optimism" should be tempered. Despite decades of attempted reform, prostitution, gambling, and opium-smoking still flourished. Communication often seemed impossible. Hope usually ended in frustration. Americans, the *Nation* observed, were just "drifting along, building a few roads, cleaning the towns." Even Charles Crane thought that "it would be ages before China will come into her own."[63] Perhaps, *Harper's Weekly* had once mused, Napoleon was right when he worried about China that "if she wakes, she will shake the world."[64]

Throughout the 1920s and 1930s such scepticism signaled the need for more rather than less American action in China. All that seemed to be needed was renewed dedication and stronger organization to achieve the goal of the American Century, a frictionless, efficient Open Door. In the 1940s, however, the tactics and goals of that policy received two successive jolts. By the end of the decade, Americans were convinced that their earlier fears had been well taken, that indeed Fu Manchu and not Charlie Chan was the characteristic Chinaman.

The first jolt came with American involvement in another world war, this one fought almost exclusively at the outset in the Pacific. Still the Second World War could be seen as a failure of methods in dealing with Japan and not of goals. In addition, the war had produced the resolve Henry Luce thought America needed. John Chinaman was never more courageous, the goals of the Open Door never

62. For examples of the negative stereotype see Herbert Hoover to the Department of Commerce, Oct. 18, 1917, SDDF 102.8/268, and George Creel's anonymous publication of *Uncle Henry, Anonymous* (New York: Reynolds, 1922) in which he spoofs the Yellow Peril and what he refers to as the "Open Sore."

63. Fletcher Brockman expressed disillusion in a note dated 1923 and found in the John R. Mott Papers, B554. See Crane to Eliot, Nov. 7, 1920, Crane Papers, and *Nation*, CX (Feb. 21, 1920), 226, making an interesting link between American adventures in Haiti and in the Far East.

64. *Harper's Weekly*, LIX (Oct. 17, 1914), 362.

clearer. After the war, as in 1919, eyes turned West again to the last unexploited Eldorado, now the one America had saved from the Japanese. Despite civil war raging in China as late as 1948, the famous four hundred million customers remained an impressive and important image for Americans, including former Philippine High Commissioner Paul McNutt and Progressive party presidential candidate Henry Wallace.[65]

With opportunity seemingly closer than ever, suddenly it was snatched away. The revolution begun in 1911 with Yuan Shih-kai had moved through successive stages with Sun Yat-sen and Chiang Kai-shek and culminated, at least temporarily, in Mao Tse-tung's Communist victory. First reactions in America were illustrative. As always, China hands, now restyled the China lobby, argued aggressive American action and aid would stem the tide and preserve Chiang's rule.[66] Yet by the beginning of the 1950s, for the first time in half a century, perhaps for the first time in all of American history, the goals of United States policy in China were entirely remote. Though similar goals might be pursued in other parts of the world, in China the door was closed and only Chiang's peephole in Taiwan remained.

Myth and Reality of the Open Door

With the unquestioned goals suddenly gone, all that was left was a tragic sense of failure. Looking purely at empirical evidence, it might be argued that China had always been a myth not a market, that it did not really matter and had never been recognized in any real sense by "John American." In fact, of course, the myth, like that of the American West, mattered greatly. What had gone wrong?[67]

Early explanations and experts were what the sociologists of the

65. Paul V. McNutt, "America's Role in the Orient," *Annals of the American Academy of Political and Social Science*, CCLVIII (July 1948), 53. See also *New York Times*, May 22, 1948, p. 5, for Wallace's 1948 China position. I am indebted to the excellent research of Theodore Rosenof whose senior honors paper, "Henry Wallace, A New Dealer's Ideology, 1933–48," was done at Rutgers University in 1965.

66. For an examination of these attitudes see A. T. Steele, *The American People and China* (New York: McGraw-Hill, 1966), pp. 34–35.

67. See the challenging, Paul H. Clyde, "Historical Reflections on American Relations With the Far East," *South Atlantic Quarterly*, LXI (Autumn 1962), 437–49.

1950s might call other directed. The idea that outright conspiracy, or at least duplicity on the part of well-known China hands, such as those in the Institute for Pacific Relations, had been the cause of Communism's success in China, satisfied some of failure's frustration. More reasonable experts such as George Kennan went back to the well-known shortcomings of America's tactics, which he found too legalistic and idealistic.[68] Kennan's answer was more interesting for its implications than its explanations. John Dewey and Charles Evans Hughes had applied the goals of the Open Door to supply the answer to a tactical dilemma they did not understand. With these goals now having failed, Kennan reversed the process and blamed the failure on the unresolved tactical debate. No one questioned whether the goals themselves needed reexamination. Kennan's was the response of a man who had studied and believed the goals of the Open Door and could not find them wanting. Like so many others, he questioned only the tactics and would have replaced them with more realistic ones. Each time American policy failed before successful Communist revolution in China, other reasonable men debated the methods used, often revised one detail or another and started again, sincerely in search of goals they never questioned. The only unrealistic side of American policy, if that term has any meaning, was what Kennan symbolized, not what he uncovered. Given a framework and a perception rooted in the American Century at home and abroad, Kennan and America had operated as intelligently as they could. Nothing had suddenly gone wrong. Debate and compromise over tactical decisions in the power politics of the Far East had been conscientiously conducted at a serious level. The crucial question was not, What had gone wrong? Rather it should have been, Why had it not been seen long before that something drastic would, in fact, happen?

With the advantages of historical hindsight other explanations, or studies which may be used as such, stress determinism and the inevitability of an American failure. The back-and-forth "ying and yang" periodization of Chinese history and the persistent and exaggerated good/evil Chinese image in the American mind, guaranteed that an age of treachery would replace one of benevolence. Sinologists have gone furthest in showing any number of factors such as China's

68. The famous Kennan arguments appear in his *American Diplomacy, 1900–1950*, Charles R. Walgreen Foundation Lectures (New York: New American Library, 1951), ch. 3, "America and the Orient."

vast area or huge population or feudal economy which naturally eroded attempts at Westernization.[69] In a perceptive piece, "Open Door or Great Wall," written in 1934, Owen Lattimore disputed the logistics of Admiral Mahan. The Open Door might allow for the maritime domination of China's coast, but the Great Wall provided a barrier to penetration from the sea and a vulnerability to land powers from the West.[70] Those who emphasize more basic biological and anthropological abstractions agree that the nature of the national space instilled in the Chinese, as in all living things, a desire to defend the territory from what was recognized as an outside threat.[71] Certainly historians have recognized that since Friars John of Piano Carpini and William of Rubruch visited the seat of Mongol power in the thirteenth century, Westerners had sometimes subdued but never conquered China.[72]

The Open Door was surely part of the long history of western commercial and intellectual invasion of the Orient. While this seems to determine America's failure, it actually makes the question of early twentieth-century American attitudes more profound. Hardly any Americans were experts or even students of China's history. Yet those, like W. W. Rockhill, who were knowledgeable about the East, believed that the American experiment was different. What made these men believe or want to believe that the United States could succeed where others had failed?

69. Among the best of such pieces are: Irene B. Taeuber, "China's Population: Riddle of the Past, Enigma of the Future," *Antioch Review,* XVII (Spring 1957), 7–18; Chi-Ming Hou, "Some Reflections on the Economic History of Modern China," *Journal of Economic History,* XXIII (Dec. 1963), 595–605. See also the older, but excellent, Carl Whiting Bishop, "Geographical Factors in the Development of Chinese Civilization," *The Geographical Review,* XII (Jan. 1922), 19–41.

70. Owen Lattimore, "Open Door or Great Wall," *Atlantic Monthly,* CLIV (July 1934). This essay is one of many in the book by the same author, *Studies in Frontier History: Collected Papers, 1928–58* (London: Oxford University Press, 1962).

71. See Theodore Herman, "Group Values Toward the National Space: The Case of China," *Geographical Review,* XLIX (April 1959), 164–82, and the highly provocative Robert Ardrey, *The Territorial Imperative: A Personal Inquiry into the Animal Origins of Property and Nations* (New York: Atheneum, 1966), pp. 229–32.

72. Charles E. Nowell, "The Discovery of the Pacific: A Suggested Change of Approach," *Pacific Historical Review,* XVI (Feb. 1947), 1–11.

The Central Significance of Progressivism

In part, the only thing unique about the Open Door policy, as with so much else in American history, was that Americans thought it was unique. The United States would remain free from the traditional European political and military entanglements in the Far East, simply because it was aware of them. The passage to the riches and rewards of the Orient was chartered on the belief that the United States could navigate the narrows between the Scylla of isolation and the Charybdis of imperialism. In this stretch, America would build a permanently open door by remaking China in its own image, using forms and designs successful at home. Such an architectural structure had serious shortcomings.

By attempting to avoid Europe's mistakes, Americans were denying the impact prior western invasions had on China. For all its supposed uniqueness, American penetration was part of a revolutionary process the West had begun in order to transform a traditional feudal society into a modern industrial one.[73] The "forced feeding" of western civilization into China was indeed an experience requiring revolutionary changes in attitude as well as technique. Yet such drastic revolution was the one thing Americans could not tolerate, for they felt it threatened the roots of the society they would export to China, which was a mirror-image of American society at home. In an understatement Charles Crane explained, "I have never been enthusiastic about revolution as a mode of progress."[74]

It is not surprising that after 1917, bolshevism became the great threat to the goals of the Open Door. It was of course the antithesis of those goals. At home, it threatened the basis of the capitalist

73. The dynamics of intercivilizational contact and the internal workings of Chinese society need much sophisticated study; see Meribeth Cameron, "The Periodization of Chinese History," *Pacific Historical Review*, XV (June 1946), 171–77, John K. Fairbank, "China's Response to the West: Problems and Suggestion," *Journal of World History*, III (1956), 381–406, and the introductory study of the American sense of uniqueness even after the Communist victory, Tang Tsou, "The American Political Tradition and the American Image of Chinese Communism," *Political Science Quarterly*, LXXVII (Dec. 1962), 570–600. Chi-Ming Hou, "Some Reflections on the Economic History of Modern China," p. 602, suggests that though the West may have slowed and changed China's economic growth, scholars need to study its "political, social, psychological and other impacts on Chinese society and institutions."

74. Crane to David Houston, July 19, 1920, Crane Papers.

economy. Its acceptance in China would double the danger of eliminating America's symbolic frontier. Crane hoped that the threat was merely a mirage. "Having gone through Bolshevism in the twelfth century," he told the Chicago City Club upon his return in 1922, "China is not in the slightest danger of repeating the experiment." Using very similar language, Robert McElroy of the China Society of America could not hide his fears. "In China for the first time our type of government is on trial in Asia. Should it fail, but it will not fail," he resolved, "the next experiment will probably be Bolshevism."[75]

The Russian experiment was as much a product of western civilization as the American but it provided the revolutionary sympathy and spirit necessary for the drastic transformation underway of Chinese society.[76] The crux of American policy in China, the key to the link between progressivism and the Open Door and the answer to the question of why Americans could not recognize that something would go wrong lies in the fact that the United States found it possible to export only what it was hoping and sometimes achieving at home. Progressivism's answers to industrial changes in America were organization, efficiency, technology, education, and democratic political institutions—the very things Americans had long sought.[77] Applied in China, where there was a very different tradition, they failed, save to alienate nationalists who sought a philosophy as well as a technology by which to order their new society.

Awareness of China began with the thrust of private economic interests. Drawing on the symbol of settling the American continent, this expansion soon became cultural as well as commercial and received the active support of the government. Constantly concerned,

75. Crane address to the City Club of Chicago, Jan. 2, 1922, Crane Papers, appendix X, no. 19. Robert McElroy to William E. Griffis, Oct. 17, 1923, Griffis Papers, box 28–8, Rutgers University Library, New Brunswick, N. J. An interesting turn-around available in English is John Albert White, "As the Russians Saw Our China Policy," *Pacific Historical Review,* XXVI (May 1957), 147–60, stressing the writings of G. V. Astafev.

76. *Nation,* CX (April 10, 1920), 454–56, and once again the article of Warren Cohen, "America and the May Fourth Movement."

77. It is here that the recent work of American historians such as Gabriel Kolko, Robert Wiebe, and Samuel Hays (see introduction) is most useful to a study of foreign policy. Even Richard Hofstadter, *The Age of Reform* (New York: Alfred A. Knopf, 1956), agrees in a later chapter that organization was the key to the period.

as all governments are, with the preservation of its own society at home, America by the end of the nineteenth century was equally concerned with building and maintaining similar societies abroad. In the early twentieth century this policy was progressive, as Prof. George E. Taylor has written, for "it assumes that the more the peoples of the East are westernized . . . the greater will be the prosperity and safety of the American republic."[78] To succeed in China was to succeed at home. To fail there was, however, to fail at home. Thus to admit faulty goals in the Far East was to confess them in the United States as well.

On the same faculty as John Dewey at Peking University, English philosopher Bertrand Russell expressed what Dewey and America did not or could not understand.[79] For all the tactical debate over cooperation or competition, "if America is victorious in the Far East, China will be Americanized and though the shell of political freedom may remain, there will be an economic and cultural bondage beneath it." That is, after all, what Charles Crane implied when he suggested that the lesson of Chicago be applied in Canton. To Americans at the beginning of the twentieth century, they and only they could solve what Russell called the problem of China. The American answer amounted to simply "substituting mechanics for Confucius."[80] Somehow, John Chinaman, whose stereotypes were well catalogued, found the uncharacteristic imagination and resolve to challenge the American role and dismiss the American answer.

78. This conclusion is my own but naturally is based on the conceptualization of others. In particular, I think the following people and books have influenced me most: Charles A. Beard, *The Open Door at Home* (New York: Macmillan, 1935) and the same author's *The Idea of National Interest* (New York: Macmillan, 1934); John King Fairbank, *The United States and China* (Cambridge: Harvard University Press, 1948, 1958); perhaps most, George E. Taylor, "America's Pacific Policy: The Role and the Record," *Pacific Affairs*, XIV (Dec. 1941), 430–47, and the same author's *America in the New Pacific* (New York: Macmillan, 1942). Taylor, of the University of Washington, has been writing on the Far East since the 1930s, spanning the gap from the Institute for Pacific Relations to the 1960s Council on Foreign Relations. In the students he has trained and the ideas he has expressed, Taylor has made a significant contribution.

79. Bertrand Russell, *The Problem of China* (London: George Allen and Unwin, 1922), p. 147.

80. H. Strong to Crane, 1909, Crane Papers; see ch. 3.

Bibliography · Index

Bibliography

DETAILED documentation for this study may be found in the notes to each chapter and in the extensive bibliography in the dissertation from which this work grows, "Progressivism and the Open Door, America and China, 1901–1921" (Rutgers University, 1967). Relevant historiographical and bibliographical patterns are traced in the introduction to this book.

This bibliography is a handy catalogue of those primary sources, unpublished, governmental, and periodical, upon which this work rests. It should be noted that the author, like all students of United States Asian policy, is greatly indebted to the work of Kwang Ching Liu, *Americans and Chinese: A Historical Essay and a Bibliography* (Cambridge: Harvard University Press, 1963).

MANUSCRIPT SOURCES, LISTED BY REPOSITORY

Personal

In the Library of Congress
Newton D. Baker Papers
Ray Stannard Baker Papers
Wharton Barker Papers
Mabel Boardman Papers
William Borah Papers
William Jennings Bryan Papers
Bainbridge Colby Papers
George Creel Papers
Norman Davis Papers
Walter Fisher Papers
Henry Fletcher Papers
John Hay Papers
George Kennan Papers
Philander Knox Papers
Robert Lansing Papers
Breckinridge Long Papers
George B. McClellan, Jr., Papers

Elihu Root Papers
Theodore Roosevelt Papers
Oscar Straus Papers
William Howard Taft Papers
James Wilson Papers
Woodrow Wilson Papers

In the Library of Cornell University
Frederick McCormick Papers
Willard Straight Papers

In the Missionary Research Library
James Bashford Papers
John F. Goucher Papers
D. Willard Lyon Papers

In the New York Public Library
Horace Allen Papers
Lillian Wald Papers

In the Library of Rutgers University
William Elliot Griffis Papers

In the Library of Ursinus College
Huntington Wilson Papers

In the Library of the State Historical Society of Wisconsin
Paul Reinsch Papers

In the Library of the Yale Divinity School
John R. Mott Papers

In the Library of Yale University
Edward M. House Papers
William Kent Papers
Frank Polk Papers
Henry L. Stimson Papers

In the possession of John O. Crane, New York and Woods Hole,
    Massachusetts
Charles R. Crane Papers

In the possession of Mrs. Martin Egan, New York
Martin Egan Papers

In the Library of Columbia University—Oral History Research Project
Lloyd Griscom Recollections
Nelson T. Johnson Recollections
William Phillips Recollections
DeWitt C. Poole Recollections
George Rublee Recollections
Upton Sinclair Recollections

Organizational

In the American Red Cross National Headquarters Library
  American Red Cross China Famine Relief Papers

In the Missionary Research Library
  World Missionary Conference Papers

In the Library of Yale University
  The Inquiry Papers
  Yale-in-China Papers

In the Young Men's Christian Association Headquarters Library
  International Commission Papers
  World Service Papers

Official

In the National Archives
  State Department Files, Record Group 59, 1901–1921
  Committee on Public Information Files, Record Group 63, 1917–1919
  War Trade Board Files, Record Group 182, 1918

GOVERNMENT DOCUMENTS

Clyde, Paul H. *United States Policy Toward China: Diplomatic and Public Documents, 1839–1939.* Durham: Duke University Press, 1940.
Congressional Record, 1900–1922.
MacMurray, John V. A. *Treaties and Agreements With and Concerning China, 1894–1919.* New York: Oxford University Press, 1921.
United States, Department of State. *Papers Relating to the Foreign Relations of the United States, 1900–1922,* including supplements and Appendix, *Affairs in China, 1901.* Washington: Government Printing Office, 1903–1936.
———. *Papers Relating to the Foreign Relations of the United States: The Lansing Papers, 1914–1920,* 2 vols. Washington: Government Printing Office, 1939–1940.

CONTEMPORARY SPEECHES AND PAMPHLETS

Angell, James B. "The Widening Horizon," baccalaureate address, June 17, 1900, University of Michigan.
Bashford, James W. "Opportune Investments in China," 1907.
———. "The Awakening of China," 1907.
———. "American and World Democracy," 1917.
Beach, Harlan P. "The Findings of the Continuation Committee Conferences Held in Asia, 1912–1913, Arranged by Topics," 1913.
Bryan, William J. "British Rule in India," 1906.
Davidson, John. *A Crossroads of Freedom: The 1912 Campaign Speeches of Woodrow Wilson.* New Haven: Yale University Press, 1956.

Fahs, Charles H. "America's Stake in the Far East," 1920.

Foreign Policy Association. "The Conflict of Policies in China," Pamphlet no. 36, 1925.

Gary, Elbert H. "Addresses and Statements," 8 vols. Collected and Bound by the Museum of the Peaceful Arts, 1927.

Hammond, John Hays. "The Business Man's Interest in Peace—Why Not Neutralize China," *Maryland Quarterly* of the Maryland Peace Society, 1911.

Hornbeck, Stanley K. "The Most-Favored-Nation Clause in Commercial Treaties," *Bulletin of the University of Wisconsin Economics and Political Science Series*, VI (1910), 327–448.

————. "Trade, Concessions, Investments, Conflict and Policy in the Far East," National Conference on Foreign Relations of the United States, Long Beach, New York, 1917.

Latourette, Kenneth S. "China, the United States and the War," *League of Nations, World Peace Foundation*, II (1919), 168–91.

Lyon, D. Willard. "The First Quarter Century of the Young Men's Christian Association in China, 1895–1920," 1920.

Powell, John B. "Newspaper Efficiency in the Small Town," *University of Missouri Bulletin*, vol. XVI (April 1915).

Roosevelt, Theodore. "Japan's Part," J. B. Millet, 1918.

————. "The Strenuous Life," in *Essays and Addresses*. New York: The Century Company, 1902.

Root, Elihu. *The Military and Colonial Policy of the United States. Addresses and Reports*. Cambridge: Harvard University Press, 1916.

World Missionary Conference. *Reports of Commissions III, VII and VIII*. New York: Fleming H. Revell, 1910.

World Peace Foundation. *Proceedings of the Conference on International Relations*. 1916.

PERIODICALS

Journals of Special Interest

American
Arena
Asia
Atlantic Monthly
Century
Chautauquan
Collier's Weekly
Cosmopolitan
Educational Review
Engineering Magazine
Forum
Harper's New Monthly
Harper's Weekly

Independent
Journal of the American Asiatic Association
Judge
La Follette's Weekly Magazine
Literary Digest
Living Age
McCall's
McClure's
Munsey's
The Nation
National Geographic Magazine
The New Republic
North American Review
Overland Monthly
Outlook
Popular Science
Review of Reviews
Scientific American
Scribner's
Success
World Today
World's Work

Contemporary Articles

Adams, Brooks. "John Hay," *McClure's*, XIX (June 1902), 173–82.

Allen, Horace. "An Acquaintance With Yuan Shih-kai," *North American Review*, CXCVI (July 1912), 109–17.

Anderson, George E. "The Wonderful Canals of China," *National Geographic Magazine*, XVI (Feb. 1905), 68–69.

Arnold, Julean. "Advancement of American Trade Interests in China," *Overland Monthly*, LVII (May 1911), 467–68.

Baker, Ray Stannard. "The Measure of Taft," *American*, LXX (July 1910), 366.

Barrett, John. "America in the Pacific," *Forum*, XXX (Dec. 1900), 478–91.

Bashford, James. "Chinese Guilds," *The Survey*, XXIII (Jan. 1, 1910), 481–84.

Bent, Silas. "The China Consortium and the Open Door," *The Nation*, CX (March 20, 1920), 379–81.

Beveridge, Albert. "The White Invasion of China," *Saturday Evening Post*, CLXXIV (Nov. 16, 1901), 3–4.

Bishop, Carl Whiting. "Geographical Factors in the Development of Chinese Civilization," *The Geographical Review*, XII (Jan. 1922), 19–41.

Boardman, Mabel. "An Audience with the Dowager Empress of China," *Outlook*, XC (Dec. 12, 1908), 824–28.

Brailsford, H. N. "A New Technique of Peace," *The New Republic*, XXIX (Nov. 30, 1921), 12–15.

Chaille-Long, Charles. "Why China Boycotts Us," *World Today*, X (March 1906), 309–14.

Chamberlain, T. C. "China's Educational Problem," *Independent*, LXIX Sept. 22, 1910), 646–49.

Denby, Charles. "Our Relations with the Far East," *Munsey's*, XX (Jan. 1899), 515–20.

Dewey, John. "The American Opportunity in China," *The New Republic*, XXI (Dec. 3, 1919), 14–17.

Edmunds, Charles Keyser. "China's Renaissance," *Popular Science*, LXVII (Sept. 1905), 387–98.

Graves, Ralph A. "Fearful Famines of the Past," *National Geographic Magazine*, XXXII (July 1917), 89.

Hammond, John Hays. "American Commercial Interests in the Far East," *Annals of the American Academy of Political and Social Science*, XXVI (1905), 85–88.

————. "The Menace of Japan's Success," *World's Work*, X (June 1905), 6273–75.

————. "Why I Am for Taft," *North American Review*, CXCVI (Oct. 1912), 449–50.

Jenks, Jeremiah. "China, America's Silent Partner," *World's Work*, XXXIII (Dec. 1916), 165–71.

————. "The Japanese in Manchuria," *Outlook*, XCVII (March 11, 1911), 549–54.

————. "Japan's Acts in China," *World's Work*, XXXIII (Jan. 1917), 312–28.

King, F. H. "The Wonderful Canals of China," *National Geographic Magazine*, XXIII (Oct. 1912), 931–58.

Klyce, E. D. H. "Scientific Management and the Moral Law," *Outlook*, XCIX (Nov. 18, 1911), 659–63.

Kuo, P. W. "The Effect of the Revolution Upon the Educational System of China," *Educational Review*, XLV (May 1913), 457–70.

Latane, John. "American Foreign Policy," *World's Work*, XLI (May 1921), 36–48.

Lenz, Frank B. "China's Next Revolution—What Part Will America Play," *Overland Monthly*, LXX (Oct. 1917), 313–22.

Low, Seth. "The Position of the United States Among the Nations," *Annals of the American Academy of Political and Social Science*, XXVI (July 1905), 1–15.

Martin, W. A. P. "China Transformed," *World's Work*, XII (Aug. 1906), 7844–48.

Marvin, George. "An Act of International Friendship," *Outlook*, XC (Nov. 14, 1908), 582–86.

McCormick, Frederick. "Present Conditions in China," *National Geographic Magazine*, XXII (Dec. 1911), 1120.

————. "Has the War Eliminated America From the Far East?" *Outlook*, LXXXIV (Oct. 6, 1906), 318–24.

Millard, Tom. "Blundering in the Far East," *American*, LXX (July 1910), 413–25.

————. "China's Case at the Peace Conference," *Century*, XCVII (April 1919), 797–802.

Miner, Luella. "American Barbarism and Chinese Hospitality," *Outlook*, LXXII (Dec. 27, 1902), 984–88.

Parsons, William Barclay. "The American Invasion of China," *McClure's*, XIV (April 1900), 499–510.

Reinsch, Paul. "China Against the World," *Forum*, XXX (Sept. 1900), 67–75.

Rockhill, W. W. "The Outlook in China," *Collier's Weekly*, XXVIII (Jan. 1902), 9.

Ross, E. A. "Christianity in China," *Century*, LXXXI (March 1911), 754–64.

————. "The Overturn in China," *La Follette's Weekly Magazine*, III (Dec. 2, 1911), 7.

————. "Race Mind of the Chinese," *Independent*, LXXI (Sept. 7, 1911), 526–28.

Roosevelt, Theodore. "Progressive Nationalism," *Outlook*, XCVII (Jan. 14, 1911), 58.

Simpson, Bertram-Lenox. "What the American Fleet Could Do for China," *North American Review*, CLXXXVIII (Oct. 1908), 481–94.

Simpson, Thomas H. "Restoring China's Forests—A New American Influence in the Empire," *Review of Reviews*, LIII (March 1916), 337–40.

Twain, Mark. "To My Missionary Critics," *North American Review*, CLXXII (April 1901), 520–34.

————. "To the Person Sitting in Darkness," *North American Review*, CLXXII (Feb. 1901), 161–76.

Williams, F. W. "China and Future Peace," *The Nation,* CV (Nov. 22, 1917), 561–63.

Wu Ting Fang. "Chinese and Western Civilization," *Harper's Monthly Magazine*, CVI (Jan. 1903), 190–92.

UNPUBLISHED DISSERTATIONS

Bocage, Leo J. "The Public Career of Charles R. Crane." Fordham University, 1962.

Gardner, John B. "The Image of the Chinese in the United States, 1885–1915." University of Pennsylvania, 1960.

McClellan, Robert F., Jr. "The American Image of China, 1890–1905." Michigan State University, 1964.

Seager, Robert, II. "The Progressives and American Foreign Policy, 1898–1917: An Analysis of the Attitudes of the Leaders of the Progressive Movement Toward External Affairs." Ohio State University, 1957.

Vevier, Charles. "The Progressives and Dollar Diplomacy." M.A., University of Wisconsin, 1949.

Whitaker, Urban G., Jr. "Americans and Chinese Political Problems, 1912–1923." University of Washington, 1954.

Index